T0330646

Understanding Complexity in Organizations

Organizations are complex entities that must adapt the practices of their employees and management to meet the demands of a dynamic environment. Organizations are behavioral systems that coordinate interactions among its members and environment. Changing practices in one area of an organization can generate a reaction throughout the entire system, thus affecting the behaviors of those working within other areas, the experience of customers, and important organizational results. Behavioral Systems Analysis (BSA) focuses on these complex contingencies from the macro system all the way down to individual behavior.

This book contains articles by internationally recognized experts in Behavioral Systems Analysis who discuss the role of organizational practices in their study of performance improvement and cultural change from both practical and conceptual perspectives. Business and non-profit managers will find tools and case studies to help understand and diagnose their organization's dynamics. Scholars will appreciate articles' theory and real-world descriptions when considering their own research direction. Finally, all students of management theory, behavior analysis, and human resources will find this collection a thought-provoking tool for their understanding of behavioral systems and their application in organizations.

This book was published as a special issue in the *Journal of Organizational Behavior Management*.

Timothy Ludwig is a professor at Appalachian State University as a University Deans' Distinguished Graduate Faculty in their Industrial/Organizational Psychology and Human Resources Management Masters program. He is the current editor of the *Journal of Organizational Behavior Management* and the author of *Intervening to Improve the Safety of Occupational Driving*. His research aims to empirically document the successes of methods to improve safety and quality in industry through behavior-based management.

Ramona Houmanfar currently teaches introductory and organizational psychology at the undergraduate level, behavioral systems analysis at the graduate level, trains graduate students in organizational consultation, and conducts research in the areas of instructional design, productivity improvement, rule governance, communication networks, and bonus compensation systems. She has co-published the book, *Organizational Change* (Context Press, 2001).

Understanding Complexity in Organizations

Behavioral Systems

Edited by
Timothy Ludwig and Ramona Houmanfar

Routledge
Taylor & Francis Group
LONDON AND NEW YORK

First published 2010 by Routledge
2 Park Square, Milton Park, Abingdon, Oxon, OX14 4RN

Simultaneously published in the USA and Canada
by Routledge
711 Third Avenue, New York, NY 10017

Routledge is an imprint of the Taylor & Francis Group, an informa business

First issued in paperback 2012

© 2010 Taylor & Francis

This book is a reproduction of a two-part special issue of the *Journal of Organizational Behavior Management*: 29.2 and 29.3/4. The Publisher requests to those authors who may be citing this book to state, also, the bibliographical details of the special issue on which the book was based

Typeset in Garamond by Value Chain, India

All rights reserved. No part of this book may be reprinted or reproduced or utilised in any form or by any electronic, mechanical, or other means, now known or hereafter invented, including photocopying and recording, or in any information storage or retrieval system, without permission in writing from the publishers.

British Library Cataloguing in Publication Data
A catalogue record for this book is available from the British Library

ISBN13: 978-0-415-57671-0 (hbk)
ISBN13: 978-0-415-63394-9 (pbk)

Contents

Introduction: Understanding Complexity in Organizations*

TIMOTHY D. LUDWIG

Appalachian State University

RAMONA HOUMANFAR

University of Nevada, Reno

Organizational systems are adaptive entities that survive by meeting environmental demands (consumers, competition, economy, governmental policies, etc.) through the development and maintenance of subsystems ultimately designed to manage behavior. Thus, organizations are behavioural systems that encompass complex patterns of behavioral interactions among their members and the environment. For instance, a change in practices of one area of the organization may bring about a ripple reaction throughout the entire system, thus affecting the behaviors of those working within one department. Behavioral Systems Analysis (BSA) focuses on these complex response patterns, and seeks to understand the critical aspects of the system involved in the controlling relationships between the organization and contingencies. Behavioral systems analysts also analyze the role of organizational practices in their study of performance improvement and cultural change.

Even though the literature and technology associated with the behavioural systems perspective can be traced back to the early 1960s, the development of conceptual as well as experimental work in this area has not evolved as rapidly as other areas of Organizational Behavior Management (OBM). The last decade, however, has seen a reengagement of interests in behavioural systems analysis through an increased demand by practitioners and leaders in organizations as they experience these complex phenomena.

In that regard, this book serves not only as a tribute to the work of our pioneering colleagues (Brethower, 1982; Malott, 2003; Rummler, 2004), but also as a source of inspiration and ideas for future research and practice. We have drawn well-known theorists, researchers, and practitioners from around the world together to present their most recent work on behavioral systems.

---

*We dedicate this book to the memory of Dr. Geary Rummler, a pioneer in the field of Behavioral Systems Analysis and inspiration for many generations to come.

This book is divided into two parts. In Part 1, the interrelated themes of behavioural systems range from analysis of multiorganizational contingencies to case studies, from practical processes to measurement tools of systems analysis. The issues discussed in Part 2 range from analysis of leadership practices in organizations to behavioral systemic views of our scientific field.

Part 1 starts with Diener, McGee, and Miguel's overview of BSA as a technology for organization-wide improvement by offering a series of practical process analyses and measurement tools. Krapfl, Cooke, Sullivan, and Cogar offer a view on engineering the reciprocal relationship between those who would intervene in a system and the behavioral systems, a world in which the behaviorist is not only the observer but the participant. This analysis is demonstrated through an organizational case study. Next, Mihalic and Ludwig offer a field report depicting a measurement system failure and its systemic and behavioral implications in a distribution organization. The next chapter by Cloyd Hyten sets the stage for a systems-oriented and results-focused approach to Organizational Behavior Management that meets the demands of the business world.

William Abernathy's chapter reviews BSA in light of Skinner's *Walden Two* classic and promotes the use of organizational systems instead of social communes as a way of realizing this utopian vision of behavioral science. Part 1 closes with the examination of interrelations among individual behavior, group alignment, and eventually organizational performance in longitudinal analyses of self-insurance systems by Alavosius, Getting, Dagen, Newsome, and Hopkins.

Part 2 opens with Anthony Biglan's analysis of the cultural practices proposed to change government's influence on costs (externalities) that corporations' actions impose on society. In line with this approach on socially appropriate organizational practices, Thomas C. Mawhinney provides a behavioral systemic view of ways by which dysfunctional and latent deadly practices may be replaced by functional practices.[1] With regards to functional organizational practices, Houmanfar, Rodrigues, and Smith offer an analysis of effective leadership in relation to communication networks in organizations. Ingunn Sandaker discusses how different processes and communication structures in the organization serve as environmental contingencies favoring variability of performance in organizations.

Next, Tosti and Herbst provide a behavioral systems approach toward customer-centered organizations by using examples and reports from the field. The final chapter by Hayes, Dubuque, Fryling, and Pritchard offers a behavioral systemic overview of behavior analysis as a scientific discipline with a focus on ways to increase its share of the psychological market, sustain its veracity, and assure its long term.[2]

ENDNOTES

1. We would like to thank our guest editor, Cloyd Hyten, for his contribution to the editorial process on Tom Mawhinney's contribution.
2. We are indebted to the contributors of this book for inspiration and ideas for future research and practice. We welcome commentaries on the concepts and tools presented in these chapters as submissions for further dialog on behavioral systems in the pages of the *Journal of Organizational Behavior Management*.

REFERENCES

Brethower, D. M. (1982). The total performance system, In R. M. O'Brien, A. M. Dickinson, & M. P. Rosow (Eds.), *Industrial behavior modification: A management handbook* (pp. 350–369). New York: Pergamon Press.

Malott, M. E. (2003). *Paradox of organizational change.* Reno, Nevada: Context Press.

Rummler, G. A. (2004). *Serious performance consulting according to Rummler.* Silver Spring, MD: International Society for Performance Improvement.

An Integrated Approach for Conducting a Behavioral Systems Analysis

LORI H. DIENER

Performance Blueprints, Rochester, New York, USA

HEATHER M. McGEE

Western Michigan University, Kalamazoo, Michigan, USA

CAIO F. MIGUEL

California State University, Sacramento, California, USA

The aim of this paper is to illustrate how to conduct a Behavioral Systems Analysis (BSA) to aid in the design of targeted performance improvement interventions. BSA is a continuous process of analyzing the right variables to the right extent to aid in planning and managing performance at the organization, process, and job levels. BSA helps to build alignment among activities within an organization to better provide value-adding products or services to the organization's consumers, which ultimately determines its survival. This paper provides an overview of the BSA approach, a Behavioral Systems Analysis Questionnaire (BSAQ) to guide the performance analyst, and an example of the BSAQ applied to an organization.

The authors thank Drs. Geary Rummler and Dale Brethower for providing the foundation upon which our Behavioral Systems Analysis Questionnaire was built and for their invaluable feedback and encouragement. We also thank Dr. Timothy Ludwig for his editorial assistance and for implementing and refining the question sets in his OBM graduate course.

AN INTEGRATED APPROACH FOR CONDUCTING A BEHAVIORAL SYSTEMS ANALYSIS

Businesses in nearly all industry sectors are continuously faced with competitive pressures influencing customer service expectations, resulting in increased organizational complexity (McElgunn, 2007). Organizations adapt to these pressures by changing their systems and processes to add value for their consumers. However, these changes can be costly when organizations focus on the wrong part(s) to "fix" or neglect to design the necessary behavior change of individuals who participate in the processes and systems being changed. The Behavioral Systems Analysis (BSA) approach to performance improvement described in this article provides the "how-to" for viewing an organization as a whole system and understanding how its many parts interact. By taking this approach, the performance analyst will be able to help his or her organization target its efforts and adapt more readily to change, which could lead to increases in profitability, customer satisfaction, market share, and more (Redmon & Mason, 2001).

BSA sets itself apart from other approaches to performance improvement by focusing on sustainable results through analyses of all components of the system that could impact performance (Brethower, 1982, 2000, 2001, 2002; M. E. Malott, 2003; Sulzer-Azaroff, 2000). BSA can be contrasted with the more commonly applied organizational behavior management interventions also known as Performance Management (PM). PM involves improving individual or group performance by directly manipulating the environment. The PM process typically involves the analysis of antecedents and consequences supporting the behaviors of individuals (or groups of individuals) within the organization and altering these variables to either decrease unproductive or increase productive performance (Austin, 2000; Daniels & Daniels, 2004). PM is consistent with the science of behavior analysis whose principles have been developed over the last 50 years (Skinner, 1953). Common PM interventions include goal setting, feedback, job aids, token systems (earning points that can later be redeemed for valued items), lottery systems, and so on (Redmon & Wilk, 1991). Although PM interventions have been shown to deliver robust results in the near term, there has been little evidence to show that their positive impact can sustain over long periods of time (Redmon, 1991; Sigurdsson & Austin, 2006). It is critical to build PM interventions that sustain behavior change since it is ultimately the behavior of individuals within an organization that carries out organizational goals (Brown, 2000; Daniels, 2009; M. E. Malott, 2003).

There are two primary aspects of PM interventions that affect sustainability: (a) the environment—of which the PM intervention is a part—experiences constant change; and (b) the PM intervention participants may change and/or managers, coworkers, and external customers of the organization may desire different products and services as an outcome of the intervention.

Thus, PM interventions should be considered in context of the overall organizational system to which they belong, so they can be adapted as changes in the organization occur. The design of a PM structure that adapts to shifting demands on the organization is one that will be sustainable because it can account for changes in individual and team contingencies due to variance in the greater organizational system.

The BSA method involves outlining how the components of the system interact, including how each individual contributes to the overall functioning of the system. BSA involves multilevel solutions that may include PM interventions, but also process design, automation, changes in policy, changes in resource deployment, strategy development and/or realignment, development of incentive systems, organizational restructuring, and managing the manager initiatives, to name a few (McGee, 2007). The value of BSA is that it allows us to analyze the organization outside the basic three-term contingency of antecedents, behaviors, and consequences to identify variables that can significantly impact individual and organizational performance. By analyzing the entire organization as a system, one can identify areas of improvement that will produce the largest positive impact on the organization and focus on planning and managing the variables that support desired performance.

In sum, the BSA approach to performance improvement can be characterized by the analysis of multiple levels of the organization through a set of specific tools, helping to facilitate the process of information gathering and sharing, identification of goals, problem identification, and solution development. Because the BSA process is typically quite complex (Glenn, 1988; M. E. Malott, 2003), integrative analysis tools are necessary to target the appropriate organizational variables. The BSA framework and an integrated approach for conducting a Behavioral Systems Analysis are described next.

BSA FRAMEWORK

BSA is based on a common framework for analyzing any organizational system and has evolved through the work of many pioneers in the field (Austin, 2000; Brethower, 1982; Daniels & Daniels, 2004; Gilbert, 1978; M. E. Malott, 2003; R. W. Malott, 1974; Rummler, 2004; Rummler & Brache, 1995). This common framework identifies relevant components of the organization in context of how value-adding work is (and should be) done. Using such a framework makes work visible (Rummler, 2008), which helps different performers within the organization observe work from a similar viewpoint and talk about it accurately among themselves. This facilitates agreement on where disconnects lie within the system, which performance areas need to be improved, and ultimately the priorities and resources that should be allocated to resolving those identified disconnects. Armed with a clear direction, work can be organized, performed, and managed effectively.

Since organizations are affected by multiple variables, day-to-day activities are constantly providing distractions, and it may be easy to lose sight of the bigger picture. Thus, staying focused on value-adding results throughout this perceived chaos requires determining (a) what the organization is ultimately trying to achieve; (b) how work gets done; and (c) what is necessary to get the work done (Brethower, 2000; M. E. Malott, 2003). To guide this focus, we have created a Behavioral Systems Analysis Questionnaire (BSAQ) that addresses each level of the organization as a Total Performance System, how each system is connected to other systems, and areas in which to focus management efforts. Before introducing the tool, an overview of the key concepts included in the tool is provided next.

Total Performance System

The Total Performance System (TPS) diagram is a tool that can be used to analyze performance at all levels of the organization in order to readily place information in its appropriate context to expedite accurate decisions and actions (Brethower, 1982). The TPS provides information by highlighting necessary components of the system that contribute to its success. The TPS can be used to analyze all systems and subsystems, from an entire industry to an organization, process, group, or individual performer (M. E. Malott, 2003).

A TPS diagram includes a description of seven key components, each of which requires effective functioning for the system's survival (Brethower, 1982). These components are (a) the mission/goal; (b) outputs; (c) receiving system(s); (d) external feedback loop/data; (e) processing system; (f) inputs; (g) internal feedback loop/data. To enhance this tool's effectiveness we have added two additional components: (h) environment and (i) competition. These additional components are not directly controlled by the organization but by impact strategies and decisions and, therefore, should be considered in the analysis of any system (Rummler & Brache, 1995).

We begin with the identification of the mission or goal of the system. All other system components exist to support the achievement of the mission and, therefore, any changes to the system should be functionally consistent (or "aligned") with the mission. Inputs consist of resources needed for the system to operate and often include raw materials, money, people, information, equipment, technology, etc. The processing system consists of the actions taken to transform the inputs into outputs. Outputs are the products and services produced by the organization and received by the customers. The customers (i.e., the receiving system) are those who consume the product or service. The internal feedback loop represents information gathered about the process, a form of quality control. This feedback allows the organization to correct defective process steps before outputs reach the receiving system, thus increasing the probability that those outputs will be accepted. The external feedback loop describes the impact the product has on its consumers.

If consumers are not satisfied, products may not be consumed and the organization may perish. Arco (1993) suggested that individual performance must be functionally tied to desired customer outcomes, which is assessed through data provided through the internal and external feedback loops.

Systems within Systems

Examples of how the TPS is used can be found elsewhere (Brethower, 2002; Brethower & Dams, 1999; M. E. Malott, 2003; Redmon & Wilk, 1991; Rummler, 2004; Williams & Cummings, 2001). The basic premise of the TPS is to view how each subsystem fits into a larger system within a hierarchy of systems. One can use the TPS diagram to analyze the interconnectedness of performance from the organization level to the process level and, ultimately, to the behaviors of individuals. This approach ensures a complete diagnosis of organizational performance from the top to the bottom of the organization. Without a top-to-bottom analysis, we may focus on individual or group performance that might be not functionally consistent, or "disconnected," with the organization's mission and goals.

Figure 1 illustrates a series of TPS diagrams and how each system is contained within a larger system of which it is a part. As you review the diagram, imagine if you "double-clicked" a computer mouse on one area in the processing system of the organization you could reveal a particular process in more detail (as shown lower in the diagram). Then imagine if you double-clicked on one single process step in the process, you would then see the individual or group performance system related to that process step (lower still). Since all systems are composed of interconnected subsystems wherein change in one will inevitably impact others in various ways, a systems approach to improving and managing behavior is especially effective because it is based on the commonalities across systems.

BEHAVIORAL SYSTEMS ANALYSIS QUESTIONNAIRE

The presentation of the Behavioral Systems Analysis Questionnaire (BSAQ) will take the form of a case study of the analysis of a private consulting firm attempting to improve quality and profitability. This case is organized in the context of the BSA framework (see Figure 1), beginning at the organization level, then moving to the process level and, finally, to the performer level. We begin with a brief description of the purpose of the analysis at each level (i.e., what we were looking for), followed by the analysis, resulting BSA diagrams, and recommendations for performance improvement.

The BSAQ appears in the following tables with responses from the case organization embedded as examples. Analyses that resulted from these question sets appear within the case. Future users of the BSAQ are encouraged

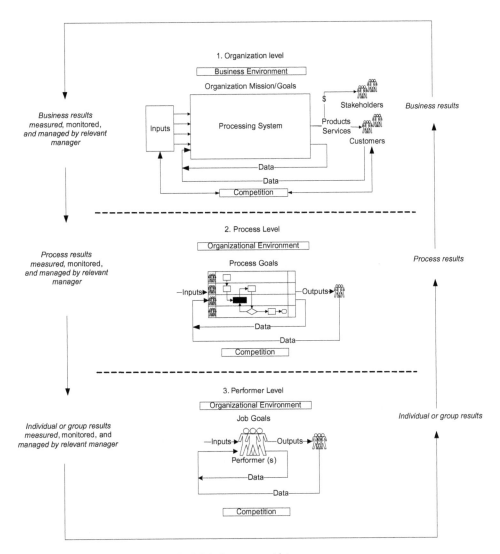

FIGURE 1 Systems within systems.

to adapt the question sets and create similar BSA diagrams (shown in figures) for their analyses. A complete copy of the BSAQ, including question sets not presented here, can be obtained by contacting the corresponding author.

Purpose of an Organizational-Level Analysis

The organizational-level analysis is where we recommend beginning, as the issues at this level are those that direct the course of all actions that follow. We begin by defining desired business results referred to in BSA as Critical

Business Issues (Rummler, 2001, 2004, 2008; Rummler & Brache, 1995; Rummler, Ramais, & Rummler, 2006b). A Critical Business Issue (CBI) is a problem or opportunity directly linked to the organization's survival. A CBI may be an actual or potential gap between the organization's performance and the competitor's performance, consumer expectations, or senior management's performance expectations.

The Total Performance System, sometimes referred to as the "supersystem" (Rummler, 2001, 2004; Rummler & Brache, 1995; Rummler, Ramais, & Rummler, 2006a), shown in the top level of Figure 1, helps to define an organization's CBI by identifying external threats and opportunities that the organization must be responsive to in order for it to survive (i.e., return on capital, net income, performance trends) and consumer measures (i.e., market share, customer satisfaction, revenue). Additionally, the TPS allows us to look at performance in the context of the products/services delivered to customers (both financial and consumer markets). Thus, the TPS helps to keep the focus on external variables that impact the organization, which should be driving all the activities within the organization's processing system.

ORGANIZATIONAL-LEVEL ANALYSIS OF PRIVATE CONSULTING FIRM

The organizational-level question set (see Table 1) is the first portion of the BSAQ. In this level of analysis, we are looking at what currently exists in each of the basic components of the overall system (e.g., mission/goals, outputs, receiving system, external feedback loop, processing system, etc.). Based on responses to the questions, we generated diagrams to make the system components visible, as shown in Figures 2 and 3. Using the organizational-level question set we were able to generate two views of the organization's processing system to gain a comprehensive understanding of where the organization needed to start their improvement efforts.

The first view, shown in Figure 2, illustrates the consulting organization's management system, core functions, and enabling functions. The primary focus of this view is to clarify how products and services are made available, sold, and delivered through the core functional areas and how those processes are measured and subsequently managed (Rummler, 2008). Ideally, the output of each critical process (i.e., Products/Services Made Available, Products/Services Sold, and Products/Services Delivered) would be monitored and managed on a regular basis and be the key driver in all management decisions. This view shown in Figure 2 was not the reality of the organization, but rather a "should" state against which to compare their current measurement and management system. The dotted lines in Figure 2 illustrate the data that the management system was missing (more details are shown in the process-level analysis next). Each component in Figure 2 is numbered to correspond with observations and recommendations provided in Table 2.

TABLE 1 Organizational-Level Question Set and Analysis

Questions	Responses
Mission	
What is the organization's mission statement?	*To passionately deliver innovative learning and communication strategies and solutions*
If the organization has a mission statement, does it pass the ACORN Test (Gilbert, 1978)?	**Accomplishment:** Does the organizational mission identify an accomplishment and not a process or behavior? *Yes*
	Control: Does the organization have control over the accomplishment identified? *Yes*
	Overall Objective: Have we identified the true purpose of the organization, or merely a subgoal? *True purpose*
	Reconcilable: If this mission were achieved, would other parts of the organization or macro system be impacted negatively? *No*
	Numbers: Is progress toward the mission something that could be measured or have we used vague/ subjective terms to describe it? *Measures need to be determined*
Do organizational goals exist? If so, what are they?	Products and services? (increase in # or quality) *No* Customer groups? (e.g., corner which market?) *No* Competitive advantages? (e.g., how to stay ahead?) *No*
Outputs	
What are the major products and services produced by the organization?	*Assessment Reports, Web based training courses, Instructor led courses, Communications, Learning Management Systems, Portals/Websites, Program/ product launches*
What are the financial outputs of the organization?	*Profit (in form of contribution Employee Shareholder Option Plan)*
Receiving System	
Who receives the products and services produced by the organization?	*Clients*
Who receives the financial outputs of the organization (e.g., Parent organization, owners/ stockholders, creditors)?	*Employees are shareholders*
External Feedback (Data)	
Does the organization receive satisfaction data about quality, timeliness, cost and customer service? How?	*30-Day Customer Satisfaction Surveys are sent the main client contact for each project when the project is closed, but questions on the survey may not be asking the right questions to provide helpful feedback to the organization. The return rate of surveys is approximately 70%. Profitability is measured by project but not tracked by product type delivered.*
Who is in charge of measuring and monitoring critical business measures related to consumer satisfaction?*	*CEO*
How is this information used to guide performance?*	*Needs to be defined*

(Continued)

TABLE 1 (*Continued*)

Questions	Responses
Does the organization receive financial data to guide appropriate allocation of resources? Examples include sales dollar volume, number of units sold, revenues and profits	*Needs to be defined*
Who is in charge of measuring and monitoring critical business measures related to financial performance?*	*CEO and President*
How is information used to guide performance?*	*Needs to be defined*

Processing System

Identify the various functions of the organization (e.g., Operations, Finance, Order Processing, Marketing, Sales) For each function listed, identify the major process areas that represent discrete actions of the function (e.g., The Operations Function may include Receiving, Quality Control, Replenishment, Selection, and Loading)	*Sales/Account Direction: generate new business, manage budget, clients and project teams*
	Creative: design, development of products
	Technology: design, development, implementation of internal and external products and services
	Instructional Design: analysis, design, development, implementation, evaluation of products
	Project Management: manage budget, clients and project teams, implementation of internal and external products and services
	Finance & Administration: internal purchasing, budgeting, reporting
Identify the major input-output relationships between the various functions. Who produces what for whom? (e.g., what is the main output of function A? What function receives it?).	*Human Resources: recruiting, hiring, training, allocating project resources*
	The organization also has five teams comprised of individuals from the functions listed above (with the exception of the President a & CEO who are part of the "management team". The goals of each team are not yet defined.
Place this information in the "Relationship Map"	*Management team: plan sales goals, oversee budget and staffing*
	Operations Team: provide process and tool updates to company
	Quality Council: provide and oversee systems and process analysis recommendations and related improvement efforts
	Products & Services: coach and guide functional areas to produce innovative products and services, develop new products and services
	Innovation: research and disseminate innovative concepts and examples throughout the organization

Inputs

| What capital is currently supporting the organization? Where does it come from? | *Revenue from projects and company investments* |
| Does the organization have sufficient human resources? Where does it come from? | *Varies* |

(Continued)

TABLE 1 (*Continued*)

Questions	Responses
Do human resources used create a competitive advantage or disadvantage to the organization? How?	*Yes and no. The organization recruits highly skilled professionals in the industry; however, turnover is high which may have a significant impact on costs related to on boarding activities*
What Materials and Equipment are needed? Where do they come from?	*Computers, hardware, software, telephones, teleconferencing equipment. Materials come from various sources and do not seem to be a perceived problem by anyone interviewed.*
Are quality standards in place for incoming resources?	*Yes, incoming human resources require referrals, work samples, and an interview screening process. Vendor/ supplier resources require referrals and work samples.*
How does the organization meet the needs of its suppliers?	*The organization meets the needs of its suppliers by paying them on time and providing feedback related to the product or service they delivered to the organization.*
Is it feasible (if necessary) to switch suppliers? Renegotiate?	*Yes, it is possible to switch suppliers and renegotiate.*
How are funds allocated for the purchase of materials/ equipment?	*Depends on internal needs or client project needs. If project needs, then funds are allocated based on the specified project's budget. Requests for internal material/equipment needs have a formal approval process that includes managers and accounting.*
Does material and equipment used create a competitive advantage or disadvantage to the organization? How?	*Yes. Materials and equipment allow for employees to work efficiently across separate offices.*
What technology is currently supporting the organization? Where does it come from?	*Each functional area uses specialized software to support their craft. The organization partners with a programming vendor to produce one of its major products (web based training courses).*
Does technology used create a competitive advantage or disadvantage to the organization? How?	*Both. The organization provides high quality solutions, but how technology is used should be looked at more in detail in context of improving efficiency (cost and timeliness).*
Internal Feedback (Data)	
What information is collected about processing system performance? (e.g., quality, quantity, timeliness, cost, safety)	*Billable hours of employees Project profitability*
How is this information measured and used? By Who?*	*Employees report hours that are analyzed monthly by every level of manager in the organization when there is an issue with project profitability*
Environment	
What environmental variables affect organizational performance (e.g., Economy, Government, Culture, Marketplace)? How?	*Needs to be defined*
Is the organization collecting information on these variables? If so, how?*	*Needs to be defined*
How does this information guide strategic and tactical decision making?*	*Needs to be defined*

(*Continued*)

TABLE 1 (*Continued*)

Questions	Responses
Competition	
Who are the organization's competitors?	*Needs to be defined*
List the relevant data:	*Needs to be defined*
▪ Comparative market share of competitors	
▪ Volume of sales and revenues	
▪ Products/Services offered.	

Consulting organization's responses appear in italics. *Questions marked by an * are those that address managing the manager issues.

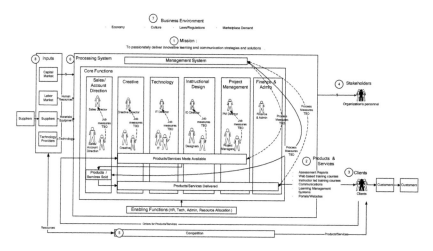

FIGURE 2 Consulting firm's total performance system.

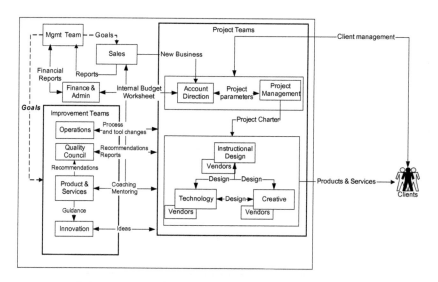

FIGURE 3 Consulting firm's functional relationship map.

TABLE 2 Organizational-Level Recommendations

System observations	Recommendations	
	Phase 1	Phase 2
1. Mission/Goals ■ Small private consulting firm formed in 1991 ■ Mission: To passionately deliver innovative learning and communication strategies and solutions ■ Organizational goals only cover revenue and sales and do not include strategic areas of product and service offerings, customer groups and competitive advantages	Define product and service offerings, consumers and competition measures and how to collect those measures (Note: more details are provided below)	After defining measures, define related process and job measures (see Processing System recommendations below)
2. Products & Services ■ Products and services are not tracked by type, which makes it difficult to (1) set strategic sales goals to target consumer groups by product type, (2) set groundwork for systematic competitive pricing, (3) Target areas for improvement in the organization (e.g., Are performance issues more likely in Web based training development or learning management systems, these require different processes) nm ■ Learning Management Systems are the only product with targeted sales goals ■ Current Product & Services Team initiatives include (1) building templates to standardize and improve the sales estimation process; (2) developing an e-newsletter to send to clients and prospects on innovative efforts within the organization; (3) developing and producing videos in-house	Gain agreement on how to define and measure products and services Develop and integrate a data collection process for products and services (See computer icons on detailed process map to integrate data collection process in existing process) Set expectations for the Quality Manager to oversee data collection process (see Performer Level analysis for details)	Evaluate how categorization is working and refine as needed Gain agreement of what constitutes a "non-conforming" product for external audit purposes Evaluate how the data management system is working and refine as needed

(Continued)

TABLE 2 (*Continued*)

System observations	Recommendations	
	Phase 1	Phase 2
3. Clients & Client Feedback		
▪ Organization continues to strive for a diversified client base, especially in past 5 years	Review Customer Satisfaction survey questions to ensure it is addressing the right questions and make refinements as needed	Evaluate how the revised customer satisfaction survey is working and refine as needed
▪ Number of new clients decreased in last two years		
▪ New clients require an upfront investment		
▪ Organization does not have unified definition of new and returning/multi-project clients which makes it difficult to assess client retention and client groups by product and service type	Gain agreement on revised Customer Satisfaction Survey	Set expectations for the Quality Manager to oversee the data collection process (see Performer Level analysis for details)
▪ Customers typically are corporate clients who deliver purchased solutions to next set of customers	Develop and integrate a data collection process for Customer feedback as part of the Project Close process (which needs to be developed and described more under "Processing System")	
▪ Customer satisfaction surveys are sent via email 30 days after project is closed and reviewed by CEO, who then passes the feedback on to the relevant project owner. No consistent system for what is done with feedback after that point.		
4. Stakeholders		
Organization has Employee Shareholder Ownership Plan (ESOP), but many employees are unaware of how system works	Conduct an ESOP training session to all company employees	Provide ESOP updates on a bi-annual basis to all employees
Employee performance and satisfaction needs to be monitored and managed regularly	Implement an internal customer satisfaction survey about systems, processes, tools, and training progress on an annual basis	Appoint a Quality Council representative to manage the internal customer feedback data collection process
		Integrate the internal customer survey as part of the performance review process

5. Competition

Organization has not identified competitors by market segment to identify threats and opportunities that would help target specific market bases in terms of product/service offerings, pricing, etc.	Develop process for conducting competitive research to determine trends, threats and opportunities	Appoint a Sales, Product & Services, or Innovation Team representative to do competition research

6. Processing System & Processing System Feedback

▪ Current management system has unclear roles and responsibilities for who reviews what data, what they are looking for, and decisions/actions to make based on data ▪ Data reviewed do not link critical business measures, critical process measures and critical job measures ▪ Goals are either missing, redundant or conflicting across the various teams the organization has put in place ▪ Sales is only process where measures are regularly measured and managed ▪ Management measures are limited to billable hours and project revenue	Define organizational measures that should be collected to cover product and service offerings, consumers, competition Revise Internal survey questions to better evaluate performance of team members and suppliers by product type Develop process to ensure data are being collected regularly	Develop and implement measurement system to collect baseline measures to further define organizational, process (made available, sold and delivered) and job level goals Appoint someone to manage the process and monitor data regularly (see Performer level analysis)
Due to timing of incoming work, resource allocation is difficult to manage with the appropriate staff that would be best suited for particular projects (i.e., availability, skills and interests aligned with type of project). Organization is currently working on developing the system to predict resources needs more readily.	n/a at current time	n/a at current time

7. Environment

Once consumer groups and products are clearly defined by organization, the marketplace and other relevant environmental variables should be analyzed to take into consideration of the impact of relevant variables in the system	n/a at current time	n/a at current time

8. Inputs

System to evaluate suppliers/vendors needs to be updated. Organization is currently working on analyzing print-production vendors.	n/a at current time	n/a at current time
HR and Products and Services team is continually maintaining and developing a talent pool.	n/a at current time	n/a at current time

Figure 3 shows the second way to view the processing system of the organization in a functional relationship map (M. E. Malott, 2003; Rummler & Brache, 1995). A functional relationship map is a useful tool to identify where goals, standards, and feedback loops should exist between supplier and customer (internal or external). This view provides a closer look into the processing system by identifying the input-output relationships between various functions (i.e., who produces what for whom). The dotted lines in Figure 3 illustrate where the consulting organization needed to focus their improvement efforts.

RECOMMENDATIONS

The recommendations based on the organizational-level TPS and Relationship Map analyses were formatted in such a way as to allow the management team of the consulting organization to assign roles and responsibilities to each improvement initiative. The recommendations focused on addressing core system issues before addressing issues that would be misguided otherwise (for example, setting strategic goals of improvement teams would be premature until a clear measurement system is defined and in place to determine where specific improvement is needed). Table 2 details the observations and recommendations we provided.

Purpose of a Process-Level Analysis

The next level of analysis involves understanding how work is done within the processing system of the organization. In the example above, strategic organizational goals could not be defined until baseline measures were established for products and services. Likewise, process measures could not be defined until those measurable business system goals were clarified. When information on how a particular process contributes to the organization's CBIs is missing, it is not recommended to continue a detailed process analysis until this information is provided since it may misguide an analyst's efforts. For example, the organization was spending time defining an innovation process, before they understood how customer satisfaction and competitive threats and opportunities were being addressed through their products and service offerings. The effort spent on figuring out the details around *how* to create those products and services was, therefore, potentially wasting time, human resources, and ultimately money because they were unable to direct change efforts in the areas that would result in the biggest positive impact. In short, the analyst must start by identifying desired results, then swiftly work backward to determine how to get those results. However, it is possible to begin a process analysis to gain tactical direction on how best to proceed with system improvement efforts, which is what was done in the current case study.

Desired business results can be achieved only through a well-planned and managed workflow, and to get there, critical process measures need to be viewed in relation to critical higher-level business measures they help achieve. If desired process results are not occurring, then the process can be broken down and specific tasks analyzed. Typically, the scale of analysis will vary depending on the complexity of the process. Viewing workflow *across* the organization is critical as it specifies the inputs and outputs that need to be measured and managed, from the beginning of a specified process to its end (i.e., when the product or service is delivered to consumers). If a work process is not effectively managed, performers may not have the right performance support, measures will be weak or unreliable, and management will spend their time focusing on unnecessary initiatives.

A process map is the tactical tool to make work manageable, since it reveals how work is actually done (e.g., who does what? what do they produce?). Process mapping shows a step-by-step diagram of how work flows across the various activities of the functional work group and the inputs and outputs of each step (see Rummler & Brache, 1995, and M. E. Malott, 2003, for descriptions of how to build cross-functional process maps). With this view, analysts can identify "disconnects" in the form of missing, redundant, or convoluted steps, standards, time, and resources involved to produce value-adding outputs. Techniques to gather this information may include interviews, observations, research, and focus groups. The process level of the BSAQ is therefore presented in the next section.

PROCESS-LEVEL ANALYSIS OF PRIVATE CONSULTING FIRM

The process-level question set (see Table 3) is the second portion of the BSAQ. In this level of analysis, we examined what was being done along the critical path of generating the consulting organization's products and services to its customers, from creating a sales plan to closing a project. In conjunction with the process-level question set, we used the *Process-Level Supplemental Tool* (shown partially in Table 4) to guide the collection of information needed for detailed process mapping. A series of interviews helped us understand the realities and barriers to successful execution of each task from the perspectives of those who performed them. An interview with several individuals representing each functional area in their work setting was helpful because they were able to show the outputs and how each task is performed. The information gathered was translated into a high-level process map, a detailed-level process map, and a disconnect analysis, shown next.

Figure 4 illustrates a high-level view of the existing processes (guidance, core, and enabling) used to achieve the organization's goals, which we learned from the organizational-level analysis and by answering the process-level question set. The ***italicized and bolded*** areas, as well the dotted

---

TABLE 3 Process-Level Question Set and Analysis

Questions	Responses
Mission	
Why does this process exist? What value does it add?	*This process exists to achieve the organization's mission: To passionately deliver innovative learning and communication strategies and solutions. The value added from this process is generating revenue by delivering the organization's products and services to keep the organization alive.*
Outputs	
What does each task in the process sequence produce?	*See Detailed Process Map Data Collection Tool and Process Map*
What is the final output of the process?	*Products and services delivered to client*
Receiving System	
Who receives the output of each task?	*See Detailed Process Map Data Collection Tool and Process Map*
Who receives the output(s) of the process overall?	*Clients and their customers*
External Feedback (Data)	
Does the process receive customer satisfaction data about quality, timeliness, cost, and customer service? How? (a process customer is the next person in the task sequence)	*Not consistently or clearly. Needs to be defined.*
Who is in charge of measuring external feedback?*	*Unclear. Needs to be defined.*
Does the process receive financial data to guide appropriate allocation of resources?	*No*
How is the information used to guide performance (related to customer satisfaction and financial performance)?*	*Unclear. Needs to be defined.*
Processing System	
When does the process start, where does it end?	*From creating a sales plan to closing a project*
Who is involved? Who does what? (i.e., What does the performer do with the input they receive to convert it to an output?)	*See Detailed Process Map Data Collection Tool and Process Map*
What are the biggest obstacles in the process?	*(1) Targeting the right product and service offerings to the right customers, (2) Balancing resources across several projects, (3) Planning and managing without clear goals/standards (see Disconnect Analysis for details)*
Inputs	
What resources, materials, equipment, and technology are used in the process?	*See Detailed Process Map Data Collection Tool and Process Map*
Which databases, operational systems and applications do the participants of the process use?	*Different functional areas use different operational systems and applications to generate their outputs (e.g., sales uses sales forecasting tools, project management uses Microsoft Project, finance uses Clients & Profits, etc)*

(Continued)

TABLE 3 (*Continued*)

Questions	Responses
What resources, materials, equipment, technology are missing, ineffective or unnecessary?	*Most financial and resource projection reports are manually created; there may be a way to reduce to simplify this resource with additional analyses (out of scope of current analysis)*
Internal Feedback (Data)	
Do standards exist for the task? Are they being met? (Quality, timeliness, quantity, cost)*	*Needs to be defined*
What is measured to know how well the process is working? What do you do with this information?*	*Needs to be defined*
Environment	
What environmental issues are occurring that are impacting the successful execution of the task?	*Unclear. Needs to be defined.*
How are these isssues being managed?*	*Unclear. Needs to be defined.*
Competition	
What organizational, process or performer issues are competing with the successful execution of the task? (i.e., task interference)	*Addressing the measurement issues above will help to determine how to better manage competing demands on functions and performers in the process.*

Note: Consulting organization's responses appear in italics. *Questions marked by an * are those that address managing the manager issues.

lines, refer to the improvement recommendations provided as a result of the analysis (both at the organizational level and at the process level).

The detailed process map generated by using the *Process-Level Supplemental Tool* is shown next (see Figure 5). The computer icons shown in the process map illustrate where and how data should be collected as part of the measurement system described in the recommendations below.

RECOMMENDATIONS

The *Process Disconnect Analysis* provided to the consulting organization is shown in Table 5. It includes tactical recommendations for improving specific areas within the process. The table includes a description of each disconnect identified, the impact of each disconnect on the overall organizational system, the measure of its impact, and a summary of possible improvements. The numbers referenced in the left column refer to the steps in the detailed process map.

Purpose of a Performer-Level Analysis

Most OBM researchers and practitioners tend to focus on individual performance as the target of their interventions (Hyten, 2009). The assumption is

TABLE 4 Process-Level Supplemental Tool

Task sequence/ steps	Activity (What is done?)	Output (What is produced?) Each output should be an input to the next task in the sequence	Measure (What do you count to know the output is meeting standard?)	Who Does It?	Who Receives It?
1	Sales plan created	Sales strategy	Goals vs. Actual prior year	President/ VP Sales	Sales
2	Leads identified	Leads	Number of leads	Sales	Sales
3	Intro call conducted	Introduction	Number of intro calls completed	Sales	Client
n/a	More information requested	Interested prospect	Number of requests	Client	Sales
4	Materials sent/ capabilities presentation conducted	Capabilities information	Number of presentations conducted	Project Management Team	Client
n/a	Proposal requested	Request for proposal/ quote	Number of requests	Client	Sales
5	New Business Alert and Project Worksheet sent	New Business Alert	Timeliness of New Business Alert	Sales	Product & Services Team Finance & Admin.

This represents a partial example from the consulting organization.

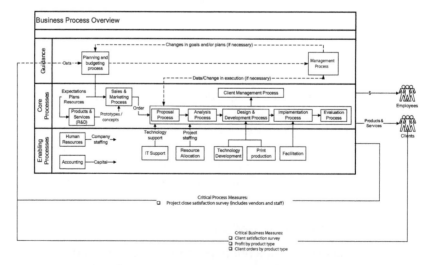

FIGURE 4 Overview of consulting firm's business process.

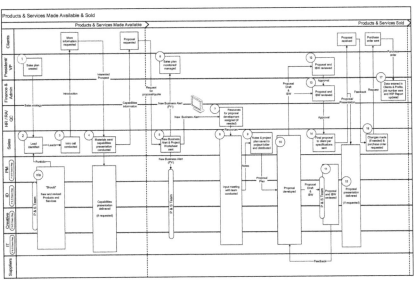

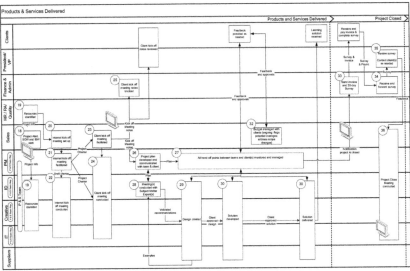

FIGURE 5 Consulting firm's detailed process map.

that organizational performance is a function of those individuals working in it. Performance, however, is not a unidirectional relation. Employees are only as good as the systems they are a part of (Deming, 1986). Since behavior is a function of its environment, it will not be maintained unless there are organizational contingencies in place to support it (i.e., reinforce it). BSA focuses on the organizational and process levels first so specific contingency support can be put in place for individuals to excel. Similarly, it is only through the performance of individual employees that well-defined processes and organizational systems can be optimized.

TABLE 5 Disconnect Analysis

Step #	Disconnect description	System impact	Measure	Possible improvements
n/a	Missing a portfolio management system for training sales team to talk about new and revising existing products and services	Products and services might not be competitive Missed sales opportunities	Number and type of customers by product type	Product & Services should measure and manage products and services to ensure that Sales team representatives can describe all product and service offerings Determine role of Innovation Team in this step
1	Sales plan goals not linked to products, services, or specific consumer targets	Missed sales opportunities	Number and type of customers by product type	Sales plan should include quantifiable goals by products and services and consumer targets
2	Process for identifying leads is not linked to products and services and specific consumer targets	Missed sales opportunities Cost of non-sales resulting activities	Number of capability presentations Number of sales by consumer group and product type	Leads should be identified based on products and services goals Competitive research process needs to be developed Sales should review data and ensure that product and services are directed toward appropriate consumer groups
9–10	Client info gathered by Sales is not a complete picture of performance improvement needs to write complete proposal	Proposed scope and budget are under priced Missed sales opportunities Clarify project expectations earlier	Number of changes to project scope after project start Profit/Loss	Equip Sales with a list of information (mini-needs analysis to obtain from client that will help proposal team analyze performance improvement needs
22	Transitions of team members from proposal phase to project start and changes in team members during project	Late handoffs Allowable hours exceeded Project team conflicts	Projects over budget Client satisfaction	Ensure that knowledge transfers from Instructional Designer and Creative resource who participated in proposal development to the Instructional Designer and Creative resource assigned to do the project
24, 28	Analysis process for gathering input for the design is inconsistent across designer and project	Inaccurate design Cost of extra design time	Number of revisions Client satisfaction	Formalize task analysis process; Include in client kick off agenda to schedule SME/ID meeting; include in project plan
34–36	Customer satisfaction survey feedback is not used in ways to effectively guide future project performance	Cost of repeated mistakes by consumer group and/or product type	Number of repeated mistakes by consumer group and/or product type	QC should review questions, ensure they're adding value, develop a roll up system to report on trends by product type
36	Post project debriefs are not occurring or not providing effective information to base improvement efforts	Innovation ideas lost Project quality and cost	Employee satisfaction Number of recurring problems on projects	Revise Project Close survey; Integrate data into Step Ahead meetings; Evaluate how system is working regularly

24

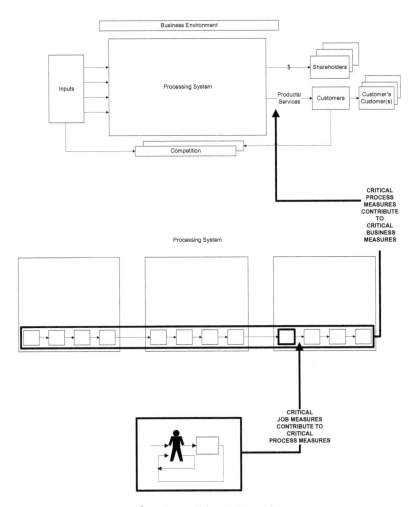

FIGURE 6 Linking all levels through measures.

To extend the analysis to the performer, managers look at critical job measures in context of critical process measures (which are in context of critical business measures). Figure 6 shows how individual performance systems contribute to the process they participate in, and how ultimately the organization, process, and performer levels are linked through critical business, process, and performer measures.

The performer level of analysis is described in context of the private consulting firm described in the previous sections. The data collected using this tool highlight the performance support necessary to design and sustain desired performance (see Table 6). Based on our process- and organizational-level

TABLE 6 Performer-Level Question Set and Analysis

Questions	Responses
Which performer(s) are we analyzing?	*Quality Manager*
Goal	
What is the performance goal?	*To ensure systems analysis recommendations are implemented, evaluated and managed*
Do this performance goal support process goals?	*Yes, this desired performance directly contributes to the processes of the Quality Council*
Outputs	
What does the performer produce?	*Plans and task specifications* *Performance support* *Quarterly updates to management team regarding system improvement results*
Receiving System	
Who receives the output(s) produced by the performer? What do they do with it?	*Individuals in the organization who perform specific tasks delegated by the Quality Manager* *Management team reviews updates and makes decisions about future actions and resources to devote toward specific initiatives*
External Feedback (Data)	
What information does the performer receive about his or her performance?*	*Management team approval*
Who provides performance feedback to the performer? How? *	*Management team*
Is performance feedback provided in relation to goals?*	*Yes*
Who is in charge of measuring and monitoring relevant critical job measures?*	*Management team*
How are critical job measures measured?*	*Quality Council reports goals met on regular basis*
How is information (critical job measures and critical process measures) used to guide performance? *	*If not meeting goals, corrective feedback will be provided*
How are deviations analyzed, causes determined and action taken? *	*If goals are not met, Management Team and Quality council Representative adjust schedule and plans as needed and works to removing any related obstacles*
Processing System	
What does the performer *DO* to achieve results?	*Plan and delegate tasks to various individuals in organization to complete initiatives* *Monitor progress of those initiatives and troubleshoot as needed* *Report on progress of those initiatives*
Does the performer have the necessary skills and knowledge to perform the job?*	*Yes*

(Continued)

TABLE 6 (*Continued*)

Questions	Responses
Inputs	
What resources are required to perform successfully (e.g., tools, equipment, information)	*Performance data, computer, Excel, PowerPoint, management calendar*
Do performance goals exist? If so, how are they communicated to the performer? By Who?*	*Yes, accountability and expectations should be set by the management team after the systems analysis review and monitored on a quarterly basis*
Are the job procedures and workflow logical?	*Yes, defined from the systems analysis report*
Internal Feedback (Data)	
Do performance standards exist?*	*No*
If yes, are standards linked to the job goals? Does performer know the desired output and performance standards?*	*Needs to be defined*
How are deviations analyzed, causes determined and action taken?*	*Quality Manager keeps an ongoing list to self manage and adjusts schedules and plans as needed to keep the initiatives moving forward despite interferences with original plan*
Environment	
What organizational issues impact performer's success?	*Other workload*
How are these issues being managed?*	*Resource allocation manager is aware and will try to keep at least 25% of the Quality Manager's time devoted toward this initiative*
Competition	
What issues are competing with the performer's success?	*Conflicting management priorities*
How are these issues being managed?*	*Quality Manager periodically attends various team meetings to stay aware of current priorities of teams and individuals and keep improvement initiatives on the forefront and integrate new challenges to address as needed*
Are there competing consequences? What are they? How will they be removed?*	*Quality Manager has other job responsibilities result in more immediate consequences. By having the Quarterly reports to management team about progress toward goals will help to keep these competing consequences from interfering with effective performance.*

Note: Consulting organization's responses appear in italics. *Questions marked by an * are those that address managing the manager issues.

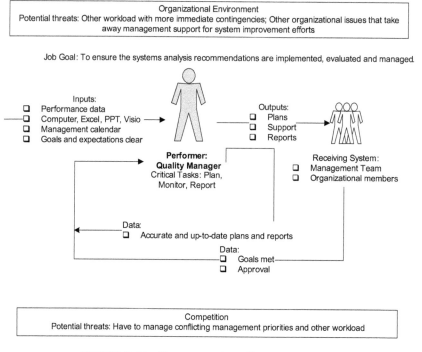

Organizational Environment
Potential threats: Other workload with more immediate contingencies; Other organizational issues that take away management support for system improvement efforts

Job Goal: To ensure the systems analysis recommendations are implemented, evaluated and managed.

Inputs:
❑ Performance data
❑ Computer, Excel, PPT, Visio
❑ Management calendar
❑ Goals and expectations clear

Outputs:
❑ Plans
❑ Support
❑ Reports

Performer:
Quality Manager
Critical Tasks: Plan, Monitor, Report

Receiving System:
❑ Management Team
❑ Organizational members

Data:
❑ Accurate and up-to-date plans and reports

Data:
❑ Goals met
❑ Approval

Competition
Potential threats: Have to manage conflicting management priorities and other workload

FIGURE 7 Quality manager's performance system.

analyses, we determined the individual whose performance was most critical to plan and manage was the consulting organization's Quality Manager, who would ultimately be responsible for ensuring the systems analysis recommendations were implemented, evaluated, and managed. Figure 7 illustrates the Quality Manager's performance system components that need to be planned and managed by the next level manager in order to ensure the Quality Manager achieves desired results. For example, if the Quality Manager does not produce results, then it is possible to see which part of the system is in need of repair.

RECOMMENDATIONS

The aim of our performer-level recommendations was to specify the performance support needed by the individual who was charged with managing the changes based on the BSA. To be successful, the manager needs to ensure change efforts are implemented and evaluated so continuous improvement efforts can be defined as the organization evolves in the changing marketplace. Since such activities would involve managing multiple people and projects, it was a difficult undertaking due to the ebb and flow of client demands that would impact this performer's dual role of an internal and external consultant. Recommendations included reporting results regularly to the president (monthly), management team (quarterly), and an external auditor (yearly). The Quality Manager's contingencies should be centered on these activities.

DISCUSSION

The BSAQ should not be viewed as rigid. It should be adapted to fit the needs of the analyst and the organization where it is used. The guided question sets were designed to help the analyst understand (a) relevant variables in an organization that impact performance; (b) the extent to which those variables are currently impacting performance positively or negatively; and (c) that the duration and intensity of the analysis will vary based on complexity of the process and access to information in the organization. We recommend starting at the organization level and working down through the process and performer levels, but the BSAQ is designed with flexibility to allow the analyst to start at any level. Many performance analysis models exist but are not typically constructed in the form of guided questions to facilitate each step of the analysis in context of the TPS. By becoming fluent in asking the right questions, even the beginner analyst will be able to accurately pinpoint where performance problems exist.

It is important to note that although several studies have used a Behavioral Systems Analysis approach similar to the one described in this article (e.g., Huberman & O'Brien, 1999; Sulzer-Azaroff, Loafman, Merante, & Hlavacek, 1990; Sulzer-Azaroff, Pollack, & Fleming, 1992; Williams & Cummings, 2001; Williams, Di Vittorio, & Hausherr, 2002) it has never been clear how the use of BSA impacted the choice of intervention and the results obtained. In addition, the lack of information on how BSA was implemented suggests that procedures may have differed across studies. The BSAQ presented here serves as the first attempt to standardize this type of analysis. The BSAQ is yet to be validated; we hope our systematic approach will inspire future research that will lead to effective application.

REFERENCES

Arco, L. (1993). Improving program outcome with process-based feedback. *Journal of Organizational Behavior Management, 13*(1), 85–112.

Austin, J. (2000). Performance analysis and performance diagnostics. In J. Austin & J. E. Carr (Eds.), *Handbook of applied behavior analysis* (pp. 321–349). Reno, NV: Context Press.

Brethower, D. M. (1982). The total performance system. In R. M. O'Brien, A. M. Dickinson, & M. P. Rosow (Eds.), *Industrial behavior modification: A management handbook* (pp. 350–369). New York: Pergamon Press.

Brethower, D. M. (2000). A systematic view of enterprise: Adding value to performance. *Journal of Organizational Behavior Management, 20*(3/4), 165–190.

Brethower, D. M. (2001). Managing a person as a system. In L. J. Hayes, J. Austin, R. Houmanfar, & M. C. Clayton (Eds.), *Organizational change* (pp. 89–105). Reno, NV: Context Press.

Brethower, D. M. (2002). *Behavioral systems analysis: Fundamental concepts and cutting edge applications.* Retrieved February 28, 2003, from http://www.behavior.org/performancemgmt.

Brethower, D. M., & Dams, P. C. (1999). Systems thinking (and systems doing). *Performance Improvement, 38*(1), 37–52.

Brown, P. L. (2000). Communicating the benefits of the behavioral approach to the business community. *Journal of Organizational Behavior Management, 20*(3/4), 59–72.

Daniels, A. C. (2009). *Oops! 13 management practices that waste time and money (and what to do instead).* Atlanta, GA: Performance Management Publications.

Daniels, A. C., & Daniels, J. E. (2004). *Performance management: Changing behavior that drives organizational effectiveness.* Atlanta, GA: Performance Management Publications.

Deming, W. E. (1986). Out of the crisis. Cambridge, MA: Massachusetts Institute of Technology Center for Advanced Engineering Study.

Gilbert, T. F. (1996). *Human competence: Engineering worthy performance.* Amherst, MA: HRD Press, Inc.

Glenn, S. S. (1988). Contingencies and metacontingencies: Toward a synthesis of behavior analysis and cultural materialism. *The Behavior Analyst, 11*(2), 161–179.

Huberman, W. L., & O'Brien, R. M. (1999). Improving therapist and patient performance in chronic psychiatric group homes through goal-setting, feedback, and positive reinforcement. *Journal of Organizational Behavior Management, 19*(1), 13–36.

Hyten, C. (in press). Strengthening the focus on business results: The need for systems approaches in OBM. *Journal of Organizational Behavior Management.*

Malott, M. E. (2003). *Paradox of organizational change.* Reno, NV: Context Press.

Malott, R. W. (1974). A behavioral systems approach to the design of human services. In D. Harshbarger & R. F. Maley (Eds.), *Behavior analysis and systems analysis: An integrative approach to mental health programs.* Kalamazoo, MI: Behaviordelia.

McElgunn, J. (2007, June). Seize the day! *Profit, 26*(3), 33, 35–38, 40. Retrieved February 25, 2008, from ABI/INFORM Global database. (Document ID: 1292777501).

McGee, H. M. (2007). An introduction to behavioral systems analysis for OBMers and non-OBMers alike. *OBM Network Newsletter, 21*(2).

Redmon, W. K. (1991). Pinpointing the technological fault in applied behavior analysis. *Journal of Applied Behavior Analysis, 14*, 441–444.

Redmon, W. K., & Mason, M. A. (2001). Organizational culture and behavioral systems analysis. In C. M. Johnson, W. K. Redmon, & T. C. Mawhinney (Eds.), *Handbook of organizational performance: Behavior analysis and management* (pp. 437–456). Binghamton, NY: The Haworth Press.

Redmon, W. K., & Wilk, L. A. (1991). Organizational behavior analysis in the United States: Public sector organizations. In P. A. Lamal (Ed.), *Behavior analysis of societies and cultural practices* (pp. 107–123). New York: Hemisphere Publishing Co.

Rummler, G. A. (2001). Performance logic: The organization performance Rosetta stone. In L. J. Hayes, J. Austin, R. Houmanfar, & M. C. Clayton (Eds.), *Organizational change* (pp. 111–132). Reno, NV: Context Press.

Rummler, G. A. (2004). *Serious performance consulting according to Rummler*. Silver Spring, MD: International Society for Performance Improvement.

Rummler, G. A. (2008). *Rummler process methodology: Reference manual*. Tucson, AZ: Performance Design Lab.

Rummler, G. A., & Brache, A. P. (1995). *Improving performance: How to manage the white space on the organization chart* (2nd ed.). San Francisco: Jossey-Bass.

Rummler, G. A., Ramais, A. J., & Rummler, R. A. (2006, November). Potential pitfalls on the road to a PMO (Part 1). *BPTrends, 4*(10). Retrieved February 10, 2007, from http://www.bptrends.com/resources_publications.cfm?publicationtypeID=DFFB9D1C-1031-D522-3AAF1211DDD4AD95.

Rummler, G. A., Ramais, A. J., & Rummler, R. A. (2006, December). Potential pitfalls on the road to a PMO (Part 2). *BPTrends, 4*(11). Retrieved February 10, 2007, from http://www.bptrends.com/resources_publications.cfm?publicationtypeID=DFFB9D1C-1031-D522-3AAF1211DDD4AD95.

Sigurdsson, S. O., & Austin, J. (2006). Institutionalization and response maintenance in organizational behavior management. *Journal of Organizational Behavior Management, 26*(4), 41–77.

Skinner, B. F. (1953). Science and human behavior. New York: Macmillan Co.

Sulzer-Azaroff, B. (2000). Of eagles and worms: Changing behavior in a complex world. *Journal of Organizational Behavior Management, 20*(3/4), 139–163.

Sulzer-Azaroff, B., Loafman, B., Merante, R. J., & Hlavacek, A. C. (1990). Improving occupational safety in a large industrial plant: A systematic replication. *Journal of Organizational Behavior Management, 11*(1), 99–120.

Sulzer-Azaroff, B., Pollack, M. J., & Fleming, R. K. (1992). Organizational behavior management within structural and cultural constraints: An example from the human service sector. *Journal of Organizational Behavior Management, 12*(2), 117–137.

Williams, W. L., & Cummings, A. R. (2001). Service review: Increasing consumer benefits by linking service outcome data to direct-care staff service delivery and decision-making. In L. J. Hayes, J. Austin, R. Houmanfar, & M. C. Clayton (Eds.), *Organizational change* (pp. 277–292). Reno, NV: Context Press.

Williams, W. L., Di Vittorio, T., & Hausherr, L. (2002). A description and extension of a human services management model. *Journal of Organizational Behavior Management, 22*(1), 47–71.

Iterative Processes and Reciprocal Controlling Relationships in a Systemic Intervention

JON E. KRAPFL

College of William & Mary, Williamsburg, Virginia, USA

JOHN COOKE

London Group, Williamsburg, Virginia, USA

TIMOTHY SULLIVAN and WILLIAM COGAR

Mariners' Museum, Newport News, Virginia, USA

This account describes the total reengineering of an organization with the attendant changes to the culture, the nature of the work, the rethinking of the organizational purpose, and the identification of a new customer base and new concepts of how the organization will reach it. The case is presented not as scientific research but as a case of behavioral engineering. A behavior theory framework is used to account for the behavior of both the interveners and those intervened upon, with all parties serving at different times in each of these roles.

ITERATIVE PROCESSES AND RECIPROCAL CONTROLLING RELATIONSHIPS IN A SYSTEMIC INTERVENTION

The following account is a description of a total systems intervention illustrating a variety of features one often confronts in a behavioral systems intervention. While this poses serious difficulties for staying within the framework of traditional operant approaches, it is entirely consistent with

The authors are indebted to the entire staff of the Mariners' Museum. We would especially like to thank members of the President's Council for their extensive participation and support.

Skinner's (1961) thinking about reciprocal controlling relations between experimenter and subject, and Sidman's (1960) distinction between experimentation and behavioral engineering in terms of control of variability.

Behavior analysts have turned to operant methodology whenever possible, but the findings of the basic science reveal little about what the relevant stimuli are or how they are to be identified in the organizational world, and, unless we know the relevant stimuli, both discriminating and reinforcing, we are functioning in a tautological world where the handles of control remain elusive. To find these stimuli, we must turn to behavior theory to provide us the frame of reference for both investigation and action. A rationale for the approach taken in this paper follows.

A case can be made that two of the most critical elements of behavior theory are, first, that behavior is continuous and therefore it is appropriate to study the individual organism in time, and second, that, as behaving organisms, the behavior of both experimenter and experimentee is subject to the laws of behavior. Therefore, when experimenter and experimentee interact, the concept of reciprocal controlling relations can apply.

The study of the individual organism in time (Skinner, 1972), may seem intuitively obvious to the lay observer, but to psychologists the framework of methodological behaviorism has been the modal method of investigation. This method is generally conceived as one in which two or more groups are treated with different independent variables to determine whether the treatment produces outcomes that are different in a statistically significant way. These strongly contrasting investigative methodologies lead one in quite different directions, both theoretically and methodologically. The point here is not about the superiority of one approach over another, but only to suggest that the operant approach seems to lend itself better to extension into the applied realm than does the methodological approach. This might seem obvious for a clinical intervention with a patient, but the case to be made here is that larger interventions involving multiple behavers across time can be studied in the same way, though the complexity is increased as a function of the mutually affecting relations that exist across both observed and observer.

Nowhere is this extension more in evidence than in the concept of reciprocally controlling relations. As Skinner so clearly articulated (Skinner, 1972), the behavior that most comes under control in the laboratory is that of the experimenter. Though publicly he never completely acknowledged it, Skinner described a universe in which causation could not be viewed as simply unidirectional, and both the experimental organism and the experimenting organism gain a mutual or reciprocating kind of control as they interact. This is a world view that was articulated by the post-Einsteinian philosophers such as Bertrand Russell (Russell, 1927), who described science as a process in which the investigator interacts with the subject matter, and not only influences behavior but is influenced by it. Causation, therefore, can no longer be viewed as linear but must be viewed as a reciprocally controlling relation in which the cause to be identified depends upon the observer's point of view. The identification of the cause in question, therefore, reflects the focus of the observer. It follows then, that the traditional concept of objective observer is viewed as myth or, at a minimum, as an incomplete account of controlling relations.

Sidman (1960) goes on to distinguish between the experimental analysis of behavior and behavioral engineering (applied behavior analysis), primarily on the basis of the extent of environmental control. In the experiment, extraneous variables are eliminated or otherwise accounted for. In applied behavior analysis, variability is not under such rigid control. Thus, in a "real world" intervention, these extraneous variables may be what affect the behavior of both the investigator and those investigated. In such an environment, the articulation required is one that describes the controlling relations and controlling reciprocal relations as they continue to evolve. The study described below is one example where the controlling environments evolved dramatically, and the investigators very often had to react to multiple changing environments.

One final aspect of behavior theory is required to set the basis for this investigation. When behavioral studies are carried out in organizations, behaviorists view the organizations as cultures (Krapfl, 2003), and systems analysis is added to behavior analysis to support the investigation. Cultures are systems of behavioral practices that evolve by selection. These organizational cultures function within a larger cultural context and have subcultures nested within them. Organizational survival depends upon selection by the larger culture. When viewed in this way, the investigator takes a view across multiple levels and varieties of what might be labeled controlling variables that are affecting the performance of the organizational culture.

This is the world of the systems intervener, a world in which the behaviorist not only observes but enters and becomes a part of it. As the systems intervener and the system interact, their actions become ever more mutually controlling. When that world is changing rapidly, or when that world is affected by a larger universe of which it is a part, both analyst and system engage in a dance in which each of their steps change as their mutually derived relationships emerge.

Turning now to business concepts, there are several that played an important role in this intervention. The first, theory of the case, specifies the organization's fundamental understanding of its relationship with each of its constituencies: owners, employees, customers, suppliers, etc. One of these relationships, the value proposition, specifies the relationship between organization and customer in terms of what will be provided to the customer and what is taken in return. An additional concept, business strategy, is a specification of the way the organization plans to secure its survival and well-being by positioning itself among its customers, competitors, and other internal and external constituencies and environments. When the value proposition is no longer valid, the organization must move to a "sea change" strategy, which entails a fundamentally new way of positioning the organization and its value offerings among its competitors and with its customers. In this study, not only the strategy had to change, but the value proposition and the theory of the case of the business.

One final preliminary point needs to be made. The descriptions of the intervention that follow are in narrative form and not specified in specific measurement terms. Nevertheless, numbers were used in the study, especially financial numbers related to both projected and actual profit-and-loss (P&L) figures such as revenue and expense and balance sheet numbers such as investment costs and asset valuations. However, in this instance the museum under study is a privately held foundation and these numbers are proprietary. The authors had a choice between either disclosing the numbers and not naming the specific museum in question or withholding the numbers and identifying the museum. Since the museum is easily recognizable, at least by museum professionals, the first alternative was not deemed feasible. In most instances in the study, however, quantified evaluations and projections formed the basis for decisions made on the intervention. Having laid the foundations for this study, it is now possible to proceed to a description of the investigation itself.

Background

The Mariners' Museum in Newport News, Virginia, is one of the finest maritime/naval museums in the world, designated by Congress in 1998 as America's National Maritime Museum. The museum is known not only for its extensive general collection but for its outstanding library holdings of archives, manuscripts, and rare books. It is the most extensive collection of such maritime materials in North America. The museum also serves as the repository for recovered artifacts of the USS *Monitor*, the ship responsible for the revolutionary change from wood to steel hulls, first for war, and then, finally, for all ships. As part of the USS Monitor Center, a world-class conservation facility was built.

The museum was founded in 1930 by Archer Huntington, who placed the museum in the Hampton Roads area of Virginia because of the region's long (and continuing) relationship with the sea and specifically with Newport News because of its position as the major shipbuilding center in the country.

Huntington not only fully funded the museum's collections and buildings, but also a magnificent park in which it is housed. He also provided an endowment to fund the operations of the museum on an ongoing basis.

In 1987 the National Oceanic and Atmospheric Administration (NOAA) named the Mariners' Museum as the recipient of recovered items from the USS *Monitor*. In view of the historical significance of the *Monitor* and its famous battle with the ironclad CSS *Virginia*, the Mariners' Museum undertook a study to determine likely public interest in a major exhibition on the ship. Based on consulting studies that indicated a likely fourfold increase in attendance, the museum decided to add an entire wing to its facilities in order to show off the newly recovered treasures. A funding campaign was undertaken to raise $30 million, and the new wing was built.

In early 2006, the president of the Mariners', a museum professional who formerly led the Museum of Modern Art in New York, decided to retire. The board, in view of the new investments and additional operating costs, decided to replace the president with a leader with a strong background in the not-for-profit arena, but also with some business acumen and leadership skills.

In the fall of 2006, the board selected Tim Sullivan, the recently retired president of the College of William & Mary, as its new president. Tim knew little about museums and wanted to find a way to come quickly to grips with the nature of the task he faced. Aware of an organization study of the business school at the College of William & Mary by the first and second authors of this paper, he requested that we all join together to do a quick study of the museum and its staff for purposes of identifying the strengths and weaknesses of both processes and players.

This study began in January of 2007, only a few weeks after Tim Sullivan assumed his new position.

The Unfolding Intervention

As is the case with many systems interventions, both the objectives and the methods for study and intervention changed often as new information about the system emerged. For the sake of clarity, the processes and conclusions will be described in phases, though the actual processes often crossed over from one phase to another.

PHASE 1: DISCOVERY

Setting & Plan

At the inception of Phase 1, none of the authors had any knowledge of the Mariners' Museum or of museums in general beyond that of being museum visitors. Therefore, the objective of Phase 1 was to learn about the people, the organizational processes, and the culture of the organization. This was intended to provide the new president a level of familiarity with the organization in order to be immediately more effective in directing ongoing operations.

Method

The method used to become familiar with the organization was that of individual interviews. These interviews were conducted by the author consultants with each executive, manager, director, and principal player in the organization. These interviews were to be followed by interviews with all full-time employees in the organization.

Results

Some very clear patterns emerged early in the process. As a result, the interviewing process was truncated, and the organization was moved to Phase 2. The main findings of Phase 1 were as follows:

1. With a few notable exceptions, the professional staff members were well established in their respective fields and strongly committed to the museum.
2. The various operating units of the organization seemed to prefer to operate as independently as possible in an enterprise that, by its nature, calls for very close coordination.
3. There was relatively little sharing of information across functions. As a result, unit heads were unaware of the aggregate of the changing set of economic factors affecting the future of the museum.
4. The museum's leadership was most focused on the traditional curatorial and conservation functions, with only limited attention to matters of finance, marketing, or customer satisfaction. These latter functions were, at the same time, taking on increasing importance to the institution.
5. Although each function had its own objectives, there was no comprehensive plan. The organization appeared not so much rudderless as multiruddered with an attendant high level of conflict and lack of efficiency.
6. There was little relationship and very little shared perspective between the Board of Trustees, the executive director, and the staff. Each had moved, essentially, in their own respective directions, assuming that they were aligned with the others in some instances and deliberately deviating from the others in a few instances.
7. In its enthusiasm to implement the new *Monitor* exhibit and conservation facilities, many aspects of the legacy museum, i.e., those traditional parts of the museum existing before the Monitor Center, were receiving little attention. The postponement of such improvements came home to roost as the projected level of *Monitor* visitation failed to materialize.
8. The lack of attention to customer satisfaction and the deteriorating state of the museum, in part, reflected the fact that it had historically been able to maintain operations at the prevailing level of attendance given the income flow from the endowment. With rapidly rising costs, the modest returns on the endowment could no longer provide a secure financial cushion.
9. The staff was not at all well informed about the functioning of the overall organization. The only financial information they had was that budgets

were tight. The staff feared the opening of the new Monitor Center wing. Much of this was related to a fear of the unknown and to a sense of uncertainty about the prospects for a new exhibition that would involve considerably increased costs, and, for the first time, require significant increases in visitor-related revenues. No one seemed to know who was responsible for making sure that any of this happened.

When these early findings were reported to the new president, three things immediately became clear. First, there was no one in the organization who had full knowledge of the potential impact of the planned major changes occurring with the opening of the new Monitor Center. That meant it was at least possible that the organization was at risk in its new and bold venture with the Monitor Center, an undertaking that inherently involved significant expense increases and depended heavily upon increased attendance.

Second, there was a leadership vacuum. The typical role of a CEO to maintain a sense of continuity and focus between the museum's board and its employees and managers was essentially absent.

Third, there had been obvious attempts to keep the Board of Trustees from knowing much about ongoing operations. The board had insisted that the museum make expenses fit within the framework of revenues provided. This had often resulted in a short-term focus and suboptimization, such as a failure to maintain facilities, collections storage, and permanent exhibitions at a proper standard. The facilities had deteriorated to the point where some of the collection was clearly in peril.

The organization's operations and culture were operating in a manner totally foreign to the open, collaborative team orientation of the new president. Something would need to be done to bring the new president and the organization together.

PHASE 2: FIRST INTERVENTION AND CONTINUED DISCOVERY

Setting and Plan

The most disturbing feature uncovered in Phase 1 was that no one had been in overall charge. As a consequence, a museum with an internal focus and long and hidebound traditions was heading toward a future that entailed major new efforts and significant increases in expenses while also requiring significant increases in attendance and the revenue associated with that attendance. This portended danger since the organization had been maintaining its balanced budget by deferring costs for major maintenance functions for a long time. A second important discovery was that the various staff groups were isolated from one another, and no one was responsible for seeing that all the pieces came together. Another important point was that the new president did not want to run an organization characterized by lack of information and silo functioning.

So the first intervention would need to: (a) begin a process of culture change to get all of the staff fully informed on the state of the museum; (b) get staff working together in a collaborative way; and (c) create an environment in which thought and work contributions at any level would surface and have a chance for adoption.

Method

An offsite retreat for the top 25 museum managers was the method chosen for the first step of this intervention. Board members were also invited as observers but not as participants, and two did attend parts of the retreat.

The offsite retreat began with a variety of presentations that covered what was then known about the current and immediate future state of the museum, including expected changes in operations, budgets, expected revenues, and anticipated expenses for the current year, and projections of each of these over the next 5 years. The attendees were then introduced to brainstorming and force/field analysis, and managers were then organized into 5 separate teams. Each team was composed of members from different departments so that perspectives would broaden beyond silos, and managers would begin to work with one another.

The first team session was a brainstorming one in order to identify the most serious issues facing the museum. The results were reported in general session. A second brainstorming session was then held to identify proposed solutions to what were considered the most significant issues.

After the proposed solutions were reviewed and prioritized, the breakout groups again assembled to do a force/field analysis in which each team identified factors that would support successful implementation of the proposed solutions as well as factors that would impede them.

The president closed the session by congratulating everyone on a job well done. He pointed out that an open display of information with staff responding in a cooperative manner that had characterized this session was typical of the manner in which he expected the organization to function in the future.

The second step in Phase 2 was the holding of general sessions with all employees of the organization. These sessions were run by the president and consisted of informing staff of the overall operational and financial performance of the museum and a review of what had been done in the offsite retreat to identify problems and suggest solutions.

In the third step in Phase 2, the president appointed new interdisciplinary committees (see Table 1) composed of managers and nonmanagers to take the work from the retreat and carry it forward into more detailed analysis and into the design of actual steps for implementation. Each of these working groups was assigned a major initiative. In this step, the staff of the entire museum began working across discipline boundaries. The groups met weekly or more often to detail the plans and to devise the implementation steps.

TABLE 1 The Assigned Committees and their Function

Committee	Role
Mission/Vision	To update the specification of the overall museum direction
Marketing Blitz	To design near-term ways to market the museum
Web Utilization & Development	To identify Web uses for exposure and revenue
Exhibitions & Programs	To plan next three years of exhibitions
Entrepreneurial Ventures	To identify revenue potential of museum holdings
Partnering	To explore possible joint ventures
Facilities	To design models for evaluating facilities and ways to cut costs
Land Development	To explore potential revenue-generating projects
Financial Issues	To explore financial information and make better projections
Market Research	To more sharply identify existing customers and find new ones
Decision Making & Communications	To explore cross-disciplinary synergies

Results

The results of the three-step intervention in the second phase were immediate and profound. They consisted of the discovery of new information for everyone and a dramatic cultural shift in the organization. The major results of the effort are identified below, first in terms of what was learned by all, and second in terms of organizational changes and results.

What was Learned

1. The financial situation of the museum was untenable. It was operating at a level whereby all revenues projected on an annual basis would cover 85% of expenses or less. The economic threat was serious enough to become everyone's primary priority.
2. The larger cultural environment in which all history museums functioned was changing dramatically. Attendance at all history museums was on an inexorable downward trend.
3. In view of the rapidly changing external environment, the anticipated quadrupling of attendance revenues at the new Monitor Center would likely not be fulfilled, making the financial situation even more serious.
4. There was no way to cut expenses to a point where revenues would equal expenses without shutting down the museum or allowing the museum to become a mere shadow of its current operation.
5. The museum's world-class library was not only underutilized, but was in danger of serious deterioration owing to outdated and less-than-optimal

environmental conditions. Manuscripts, documents, and photographs were stored in cardboard boxes for lack of space, and the air-handling system was in such serious condition that it posed a water damage threat to library holdings. The half million dollars planned for upgrading the HVAC system was a "Band-aid" that would simply buy time for a deteriorating physical plant. The $10–15 million that would be required for a new library was not feasible in the foreseeable future.

A number of recommendations were made to bring about rapid change in the museum. These recommendations included generating revenues by leveraging existing museum and library holdings, using the Web to reach out to schools with educational programs, partnering with other organizations such as Christopher Newport University and the National Oceanic & Atmospheric Administration, examining all operations for operational efficiency, reviewing the physical plant for possible consolidation, and leveraging the extensive property holdings.

What Changed

1. The environment of fear was nearly eliminated. Interestingly, staff exhibited less fear, even while learning that the organization was in serious financial trouble. Perhaps this was because they now knew what had previously been suspected, and fear was alleviated by involvement in addressing the problems.
2. The staff rallied around the new CEO. They responded to a leader who was strong in his leadership yet interested in what they thought about turning the organization around.
3. Almost immediately the staff engaged in more collaborative efforts, and these began to produce significant opportunities for change.
4. The staff, individually and as a group, began to exhibit more customer focus. Rather than looking internally, they started focusing on identifying their customer base and finding out what their customer base wanted.
5. It became clear that the previously contemplated changes to facilities, programs, and exhibitions would have to be delayed or eliminated until the organization was put on a firmer financial footing.

At this point in the intervention three things happened that were not directly a result of the intervention. The first was that two senior managers, neither of whom was seen as a team player, were eliminated.

Second, a new manager was appointed to become, in effect, the number two person in the organization. He began to work directly with the other three authors to guide the process of rethinking the fundamental value proposition of the institution.

Third, the new Monitor Center opened to critical acclaim but to attendance and related revenues considerably below expectations, making the
financial issues even more serious. It was determined, at this point, that
continued operation at existing staff levels was untenable. All expenses considered nonessential were eliminated from the budget.

PHASE 3: FIRST BOARD INTERVENTION

Setting & Plan

Upon assuming his position, the new president had indicated to the Board
of Trustees that he would (a) endeavor to make an assessment of the organization and then (b) design a strategy for going forward, which he would
bring to the board for consideration. Very early in the analysis phase it
became clear that the board had not been well informed about what was
happening in the museum, partly because no one in the museum had a
good overall sense of what was happening, and partly because there had
been established an unwritten ethic that the board was not to be informed
about many of the operational and financial issues the museum was facing.
The dire circumstances in which the museum now functioned, however,
required that the board be informed about what had been learned in the
first two phases of the intervention.

The overall intervention was now in its 5th month, and the situation
analysis had been essentially completed. It had become clear that the
museum, though financially well endowed and staffed, was in serious financial
trouble that would likely not be resolved by the opening of the new Monitor
Center. In fact, if the Center's attendance figures did not reach projections,
the overall situation would become even more critical.

Furthermore, there had been significant changes in internal operations and culture of the organization. Up to this point, the museum's
Board of Trustees had had little involvement in the process, and they had
not been informed about the untenable financial position of the museum
going forward.

Method

A special meeting of the Board of Trustees was called. Board members
traveled from distant parts of the country, even from as far away as the
UK. A special meeting, therefore, was not a minor event. The meeting
had two major components. The first component was a series of presentations by the president and others about the state (financial and otherwise) of the museum, the untenable nature of the strategic plan that
already existed, the potential further deterioration of that position
depending on attendance at the new Monitor Center, and a review of the

changes that had already been introduced in the organization. This was followed by a presentation of the planned steps to handle the immediate crisis in the museum and the planned effort to bring about changes in the museum over the longer term. The president then asked the board for agreement on the findings and agreement to support the proposed plan of action.

The second major component of the day was a review and questioning process by the board, followed by the formation of a consensus board view.

Results

Though concerned to learn that the museum was at considerably more risk than previously known, the board expressed confidence in the process of analysis and the interventions that had already been implemented. As a result, it shared the same view of the museum that the president and staff held. Now the principal constituencies of the organization, staff, director, and board had become aligned. The board had become a partner in the process of change.

PHASE 4: SECOND ORGANIZATIONAL INTERVENTION, A NEW THEORY OF THE CASE, AND A NEW VALUE PROPOSITION

Setting & Plan

Although the museum was now operating much more efficiently and the level of cooperation had increased markedly, and despite the fact that the full staff had begun to engage enthusiastically in efforts to improve efficiency and increase customer focus, two additional pieces of information emerged that were an omen of serious trouble on the horizon.

First, one outcome of the offsite retreat was a recognition that the museum lacked information about the people who visit history museums and the general environment in which history museums functioned. Several senior staff undertook an analysis of that external environment, and the results were not encouraging. History museums have begun to see a significant decline in attendance over the past decade. The reasons for this dropoff are not known, but it was clear that a variety of changes tried in other history museums had not substantially changed attendance. The trend was clear and strong, and even major changes in other museums' approach to exhibition and display had only a marginal effect.

The second bit of evidence came from the attendance figures for the new Monitor Center. This $30 million venture was a purposely built state-of-the-art museum exhibition about one of the most famous and iconic ships in American history, studied by virtually every child schooled in the United

States. Yet early indications were that the Monitor Center attendance and sales figures were going to be far below expectations. Visitor response to the center was uniformly very positive. Articles in local and regional newspapers and reviews in the media were uniformly glowing and complimentary. Yet there was only an approximate doubling of attendance compared to prior years. This contrasted with the predictions prepared by expert professionals engaged specifically for the purpose that called for a quadrupling of attendance.

Everyone agreed that the Monitor Center was at the forefront of museum exhibition design, and nothing of any significance could be identified that should have been done differently. These two bits of information could mean only one thing. No matter what the museum spent, and no matter how good the exhibition or programs connected with it might be, it would not be enough to make the existing museum model financially viable. The theory of the case of the museum was moribund. What was called for now was fundamental change Whereas the work up to that point had been on improving existing operations, the work now would be the formulation of a fundamentally new theory of the case, a new value proposition, and a "sea change" strategy. In addition, a thorough review of each staff position was conducted, and all positions not considered essential to the future of the museum were eliminated through a reduction in staff.

Method

A president's council of 11 individuals, including the authors, was formed to engage in a process to identify a financially viable model of museum operation that would still support the basic purposes of the museum. The council met once a week to identify and review alternatives. This group took responsibility for oversight of the committees that had been organized to develop the work of the offsite retreat. These committees were reorganized. The Marketing Blitz Committee, the Financial Issues Committee, and the Marketing Committee were disbanded. Other committees were reconfigured and redirected. The committees and the president's council interacted much more frequently, and the council assumed responsibility for focusing and redirecting the entire effort. The committees were instructed to place increasing emphasis on new and "out of the box" thinking with respect to the projects they were working on. They were also instructed to think in terms of cost benefit and cost/return for each of their formal recommendations. Each week one of the committees would present a progress report that would be evaluated by the president's council. The council would then endorse, and often modify, the focus of each planning committee, placing significant emphasis on the likely cost and return of each of the presented alternatives. What was actually happening was a searching and hypothesis-testing process in a variety of areas to see what breakthroughs might emerge from anywhere within the purview of each of the committees.

Results

By the end of the summer a good deal more had been learned, some decisions made, and some portions of a new direction were already being implemented. The following is an overview of our findings.

What was Learned

1. Given that there was no way to make the ongoing operations financially viable by themselves, it would be necessary to secure a larger potential audience for museum offerings. This meant reaching out on a national or international scale rather than focusing on a regional audience.
2. Outside funding in the form of grants and gifts would need to increase substantially. The development office would therefore require significant upgrading and would need to appeal to a new and larger audience beyond the local and regional audiences that now supported the museum.
3. Partnering relationships would need to be developed with other organizations where there was a potential for mutually beneficial synergies.
4. The internet would allow the museum to reach a national, even international audience, and would need to be developed in such a way as to contribute revenues to the museum. Research data indicates that of every 100 persons who visit a Web site, at least one of them makes a purchase.
5. New revenue-generating functions would have to be formed in the museum.
6. A new mission and vision statement would be needed to inform employees of what was expected of them in the absence of specifically formulated rules and directives.
7. Every employee and every operation of the museum would have to be cost justified in terms of efficiency and relevance to the new strategic plan.
8. The museum would need to consolidate and reconfigure its physical plant so as to reduce the actual costs incurred for operating the museum.
9. The hundreds of acres of land upon which the museum was located were an expense-generating asset that had to produce revenue or be eliminated.

What was Planned

1. Every element of change would need to be evaluated in terms of investment costs, likely revenue and expense generation, and likely profit.
2. The museum would move toward the virtual world. The existing museum would not be shut down, but the focus would be on putting the collections, exhibitions, programs, and products on the World Wide Web.
3. While casual perusal of the collection on the internet would entail no cost, detailed and scholarly pursuit by visitors would carry a charge.

4. The museum shop would expand its offerings considerably and make them available on the Web.
5. Partnering arrangements with Christopher Newport University, which had an adjoining campus, and NOAA, the National Oceanic and Atmospheric Administration, would be pursued.
6. A committee of the Board of Trustees was formed to pursue possible revenue-generating uses of the property.
7. The mission of the development office was to be modified to align with the new strategic plan.
8. Marketing was to be aligned with the new strategy.
9. The museum would close several of its exhibition halls and eliminate two rented storage units located off campus. The museum holdings in these storage units would be transferred to onsite spaces.
10. A rationalization of staff and functions would be undertaken.
11. A revised budget, a new theory of the case, a new value proposition, a new strategy, and a financial plan would be sold to the board.

PHASE 5: SECOND BOARD INTERVENTION

Setting & Plan

While the board had been made aware of the severity of the operating deficit of the organization and understood that changes would need to be made in museum operations, they were not fully aware of the changing environment for history and maritime museums. Further, they needed to be convinced of three fundamental concepts that the president's council considered crucial to future success.

First, no improvement of existing operations could make up the existing and likely future deficits. Second, the museum needed a fundamentally new theory of the case that had three critical elements: (a) a focus on customers that would drive the design of museum programs, exhibitions, and other functions; (b) the redefinition of customers to include a national visitor and donor base instead of the current local and regional audiences alone; and (c) a move to engage in partnering arrangements with other organizations to achieve the newly defined mission.

Third, there had to be a change in the value proposition which basically applied to an older audience and offered physical access to a local/regional audience for an admission fee. The new value proposition was intended to reach the national/international audience and to tap into the way persons under 30 go about searching out interests and learning something new would require that the museum go virtual. In doing so, the museum holdings would be accessible on the internet for no charge. Revenue would be based on purchases in the Web museum shop and on charges for extensive review of museum holdings by scholars or other persons with serious interests in maritime culture.

Museums are similar to academia in that they are conservative places that do not accept change readily. Typically this is characteristic of museum and academic boards as well, plus there is the additional fiduciary responsibility that falls on a board. The museum's board would not only be required to endorse the changes, but they would need to fund them over the next 3 to 5 years since it would take that long to put the new features in place.

Method

The method used was simple and straightforward. The president and other members of his council made presentations designed to accomplish three objectives. The first was to review projected revenues and expenses for the coming 5 years to confirm the need for change. The second was to present a new theory of the case, a new value proposition, and a new strategy, each designed to turn the financial picture around in 5 years. The third was to identify the initiatives that were underway or would get underway, if the board adopted the recommendations of the president.

Results

The Board accepted the recommendations in their entirety. They demonstrated an understanding of the new environment that the museum faced and expressed confidence in the museum's leadership, staff, and plans for the future. Most importantly, they agreed to underwrite the proposed changes, recognizing that they could not be achieved within a short timeframe.

What was Implemented

The museum, as of January 2008, has started to act upon its new plans. Early signs are encouraging. One initiative, a relatively minor one involving using paddle boats on the museum lake, has already failed, but in another initiative, the securing of a new library facility has been successfully executed and the physical move of the library will take place later this year when upgrades to museum status are completed in the new library's physical plant. Others are underway and show promise. Here is what else is being done.

- Every initiative is viewed in terms of its potential return, financial or otherwise, to the museum. These returns are evaluated against projected expenses before adoption.
- A new theory of the case recognizes the need for all future professional actions of the museum to be evaluated in terms of their likely appeal to customers, and a value proposition is adopted that will allow access to the

museum on the Web for no charge, but sale of museum-related articles and services is expected to yield significant revenues.

- A new vision statement has been adopted.
- The museum has started to place all of its holdings in the virtual museum, which will be available on the Web. With such a large and diverse collection, it will take several years to get everything on the Web.
- The arrangement with Christopher Newport University to house the Mariners' Museum Library in their brand-new, state-of-the-art library will save the museum $10–15 million in construction costs and immediately prevent any damage occurring to the collection. The museum still owns the collection and the university significantly increased its holdings, plus it gained complete access to the finest collection of maritime library holdings in North America.
- Further negotiations are pursuing potential joint degree offerings plus academic uses of Mariners' Museum property, facilities, and holdings to support a variety of courses, programs, and educational initiatives across a wide array of departments at Christopher Newport University. These services will be compensated for by the university.
- An exhibition is being planned for some of the museum's significant paintings. These paintings are very valuable, and art museum curators have stated that they will have significant appeal. Prints of these paintings and framing will be available for purchase.
- The photography initiative is getting underway. This involves both the sale and licensing of photographs.
- The closing of several of the museum's galleries is planned for the immediate future. This will allow for an expense reduction because the offsite rented buildings housing museum holdings will be eliminated. Further, the consolidation of all holdings to a single location will decrease operational costs for security and maintenance and will allow for access to all of the pieces that are to be available in the virtual museum.
- A process was put in place to develop further partnering relations with NOAA. Both sides expressed interest and commitment, but specific plans remain to be developed.
- The board committee is actively pursuing the development of a piece of the museum property for construction of a new medical office facility. This single action can account for as much as a third of the museum's annual operating deficit.

SUMMARY & CONCLUSION

This account describes the total reengineering of an organization with the attendant changes to the culture, the nature of the work, the rethinking of the organizational purpose, and the identification of a new customer base and new concepts of how the organization will reach them. The case is presented not as scientific research but as a case of behavioral engineering with no attempt to maintain artificial controls or to hold environmental conditions constant. Rather, a behavior theory framework is used to account for the behavior of both the interveners and those intervened upon, with all parties serving at different times in each of these roles (Sidman, 1960).

What started as an investigation of individual staff strengths and weaknesses revealed a dysfunctional culture. Observing that individuals were functioning competently but ineffectively served as the stimulus to drive the authors from an observation study to an intervention that would align the board, the CEO, and the various operating functions in a direction that would ensure the survival and success of the organization in the larger culture of which it was a part (i.e., its visitors and donors) This intervention upon the entire staff by the behavioral interveners resulted in integrated organizational performance but not effective performance. A change to effective practices revealed that no amount of effective practice could produce enough revenue to ensure the survival of the organization. Thus, the changed behavior of the staff once again required a change of behavior on the part of the interveners, who now realized that a "sea change" strategy would need to be put into place that required a new theory of the case and a new value proposition. The new theory of the case, value proposition, and attendant "sea change" strategy resulted in yet another intervention on the staff to fundamentally redesign nearly every aspect and every position in the museum.

It is here that the story of the intervention ends, but not the story of the museum. The museum is implementing its new vision and will be doing so for the next 3 years according to plan. So far the change is moving along successfully.

Can this study be replicated? In point of fact, I think that this study is replicated often by behavioral consultants who are involved at the highest levels of an organization. Behavior is continuous, and environments, internal and external to the organization, are constantly changing (Krapfl, 2003). Just like Skinner standing over a pigeon pecking a key, the behaviorist consultant moves and is moved by the world around him. The case made here is that the success of behavioral engineering is not determined by adhering to the requirements of scientific rigor. Rather it is ultimately the quality and magnitude of the change and its attendant support by the natural environment; in this case, visitors and donors.

REFERENCES

Krapfl, J. E. (2003). Corporate cultures. In Lattal, K. A., & Chase, P. N. (Eds.), *Behavior theory and philosophy*. New York: Kluwer Academic/Plenum Publishers.

Russell, B. (1927). *An outline of philosophy*. London: George Allen and Unwin. (Reprinted as *Philosophy*, New York: W. W. Norton)

Sidman, M. (1960). *Tactics of scientific research*. New York: Basic Books, Inc.
Skinner, B. F. (1956). A case history in scientific method. *American Psychologist,*
    11, 221–233.
Skinner, B. F. (1961). The design of cultures. *Daedalus, 90*, 534–546.

Behavioral System Feedback Measurement Failure: Sweeping Quality Under the Rug

MARIA T. MIHALIC and TIMOTHY D. LUDWIG

Appalachian State University, Boone, North Carolina, USA

Behavioral Systems rely on valid measurement systems to manage processes and feedback and to deliver contingencies. An examination of measurement system components designed to track customer service quality of furniture delivery drivers revealed the measurement system failed to capture information it was designed to measure. A reason for this failure was an inadequate design, which resulted in sabotage of the measurement system by agents in the organization. The failure of this measurement system led to the ineffective operation of business processes and related systems. For example, a bonus pay system and a disincentive system were disabled due to the faulty measurement system. Suggestions for the development of a valid measurement system are offered.

BEHAVIORAL SYSTEM FEEDBACK MEASUREMENT FAILURE: SWEEPING QUALITY UNDER THE RUG

Behavioral Systems Analysis (BSA) involves analyzing components of interconnected processes that impact individual and organizational performance (Brethower, 1982, 2000, 2001, 2002; M. E. Malott, 2003; Sulzer-Azaroff, 2000). According to Malott (2003), individuals behave in ways that should be consistent with the goals and mission of their organization. Individuals working together toward goals do so in organized processes that include the sequenced behaviors of individuals (or machines) across different functions and levels of the organization (Rummler, 2004). Brethower (2000) argues that these processes must be monitored via process and customer feedback to better align the processes with the system goals.

Measurement is a key component of a healthy behavioral system. Techniques used in BSA require effective monitoring through measurement systems focusing on critical steps across organizational levels (Abernathy, 2000; Glenn, 1988; R. W. Malott, 1974, 1999; Rummler, 2004). When process data are collected and analyzed they can then provide feedback to individuals responsible for the process (Brethower, 2000). Process feedback can be used to shape behaviors necessary to accomplish the organization's mission (M. E. Malott, 2003). If process feedback is not available, managers of the process have little basis for improving the processes and the behavioral contingencies therein. Processes become neglected (Katz & Kahn, 1966), and other organizational systems also fail to function. Thus, measurement systems provide the process feedback necessary for system survival.

Measurement systems are used to assess employees, work groups, departments, or entire organizations with a variety of organizational measures (e.g., absenteeism, productivity, quality, etc.) that directly relate to critical business issues (Rummler, 2004). Measurement systems are designed not only to assess current levels of performance, but also to provide feedback to shape performance toward goals, aid in organizational diagnosis and improvement, and provide the foundation for bonuses and promotions (Anderson & Fagerhaug, 2002). "Measurement is the first step that leads to control and eventually improvement. If you can't measure something, you can't understand it. If you can't understand it, you can't control it. If you can't control it, you can't improve it" (Harrington & McNellis, 2006).

Measurement Systems

In the measurement literature, this feedback in behavioral systems has been referred to as "organizational control systems." Organizational control is the "process of influencing members of a formal organization" (Flamholtz, 1979, p. 51). Organizational control systems are devised to increase the likelihood that members of an organization behave in ways that are consistent with organizational goals through the delivery of contingent performance feedback (see also M. E. Malott, 2003). Control systems allow leaders to regulate the activities of the organization and monitor achievement toward performance standards (Lewis, Goodman, & Fandt, 2004). Power (2004) explained that without effective measurement systems, organizations would be hindered by individuals who act in their own interests instead of those who help achieve organizational goals.

Lewis and others (2004) outline the four major components of an effective organizational control system. The first component of a control system is the establishment of organizational goals. Hall (1975) explained that goals are important because resources can be distributed and policies can be created based on them. The next component is the establishment of standards of performance. In the next component, measurement is used to evaluate performance against these standards to discover gaps. Lastly, rewards can be assigned for surpassing the standard of performance, while corrective actions address deviations from the goal that are not acceptable.

Measurement systems provide a framework from which decisions can be made and resources allocated (Anderson & Fagerhaug, 2002; Kula, 1986). Data produced by measurement systems must allow the organization to predict future performance (Bassi & McMurrer, 2005) and serve as the foundation of many business decisions such as daily operations, planning, and early warning systems (Anderson & Fagerhaug, 2002).

To eliminate situations where no contingencies exist and the behavior goes unchanged, measurement systems serve as the basis for incentive plans designed to reinforce behavior (Anderson & Fagerhaug, 2002). However, incentives can sometimes be fatal remedies when based on faulty measurement systems that create incentives for behaviors counter to the actual goals of the organization (Sieber, 1981).

Components of a Good Measurement System

To identify gaps in performance, Bassi and McMurrer (2005) state measurement systems should be "actionable," focusing only on items that are under the control of the organization; "descriptive," summarizing key system issues through statistics; and "detailed" to enable the organization to pinpoint behaviors in need of attention. A measurement system also needs to be accurate and consistent, producing unbiased, reliable data. Reliability is the degree of stability and consistency inherent in a set of data (Bernstein, Penner, Clarke-Stewart, & Roy, 2003). "Measurements are *in principle* replicable and not dependent on when, where, and by whom the measurement is done" (Power, 2004, p. 769).

A measurement system should be parsimonious enough to facilitate reliable application and results. As a measurement system becomes more complicated, the reliability of the system tends to be challenged. An increase in variables to measure leads to an increase in measurement error (such as in code entry), which reduces reliability. In turn, user friendliness will increase the reliability of the measurement system.

Bernstein and others (2003) explained that the usefulness of a measurement system is represented by the validity of the data produced. A number of factors can influence validity. The content validity of a measure is the degree to which the measure relates to the variable being assessed (Bernstein et al., 2003). Furthermore, a measure with high content validity samples all the variables related to the topic, not a small segment (Lanyon & Goodstein, 1997). An invalid measure may not sample enough aspects of the variable or may assess components not related to the variable.

A measurement system must facilitate timely delivery of feedback to employees to facilitate change and improvement in the organization (Anderson & Fagerhaug, 2002). The more proximal feedback delivery is to performance, the more effective the feedback is (Ludwig & Goomas, 2007). Feedback delivered proximal to performance allows the performer to gain access to information close to the emitting of behavior and more immediately correct errors. As time passes between behavior and feedback, the link between the behavior and its consequence is weakened, and feedback becomes less effective (Daniels & Daniels, 2004).

Finally, Garnego, Biazzo, and Bitici (2005) state that measurement systems should include a review function that allows the system to be adapted to respond to changes and to fit with the strategy of an organization. A static measurement system in a dynamic organizational environment will quickly become obsolete. To ensure continued relevance, a measurement system must be dynamic and allow for change when needed. The system should be designed to allow employees and users to provide input to improve the utility of the measures and systems (Anderson & Fagerhaug, 2002).

In summary, an effective measurement system must, first and foremost, be valid and reliable. In addition, the system needs to be dynamic enough to change with the organization. It must provide accurate and understandable feedback to employees and managers to monitor and help change behavior. Organizations that follow these guidelines measure meaningful variables accurately and are in a better position to manage control over organizational goals.

Incentive Systems

Incentive systems have been shown to decrease the amount of monitoring necessary for supervisors to maintain performance (Banker, Lee, Potter, & Srinivasan, 1996) if made contingent on performance (Bucklin & Dickinson, 2001). Pritchard, Jones, Roth, Stuebing, & Ekeberg (1988, 1989) found that the addition of feedback to measurement systems increased the productivity of employees 50% over baseline levels. Furthermore, adding incentives increased productivity 76% over baseline performance.

Incentives also serve as feedback for the performer (Goomas & Ludwig, 2007). Indeed, the effects of feedback can be strengthened with the addition of rewards (Alvero, Bucklin, & Austin, 2001; Balcazar, Hopkins, & Suarez, 1985/86; Welsch, Luthans, & Sommers, 1993). Thus, incentive systems have been found to be effective in organizations when contingent on desired behavior and paired with frequent feedback (Abernathy, Duffy, & O'Brien, 1982; Bateman & Ludwig, 2003; Dickinson & Gillette, 1993; Gaetani, Hoxeng, & Austin, 1985; Honeywell-Johnson, McGee, Culig, & Dickinson, 2002). However, if the measurements that serve as the basis of the incentive system are flawed, agents of the system may behave in ways to gain the incentive (or avoid the disincentive) that may not support the goals of the system.

CASE STUDY

The present report looked at the measurement system of a high-end furniture distribution company to identify weaknesses in design and implementation, and to interpret the causes of these weaknesses in context of a number of theories for management, economic, and psychological literature including organizational control, agency theory, and behavioral analysis.

Company Profile

This study was conducted at a furniture distribution company located in the southeastern United States that catered to high-end clientele throughout the country. This company received, stored, and distributed approximately 60,000 furniture orders per year with an average of approximately $160 million in delivered sales yearly.

Customer orders were received, and orders were placed with the manufacturer. Furniture pieces were then received from the manufacturer and stored in the warehouse. When all the pieces of a customer order were received by the warehouse, items were assembled, inspected, and repaired (if necessary). After the orders were prepared, furniture was loaded on a truck and delivered to a customer's house, office, store, or other location.

There were numerous errors that could occur during the delivery process, such as transit damages and leaving parts in the truck. When damaged or imperfect furniture was discovered after arriving at the customer location, drivers were required to call the company's Customer Service Department for authorization to fix damaged pieces, schedule an outside repair, or return the furniture to the truck. Customer Service analyzed the estimated cost of the repair performed on site versus the cost of bringing the piece back to the warehouse for repair and redelivery before giving authorization. However, drivers employed by this company were leaving damaged, imperfect, and even incorrect furniture in the customers' houses without calling Customer Service.

Left in Home Unauthorized

A Left in Home (LIH) error was defined as any piece of furniture in need of repair or return left in the delivery location without calling a customer service representative (CSR) for authorization. LIH errors also occurred when drivers waited to call CSR until after leaving the customer home or when the customers themselves called about a damaged or incorrect piece left in the home. Finally, the driver may report the LIH when the truck returned to the warehouse at the inbound docks. In each case, the damaged or incorrect piece was left in the delivery location and CSR was not called while the driver was at the customer location, therefore the driver did not receive authorization to leave the piece(s). LIH incidents resulted in the company having to contract a local professional to do the repairs at higher costs or send a truck out to pick up the furniture piece for repair and redelivery.

The company had developed an elaborate listing of error codes for their measurement database to aid in the tracking and resolution of errors in delivery. The error code, description of the problem, furniture piece identification number, and actions taken were put into the database by either a customer service representative or the manager of the inbound delivery docks. The identifying number of the furniture piece could be tracked to the customer order and delivery team.

Driver Pay System

In addition to tracking errors, the measurement system was designed to input performance data into a pay system for delivery drivers. On a biweekly basis, drivers received a "load pay" amounting to 6.2% of the revenue of each order delivered to the customer. The driver team lost the load pay for a delivery if an error was recorded. An additional 25% of the load pay was eligible for a quarterly bonus. If errors were extensive, 10% of the bonus was forfeited. Moreover, an immediate charge of $200 was assigned automatically when LIH error codes were assigned.

Major Agents of the Measurement System

In addition to the CSRs and inbound managers who entered error codes, a number of other agents had an impact on the measurement system or were subject to contingencies based on the measurement system.

DRIVER

Delivery drivers delivered customer orders, unloaded and set up the furniture in the customer home or office, and inspected the furniture for defects. If any problems with the furniture piece were discovered during installation, drivers were trained to repair the piece. If the repair could not be done, the driver was to call Customer Service to determine whether to contract a local repair person or have the piece returned to the warehouse. After all orders were delivered, drivers returned to the warehouse, turned in paperwork, and unloaded any furniture items left on the truck.

CUSTOMER SERVICE REPRESENTATIVE

If any problems arose during delivery, a CSR became the point of contact for resolving customer issues and recording errors in the Customer Service database. The CSR opened a problem slip in the database and recorded relevant customer and delivery information before describing the specific error in detail. The CSR then applied the most representative error code out of the possible 145 error codes in the Customer Service database. CSRs added information to problem slips to document steps made to fix the problem (e.g., repairs, subsequent delivery).

INBOUND MANAGER

When driver teams returned to the warehouse they were asked to recount any delivery errors that may have occurred. This information was recorded by the Inbound manager in the Inbound database with accompanying delivery and customer information. Error codes were applied from the list of 99 Inbound problem codes.

The Inbound database used a different coding system than the Customer Service database. The Customer Service database was the main measurement system designed to track errors and provide information for the company's bonus pay systems. The Inbound measurement system, on the other hand, was designed to track problem furniture pieces as they moved through the resolution process.

AUDITOR

To check for accuracy, auditors monitored the application of codes in the Customer Service database. The audit procedure required that full records of errors affecting driver pay be reviewed. Written information in this database was compared to the CSR error code list to ensure the error code applied was accurate prior to bonus pay periods.

QUALITY SERVICE MANAGER

Quality service managers combined the Customer Service database and the Inbound database. The data from each database were extracted, combined, and aggregated to generate reports for various levels of management. These reports summarized the number of each error code monthly and were used to monitor error rates across variables of interest (e.g., driver, furniture brand, and store). Quality service managers also monitored both databases for irregularities and inconsistencies in reporting.

VICE PRESIDENT OF OPERATIONS

Among other responsibilities, the vice president of operations was in charge
of monitoring and managing the performance of the drivers. Thus, the measurement and bonus pay systems were under his direct control. Reports
generated by this measurement system were used to make his managerial
decisions regarding personnel, customer service, and financial investments
or cost cutting. It was the vice president who initially developed the disincentive system designed to reduce driver errors, including LIH.

INVESTIGATION

An investigation of the company's measurement system data was undertaken to further pinpoint the variables of interest. This investigation specifically centered on the Customer Service database as the primary source used
by the pay systems to evaluate driver performance and to dispense bonuses
and penalties. This database housed the problem slips opened by the CSRs
to document errors.

Data were evaluated to examine error trends over a 7-year period, from
2000–2006. During 2000 and 2001 the number of LIH errors went from 4,732
to only 44. The number of authorizations (where drivers got permission to
leave defective pieces in homes) went from 0 in 2000 to 3,235 in 2001. Very
low levels of LIH were maintained through 2006 (see Figure 1). A preliminary

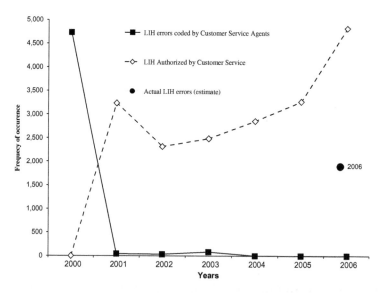

FIGURE 1 LIH Errors: 2000–2006. Filled squares represent annual LIH errors coded by CSRs.
Open diamonds represent annual authorizations of LIH by CSRs. The filled circle represent
an estimate of actual LIH errors for 2006 based on our quality service audit.

hypothesis was that the substantial decrease in LIH errors was due to the implementation of the two disincentives (i.e., $200 charge in load pay and forfeiture of bonus pay) within the bonus pay system in October 2001. The initiation of the disincentive system was credited by the vice president to help alleviate an expensive problem for the company. It is also noteworthy that, from its inception in 2001, the measurement system seldom resulted in applying any disincentives to drivers for LIH errors.

After further analysis it became apparent that the decrease in the number of LIH errors could not have been due to the disincentive. The disincentive was put in place in October of 2001; however, the decrease in the number of LIH errors seemed to begin in the first week of 2001. The question then became, "What happened at the beginning of 2001 that could account for such a drastic decrease of errors?"

Interviews with management revealed that a new measurement system had been put in place at the beginning of 2001 to more accurately capture, report, and control errors. Year 2000 errors were not recorded by CSRs. Instead, reports were generated by reading the original customer service records, and errors for the year 2000 were recoded according to the new measurement coding system implemented in 2001. This post-hoc coding resulted in the wide discrepancy in the frequency of LIH errors between the years 2000 and 2001 (see Figure 1).

Additionally, there was a consensus among employees consulting with the project that LIH errors were not being accurately captured. Interviews with various staff members revealed that employees had learned to manipulate the measurement system. Thus, a more thorough investigation was undertaken to reevaluate the data.

For this investigation the quality service manager and another colleague analyzed Customer Service problem slips by hand for the month of August 2006, in the same way the year 2000 errors were coded previously. These paper records contained problem descriptions written by CSRs, including error codes assigned and details of the problems entered into a free response section. The details of the problem often revealed other errors that occurred during a delivery that were not assigned an error code. For example, an error code for "transit damage" may have been filed, but the written information stated that the furniture piece was left in the home without authorization. Thus, the error should also have been coded as LIH.

An analysis of 160 problem slips from August 2006 determined that 63 incidents (39.4% of the 160 incidents) should have been coded as LIH but were not. The Customer Service measurement system for this time period reported only 2 occurrences of LIH. Assuming that approximately 40% of the problem slips should have been recorded with an LIH code, as many as 1,901 incidents of 4,824 problem slips opened in all of 2006 should have been recorded as LIH (see Figure 1). This estimated discrepancy suggested the system was not capturing LIH errors, and the measurement system had failed.

FAILURE OF THE MEASUREMENT SYSTEM

Too Many Error Codes

Tangen (2004) explained that information overload can occur from too many performance measures, which results in inaccurate recording. As a result of the over 200 different codes, CSRs were applying only a handful of codes, mostly the general problem codes that they were most familiar with. CSRs reported in interviews that many of the codes were considered redundant, did not describe good performance, and were never used for reporting. The abundance of error codes greatly reduced the reliability of the data because different CSRs picked different error codes given the same information. No real operational definitions of these codes existed for the CSRs. Even employees who developed the system had differing opinions during interviews about what constituted various errors.

To complicate matters, new codes could easily be created in the system with no prior approval. The system was designed to describe the error from the broadest category (i.e., what the error was) to the most precise (i.e., who did it, what furniture pieces were damaged, etc). However, the system had not maintained this order, nor was it ever clearly established according to this goal. Yet the system administrators and executives in the organization refused to simplify the system and reduce the number of codes used, even though it was common knowledge that fewer than 10 codes were being applied routinely. After all, "it is a waste of time to collect data if they are being ignored" (Tangen, 2004, p. 728).

Inaccurate Feedback

The company's measurement system, designed to provide feedback for correcting gaps in performance, could not accurately or consistently identify performance errors. The reduced reliability and validity of the data resulted in inaccurate feedback. As a result, the employees monitored under this measurement system were incorrectly being told that they were behaving correctly. Similarly, reports using the system misled management by suggesting that customers were being left with high-quality furniture nearly 100% of the time.

Misapplied Incentive Systems

The failure of the measurement system led to a failure in the incentive system. Latham and Dossett (1978) explained that failure of incentive systems can be linked to money not being made contingent on verified performance. Additionally, the lag time between when data were entered and when drivers got feedback was often months. Drivers were supposed to be notified of errors via biweekly paychecks, when disincentives related to specific error codes were withheld from their pay. The majority of the time, however, drivers were made aware of errors only in an aggregated report in quarterly bonus. This lag time and the aggregation of target errors made it improbable if not impossible for drivers to link specific instances of errors to their feedback and incentive pay.

Undermining the Measurement System

Our investigation revealed that the measurement system seriously underreported thousands of LIH errors that may have been occurring each year. Thus, the incentive system may have ended up reinforcing behaviors that manipulated the system to avoid error code assignments. Indeed, drivers interviewed said they learned to call CSRs after multiple deliveries to avoid the LIH code or to wait to report errors to Inbound. However, weaknesses in accountability were not limited to drivers. There were also weaknesses in the recording, checking, and reporting of error codes.

CORRUPTION OF THE MEASUREMENT SYSTEM

Agency theory (Jensen & Meckling, 1976) explores why the agents of the system begin acting in opposition to the system's goals. In concert with behavior analysis (Skinner, 1953), we can examine specific contingencies that may have encouraged the manipulation of the measurement system for each major agent in the organization.

Agency Theory

Agency theory describes problems that arise in an organization by considering what occurs when different goals exist between cooperating parties (Eisenhardt, 1989). Agency theory has been applied to economics (e.g., Jensen & Meckling, 1976), sociology (e.g., White, 1985), and organizational behavior (e.g., Eisenhardt, 1985) and has resulted in numerous literature reviews (Eisenhardt, 1989; Mitnick, 1992, 1998; Moe, 1984).

Much of the research in this area revolves around the assumption that agents are "pursuing self-interest with guile" (Williamson, 1975, p. 134). Individuals act in a self-serving manner instead of acting in the best interest of the company, often to protect themselves from risk (Shapiro, 2005). All of the major agents in this case study had a number of reasons to sabotage the system in order to protect their own interests or the interests of others.

According to Shapiro (2005), one of the problems that arise is what he calls "information asymmetries" and centers on the organization's inability to know what its agents, or employees, are doing. This is often because the information cannot be obtained without great difficulty or expense (Eisenhardt, 1989). The failure, in this case, of a measurement system to adequately inform the organization of its agents' activities resulted in unreported errors in customer service. The agents of the measurement system in this case study began acting in opposition to the goals of the system.

Behavior Analysis

Behavior analysis examines the relationship between behavior and the environmental consequences of behaviors (Rogers & Skinner, 1956; Skinner, 1953). An important consideration is the response cost of the desired versus actual behaviors. Response cost is the effort required to do the behavior or to obtain a result based on the behavior(s) (Gormezano & Wasserman, 1992). The more effort required to achieve a result, the less likely the agent is to perform these behaviors. Response cost can punish responding when the consequence, or cost, of performing is increased effort on the part of the agent. In the present case, error reporting was laborious and, as a result, LIH data were not collected.

In the context of the behavioral system, each agent had a variety of contingencies that could easily be used to explain their resistance to using the system as it was designed. Descriptions of the contingencies on each agent are detailed below.

DRIVERS

While delivery drivers were to call in and report LIHs, there was almost no reinforcement for doing so. Instead, if the drivers called in to report an error, they lost the pay they earned for that delivery. The load pay for the trip was paid to the driver teams only if the delivery was carried out without any error. Thus drivers began calling in to report the error after leaving the delivery location or reporting the error at Inbound to avoid the disincentive.

In addition, drivers experienced response costs by making phone calls to Customer Service and going through the process of obtaining approval. By not calling from the customer's home, drivers could avoid having to move the furniture piece back into the truck, reshuffling the rest of the day's deliveries to make room, and unloading it at the warehouse.

CUSTOMER SERVICE

The correct application of the error codes by CSRs would have led to accurate records and reports, which may have resulted in praise from supervisors. However, these consequences were not salient to CSRs because reinforcement resulting from accuracy may never have occurred. In contrast, applying multiple error codes incurred response costs. So instead of opening separate problem slips for each separate error that occurred during a delivery, the CSR tended to report only one error and document the details of the delivery error in the trip detail section of the single problem slip. The LIH error did not get coded, and the text describing it became buried in the paperwork, which was not easily searchable and did not inform any of the measurement or pay systems.

Further, incorrect error coding allowed CSRs to avoid uncomfortable social situations. The CSRs were being asked to help in administering the $200+ punishment to drivers. CSRs reported that the male drivers would boisterously cajole the female CSRs to change the code after the fact. Thus, recording errors resulted in arguments with drivers, which socially punished CSRs for applying the correct codes. Thus, CSRs learned over time that incorrectly coding these errors saved time, effort, and social unpleasantness.

AUDITORS

To verify the validity of the data produced by the measurement system, the organization appointed auditors to review Customer Service records for inaccurate error codes before issuing quarterly bonuses. This entailed the review of thousands of records for the quarter, which auditors reported as "tedious and boring." In order to avoid the response costs auditors would procrastinate. According to interviews, auditors tended to wait until the last minute to perform the audits because these duties interfered with regular tasks required in their job. In practice, auditors put off the task for so long others had to review the records for them. Sometimes extensions were applied for and/or the review was never completed. Thus, there were not sufficient reinforcers to offset the response costs of correctly doing the audits, and this eliminated the only source of data verification.

QUALITY SERVICE MANAGER

Quality service managers were supposed to monitor the database on a daily basis to ensure accuracy and resolve problems. Additionally, the separate Customer Service and Inbound databases were supposed to be merged by quality service managers. Instead of continued monitoring and improvement, quality service managers complicated the measurement system by adding unnecessary codes and restrictions. If the different Inbound and CSR databases were combined and the coding system simplified, the result may have been a decreased need for the quality service manager position to exist. However, the continued growth of the measurement system made the position important, thereby reinforcing behaviors that may have led to increased complexity and confusion.

VICE PRESIDENT

Ultimately, the vice president for operations used the reports generated by the measurement system to make business decisions. However, the flawed system led the VP to conclude LIH errors due were not a problem. Because he designed the measurement and incentive systems, the VP received praise for seemingly addressing the costly problem of LIHs. With errors averaging approximately $5 per incident, the resolution of one of the most prevalent errors was a major accomplishment. This resulted in positive consequences such as increased responsibility, career growth, and recognition. Repairing the measurement system after it was obvious that it was flawed would have drawn scrutiny of the unchecked costly errors and social disapproval from superiors.

Suggestions for a New Measurement System

The measurement system was designed to capture errors in the delivery process as they occurred and summarize trends to aid in the resolution of these problems. The other goal of the measurement system was to provide the quantitative basis for the company's incentive system. However, the lack of reinforcement for oversight resulted in invalid data remaining hidden for over 5 years and contributed to bad organizational decisions. Additionally, the contingencies surrounding the measurement system reinforced agents for manipulating the processes for their own benefit and/or the benefits of others. The likelihood that an agent will act in the interest of the organization increases when the organization has information that can be used to verify the behavior of the agents (Eisenhardt, 1989). Thus, the measurement system should be repaired by refocusing on its designed purpose.

System restructuring

A measurement system needs to capture enough detail to inform business decisions and provide information about employee performance. A redesign must pinpoint areas where the organization can make improvements. If these specific variables are captured by the system, management of performance improvement becomes more effective. Eisenhardt (1989) explained that when managers and employees are rewarded for outcomes dependent on the same behavior, the conflicts between the two parties are reduced and employees are more likely to act in the interest of the organization. A new single measurement system should be developed based on the mission and goals of the organization first, then the goals of the departments, and individuals should be considered next. The resulting goals (e.g., customer service) should then be used to develop the variables to be assessed.

Ultimately, the variables measured must be under the control of the organization and its agents (Bassi & McMurrer, 2005). The agents who use the system daily (e.g., CSRs and Inbound managers) are experts who should be consulted concerning what aspects of the system work, which codes are actually used, and which could be discarded. Consequently, using the agents in system redesign will increase buy-in, which may ensure the system will be supported and used properly. Furthermore, this redesign using the agents who will end up using the system will allow more reliability and validity in the application of codes.

Lastly, the system should be flexible and allow for change when needed. It is essential that the organization routinely review the accuracy of the system and the variables captured by auditing the system. The system must be monitored to ensure that it examines the most important variables and can accommodate any new variables needed. However, these changes should not be at the discretion of any one user. Thus, access to system design features should be limited. By creating an avenue for evaluation and improvement, the continued relevance of the measurement system can be maintained in the face of changes (Garnego et al., 2005).

PROCESS-BASED CHANGE

In the failed measurement system, driver errors could be recorded in 2 systems with almost 250 choices of codes to apply between them. The codes were housed in separate systems and applied by separate agents and had no tangible link to one another. Codes were often redundant within a single system and even more so between the systems. Codes were then merged to form a single report used to make business decisions. This report was mainly informed by the Customer Service database and was supplemented by Inbound data when errors were not captured wholly by the Customer Service data.

In a new system, all agents would enter error codes into the same system. The agents would choose from a number of error code options limited to only the most relevant. Multiple codes should be captured in one problem slip. Additional important information (i.e., agent responsible for error, furniture brand or type) could be made selectable in a searchable format. This would allow for the information needed to be more easily identified through searches without complicating the error coding process.

TRAINING

Individuals who use the system and apply the codes need to be aware of how it is to be used and what it was supposed to accomplish. Technical training will provide information required to use the system (Lewis et al., 2004), such as standardized definitions and examples of each code. Training will increase fluency in application and increase reliability and validity.

AUDITING/ACCOUNTABILITY

Coding inaccuracies were overlooked in the audit process of the current measurement system. According to Power (2004), auditing is the organizational equivalent of scientific replication in that it serves as "institutional revisiting of performance measures" (p. 770). The auditing system needs to be reworked to reduce the aversive costs associated with the process. The existence of two databases measuring the same errors resulted in unnecessary redundancies and response cost in the auditing process. Any measurement system should compile one database and build information technology to automate the audit process. The management team should reinforce frequent auditing, perhaps making it a weekly instead of a quarterly process. The reduced lag time will reduce the number of records to be audited at a given time. Moreover, the company could designate auditing as the primary responsibility of a clerical employee.

FEEDBACK

With enhanced auditing, frequent feedback could be provided. Also, a report on the accuracy of code entry would allow the company to reinforce CSRs' coding. A new measurement system should enhance the timeliness and clarity of feedback to drivers as well. Frequently verified error codes could be translated into driver feedback more often than once a quarter. Delivery performance can be made available electronically through cellular phones or computers in the delivery trucks. In addition, weekly reports should be issued, highlighting areas of success and areas in need of improvement. The feedback loop, then, provides an avenue for evaluation and improvement of the system and performance.

CONCLUSION

Purchase decisions are made on expectations rather than complete information, thus the higher a customer's expectation of product quality, the higher the price the customer is willing to pay (Goering, 1985). Indeed, an organization's competitive advantage depends on the quality of its goods and services (Gronroos, 1988). When making purchasing decisions, the two most important factors according to customers are product quality and the company's handling of service failures (Conlon & Murray, 1996). When customers are not satisfied with the service received, they may relay this information to 10–20 people (Mattila, 2001).

For the business reviewed in this case, a defective furniture piece left in a customer's home could influence future purchasing decisions by these high-end customers. Thus, special measurement systems were designed to influence deliverer behavior. However, very real and significant side effects of the faulty measurement system had gone unnoticed.

The most obvious side effect of measurement system failure was the incentive system failure. The manipulation of the system made these incentives ineffective. Drivers were being reinforced; however, it was not contingent on any accurate measure of performance. As Latham and Dossett (1978) explained, reinforcement (i.e., monetary incentives) needs to be contingent on performance to be effective. Instead, the incentive was resulting in increased expenses for the company without the benefit of managing key quality behaviors visible to the customer. The only real consequence of this system was the illusion of improvement.

REFERENCES

Abernathy, W. B. (2000). *Managing without supervision: Creating an organization-wide performance system*. Atlanta, GA: Performance Management Publications.

Abernathy, W. B., Duffy, E. M., & O'Brien, R. M. (1982). Multi-branch, multi-system programs in banking: An organization-wide intervention. In R. M. O'Brien, A. M. Dickinson, & M. P. Rosow (Eds.), *Industrial behavior modification: A management handbook* (pp. 370–382). New York: Pergamon.

Alvero, A. M., Bucklin, B. R., & Austin, J. (2001). An objective review of the effectiveness and essential characteristics of performance feedback in organizational settings (1985–1998). *Journal of Organizational Behavior Management, 21*, 3–29.

Anderson, B., & Fagerhaug, T. (2002). *Performance measurement explained: Designing and implementing your state-of-the-art system*. Milwaukee, WI: American Society for Quality Press.

Balcazar, F. E., Hopkins, B., & Suarez, Y. (1985/86). A critical objective review of performance feedback. *Journal of Organizational Behavior Management, 7*, 65–89.

Banker, R. D., Lee, S.-Y., Potter, G., & Srinivasan, D. (1996). Contextual analysis of performance impacts of outcome-based incentive compensation. *Academy of Management Journal, 39*, 920–940.

Bassi, L., & McMurrer, D. (2005). Learning from practice: Developing measurement systems for managing in the knowledge era. *Organizational Dynamics, 34*, 185–196.

Bateman, M. J., & Ludwig, T. D. (2003). Managing distribution quality through an adapted incentive program with tiered goals and feedback. *Journal of Organizational Behavior Management, 23*, 33–55.

Bernstein, D. A., Penner, L. A., Clarke-Stewart, A., & Roy, E. J. (2003). *Psychology*. Boston: Houghton Mifflin.

Brethower, D. M. (1982). The total performance system. In R. M. O'Brien, A. M. Dickinson, & M. P. Rosow (Eds.), *Industrial behavior modification: A management handbook* (pp. 350–369). New York: Pergamon Press.

Brethower, D. M. (2000). A systematic view of enterprise: Adding value to performance. *Journal of Organizational Behavior Management, 20*(3/4), 165–190.

Brethower, D. M. (2001). Managing a person as a system. In L. J. Hayes, J. Austin, R. Houmanfar, & M. C. Clayton (Eds.), *Organizational change* (pp. 89–105). Reno, NV: Context Press.

Brethower, D. M. (2002). Behavioral systems analysis: Fundamental concepts and cutting edge application. Retrieved February 28, 2003, from http://www.behavior.org/performancemgmt.

Bucklin, B. R., & Dickinson, A. M. (2001). Individual monetary incentives: A review of different types of arrangements between performance and pay. *Journal of Organizational Behavior Management, 21,* 45–137.

Conlon, D. E., & Murray, N. M. (1996). Customer perceptions of corporate responses to product complaints: The role of explanations. *Academy of Management Journal, 39,* 1040–1056.

Daniels, A., & Daniels, J. (2004). *Performance management: Changing behavior that drives organizational effectiveness.* Atlanta, GA: Performance Management Publications.

Dickinson, A. M., & Gillette, K. L. (1993). A comparison of the effects of two individual monetary incentive systems on productivity: Piece rate pay versus base pay plus monetary incentives. *Journal of Organizational Behavior Management, 14,* 2–82.

Eisenhardt, K. M. (1985). Control: Organizational and economic approaches. *Management Science, 31,* 134–149.

Eisenhardt, K. M. (1989). Agency theory: An assessment and review. *Academy of Management Review, 14,* 57–74.

Flamholtz, E. G. (1979). Effective organizational control: A framework, applications and implications. *European Management Journal, 14,* 596–611.

Gaetani, J. J., Hoxeng, D. D., & Austin, J. T. (1985). Engineering compensation systems: Effects of commissioned versus wage payment. *Journal of Organizational Behavior Management, 7,* 51–63.

Garnego, P., Biazzo, S., & Bitici, U. S. (2005). Performance measurement systems in SMEs: A review for a research agenda. *International Journal of Management Reviews, 7,* 25–47.

Glenn, S. S. (1988). Contingencies and metacontingencies: Toward a synthesis of behavior analysis and cultural materialism. *The Behavior Analyst, 11*(2), 161–179.

Goering, P. A. (1985). Effects of product trial on customer expectations, demand, and prices. *Journal of Consumer Research, 12,* 74–82.

Goomas, D. T., & Ludwig, T. D. (2007). Enhancing incentive programs through proximal goals and immediate feedback: Engineered labor standards and technology enhancements in stocker replenishment. *Journal of Organizational Behavior Management, 27,* 33–68.

Gormezano, I., & Wasserman, E. A. (1992). *Learning and memory.* Hillsdale, NJ: Erlbaum.

Gronroos, C. (1988). Service quality: The six criteria of good perceived service quality. *Review of Business, 9,* 10–13.

Hall, F. S. (1975). Organizational goals: The status of theory and research. In J. L. Livingstone (Ed.), *Managerial accounting: The behavioral foundations* (pp. 1–32). Columbus, OH: Grid.

Harrington, H. J., & McNellis, T. (2006). *Mobilizing the right lean metrics for success.* Retrieved September 2, 2007, from http://www.qualitydigest.com/may06/articles/02_article.shtml

Honeywell-Johnson, J. A., McGee, H. M., Culig, K. M., & Dickinson, A. M. (2002). Different effects of individual and small group incentives on high performance. *The Behavior Analyst Today, 3*(1), 88–103.

Jensen, M., & Meckling, W. (1976). Theory of the firm: Managerial behavior, agency costs, and ownership structure. *Journal of Financial Economics, 3,* 305–360.

Katz, D., & Kahn, R. L. (1966). *The social psychology of organizations*. New York: Wiley.

Kula, W. (1986). *Measures and men*. Princeton, NJ: Princeton University Press.

Lanyon, R. I., & Goodstein, L. D. (1997). *Personality assessment*. Oxford, England: John Wiley & Sons.

Latham, G. P., & Dossett, D. L. (1978). Designing incentive plans for unionized employees: A comparison of continuous and variable-ratio reinforcement schedules. *Personnel Psychology, 31*, 47–61.

Lewis, P. S., Goodman, S. H., & Fandt, P. M. (2004). *Management: Challenges for tomorrow's leaders*. Mason, OH: South-Western.

Ludwig, T. D., & Goomas, D. T. (2007). Performance, accuracy, data delivery, and feedback methods in order selection: A comparison of voice, handheld, and paper technologies. *Journal of Organizational Behavior Management, 27*, 69–107.

Malott, M. E. (2003). *Paradox of organizational change*. Reno, NV: Context Press.

Malott, R. W. (1974). A behavioral systems approach to the design of human services. In D. Harshbarger & R. F. Maley (Eds.), *Behavior analysis and systems analysis: An integrative approach to mental health programs*. Kalamazoo, MI: Behaviordelia.

Malott, R. W. (1999). *Behavior analysis as world view: A worktext*. Retrieved January 8, 2008, from http://dick-malott.com

Mattila, A. S. (2001). The impact of relationship type on customer loyalty in a context of service failures. *Journal of Service Research, 4*, 91–101.

Mitnick, B. M. (1992). The theory of agency and organizational analysis. In N. E. Bowie & R. E. Freeman (Eds.), *Ethics and agency theory* (pp. 75–96). New York: Oxford University Press.

Mitnick, B. M. (1998). Agency theory. In R. E. Freeman & P. H. Werhane (Eds.), *The Blackwell encyclopedic dictionary of business ethics* (pp. 12–15). Malden, MA: Blackwell.

Moe, T. M. (1984). The new economics of organization. *American Journal of Political Science, 28*, 739–777.

Power, M. (2004). Counting, control and calculation: Reflections on measuring and management. *Human Relations, 57*(6), 765–782.

Pritchard, R. D., Jones, S. D., Roth, P. L., Stuebing, K. K., & Ekeberg, S. E. (1988). Effects of group feedback, goal setting, and incentives on organizational productivity. *Journal of Applied Psychology, 73*(2), 337–358.

Pritchard, R. D., Jones, S. D., Roth, P. L., Stuebing, K. K., & Ekeberg, S. E. (1989). The evaluation of an integrated approach to measuring organizational productivity. *Personnel Psychology, 42*, 69–115.

Rogers, C., & Skinner, B. F. (1956). Some issues concerning the control of human behavior. *Science, 124*, 1057–1066.

Rummler, G. A. (2004). *Serious performance consulting according to Rummler*. Silver Spring, MD: International Society for Performance Improvement.

Shapiro, S. P. (2005). Agency theory. *Annual Review of Sociology, 31*, 263–284.

Sieber, S. (1981). *Fatal remedies: The ironies of social intervention*. New York: Plenum Press.

Skinner, B. F. (1953). *Science and human behavior*. New York: Free Press.

Sulzer-Azaroff, B. (2000). Of eagles and worms: Changing behavior in a complex world. *Journal of Organizational Behavior Management, 20*(3/4), 139–163.

Tangen, S. (2004) Performance measurement: From philosophy to practice. *International Journal of Productivity and Performance Management, 53*, 726–737.

Welsch, D., Luthans, F., & Sommer, S. (1993). Managing Russian factory workers: The impact of U.S.-based behavioral and participative techniques. *Academy of Management Journal, 36*, 58–79.

White, H. (1985). Agency as control. In J. Pratt & R. Zeckhauser (Eds.), *Principals and agents: The structure of business* (pp. 187–214). Boston: Harvard Business School Press.

Williamson, O. E. (1975). *Markets and hierarchies: Analysis and antitrust implications.* New York/London: Free Press.

Strengthening the Focus on Business Results: The Need for Systems Approaches in Organizational Behavior Management

CLOYD HYTEN

University of North Texas, Denton, Texas, USA

Current Organizational Behavior Management (OBM) research and practice may be characterized as either behavior focused or results focused. These two approaches stem from different origins and have different characteristics. The behavior-focused approach stems from applied behavior analysis (ABA) methods and emphasizes direct observation of and intervention on target behaviors of employees. In contrast, the behavioral systems approach encourages a shift from focusing on behavior exclusively toward focusing more on business results. A systems-oriented, results-focused approach toward Organizational Behavior Management is suggested as a means of making the field more relevant to the concerns of the business world.

STRENGTHENING THE FOCUS ON BUSINESS RESULTS: THE NEED FOR SYSTEMS APPROACHES IN OBM

There appear to be variations in Organizational Behavior Management (OBM) research and practice that are sufficiently different to question the

---

The author was a faculty member of the Department of Behavior Analysis at the University of North Texas in Denton, Texas, at the time of the writing of this article. He is now with Aubrey Daniels International of Atlanta, Georgia.

very definition of OBM. Hyten (2002) described an "identity crisis" in OBM because the two major OBM variants approach their subject matter and their goals so differently. One approach, which could be called *behavior focused,* historically grew out of applied behavior analysis (Baer, Wolf, & Risley, 1968) and utilizes a similar methodology to intervene and strengthen employee behaviors thought to be important. The other approach, which could be called *results focused,* links to the writings of Brethower (1972, 1982), Rummler and Brache (1995), and Gilbert (1978/1996) on performance and systems models. At present, the behavior-focused approach is dominant within OBM based on the type of articles published in the *Journal of Organizational Behavior Management (JOBM)*. In this paper, I will argue that for OBM to grow and prosper, a systems-oriented, results-focused approach should be adopted among practitioners and academics. This does not mean throwing away expertise regarding behavior; it means incorporating this expertise as part of a larger scope of analysis that includes elements of greater relevance to the organization.

In order to evaluate the two orientations of OBM, it would first be useful to articulate indicators of success. To do this we will look to models from other, similar organizations in an effort to describe the ideal circumstances for OBM: (a) OBM should experience the growth of membership like that experienced by applications of behavior analytic therapy to autism. The explosive growth in autism applications in the last 5–10 years has reshaped the Association for Behavior Analysis (Kangas & Vaidya, 2007; Twyman, 2007a); (b) OBM should appear in popular books, and CEOs ought to actively pursue OBM applications much as they currently do with quality tools like Lean/Six Sigma (cf., Pyzdek, 2003; Wedgwood, 2007); (c) OBM competencies should be so essential in business that specific jobs require expertise in OBM equivalent to any other established business discipline such as human resources or accounting; (d) large consulting companies such as Accenture should promote OBM on a par with their other business units. In fall of 2006, Accenture had 30,000 employees in the United States alone, more than double that worldwide, and quarterly revenues in the consulting division of about $3 billion (McDougall, 2006).

The gap between the current state of OBM and the ideal described above is considerable. OBM has attracted only a moderate following (e.g., the OBM Network had 253 members in 2006; Slowiak, 2007). There are only a handful of graduate training programs in OBM of any size at American universities (see www.obmnetwork.com for a list of programs). OBM presentations have a relatively flat growth rate within the annual convention of the Association for Behavior Analysis (see Figure 1 showing the number of OBM presentations plotted against presentation counts for Developmental Disabilities & Autism; data from Kangas & Vaidya, 2007, pp. 120–121).

Despite what look like successful case studies and research into reliable behavior change techniques, OBM has generated relatively little visibility in

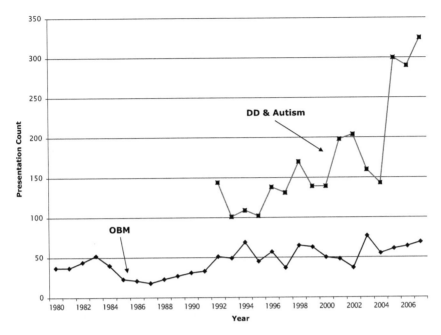

FIGURE 1 ABA conference presentations in OBM and in the area combining Developmental Disabilities and Autism from 1980–2007. Autism-related presentations were included in the DDA category until 1998 when they were identified in a separate AUT category. From Kangas & Vaidya (2007).

the business world. Job titles that specify OBM expertise are very rare. There are few OBM-based management consulting companies, and none of them approaches the size of Accenture. Few tools OBM has produced have the name recognition of Lean/Six Sigma, except for perhaps Behavior-Based Safety (see e.g., Krause, 2005; McSween, 2003).

It is tempting to blame slow growth on ineffective marketing. To be sure, behavior analysts have always been poor at marketing. In fact, applied behavior analytic autism therapy languished for years as a relatively small professional community prior to the publication of a bestselling book written not by a behavior analyst but by a parent of an autistic child (Maurice, 1993). Over the years the Association for Behavior Analysis (ABA) tried hiring public relations firms to help market behavior analysis (Twyman, 2007b). Perhaps it is time OBM examined the content of what we would market. Is OBM something that would be in demand by the business world if they were aware of it? In other words, what is it we have to sell?

The Behavior-Focused Approach

OBM has produced 30 years of data-based evidence showing that behavior principles can be applied to change human behavior in the workplace. This is continuing proof that methods of behavior analysis can be applied in a range of settings with normal adult humans (something rarely shown in the pages of the sweepingly titled *Journal of Applied Behavior Analysis*). Dickinson (2000) reconstructed the early history of OBM, noting its progenitors as well as its roots in programmed instruction and applied behavior analysis in the 1960s and 1970s. Her listing of seminal articles and events reveals much interest in "behavior modification" during this time period. Daniels (1977) opened the first issue of the *Journal of Organizational Behavior Management* with an editorial that closely identified OBM with applied behavior analysis in many respects, as defined by the Baer, Wolf, and Risley (1968) article in the first issue of the *Journal of Applied Behavior Analysis*. This view of OBM, as an area of applied behavior analysis in organizational settings, has been both beneficial and detrimental to the field.

Applied behavior analysis has a track record of precisely identifying and measuring behaviors of interest, analyzing controlling variables, and reliably changing the quality or rate of important behaviors. Eager to extend these methods to work settings, OBM practitioners have adapted methods such as pinpointing, direct observation systems, and contingency management to various behaviors in organizations. The pages of *JOBM* are full of articles ably demonstrating that employee behavior can be improved in a variety of organizations. Consulting companies such as Aubrey Daniels International (www.aubreydaniels.com) and the Continuous Learning Group (www.clg.com) have been in business for decades teaching behavior management strategies.

The expertise of OBM is in understanding and changing the behavior of individual employees by modifying the context of their behavior. OBM can direct the design and evaluation of behavioral contingencies, including antecedents and consequences supplied by management, coworkers, or the work setting. At its best, the behavior-focused approach has led to changes in management practices to emphasize positive reinforcement (e.g., Daniels, 1999). Another success may be the impact of behavior-based safety (e.g., McSween, 1995, 2003), which incorporates, as part of a companywide system, pinpointing of safe and at-risk behavior, direct observation, and peer feedback to decrease incidents of injury.

What limits us is when OBM leads only to the identification of a "target behavior" early in the discussion with the organizational client. Information about the client organization, its internal systems, and pressures from its business environment are rarely considered. In OBM publications, target behaviors are said to be significant to the organization but no real data backs up these claims. The absence of business impact data (e.g., profitability) is a severe limitation of the behavior-focused approach (Abernathy & Harshbarger, n.d.).

A casual reader of *JOBM* could get the impression from several recent articles that there is a crisis in American business involving the failure to greet customers as they enter a store. In Volume 27, Number 3 (2007) of

JOBM, three out of the four research reports included employee greeting of customers as a focal point of their articles. The fourth article focused on staff cleaning behaviors in a retail store. All of these articles reported on interventions that included behavioral feedback supplied by external observers and presented time-series graphical data on target behaviors. Not one of these articles included any results data on how the host business was affected operationally or financially. Perhaps results data would have shown that the greetings, eye contact, smiling, suggestions to buy more, or cleaning indeed added to store sales, increased customer visits, or even added to more favorable customer opinions. Alternatively, it is also possible that results data would have shown these behaviors had no impact or only marginal impact on the client organization. Perhaps a review of business data at the outset would have suggested that these employee behaviors were not the most pressing items to address to improve organizational success. Some of the articles of this type are authored by academic students, which often limits the scope. I have published such small-scale projects myself (e.g., Lafleur & Hyten, 1993) and also failed to include data about the organizational impact.

To be clear, not all behavioral-focused studies in *JOBM* fail in attempting to link to business results. In fact, in Volume 27, Number 1 (2007) of *JOBM*, Ludwig and colleagues (Berger & Ludwig, 2007; Goomas & Ludwig, 2007; Ludwig & Goomas, 2007) present studies on quality productivity improvement in warehouse operations that include cost-benefit data. However, the behavior-focused approach too often encourages us to spend little time understanding the business as a whole and its important results measures such as sales, growth, cost containment, quality assurance, or profitability. Instead we interview a manager to ask what behaviors they would like to see change. It often appears that behaviors are identified more because they are troubling to managers than because they drive business results. This parallels criticisms of ABA in the 1970s, when studies focused on annoying classroom behaviors while ignoring behaviors involved in academic learning— the central purpose of education (see Ayllon & Roberts, 1974; Winett & Winkler, 1972).

Too often in OBM, we target behaviors based on their availability for observation, deploy familiar direct observation techniques, and end up with a graph showing that employee behavior changed as a result of feedback. This problem was noted by Lee Frederiksen, then the Editor of *JOBM*, over 25 years ago (Dickinson, 2000). In an editorial, Frederiksen (1982, p. 2) observed with lament that OBM focused on "increasing the performance of a single, routine task or compliance to specific procedures or rules," and that OBM could be described "as a technique for solving isolated problems rather than as an approach to managing the human resources of the whole organization." Thus, the behavior-focused approach is adequate for demonstrating that employee behavior can be changed (something we have known for decades) but weak in demonstrating the impact on business results.

And it is improvement in business results that matters most to corporate leadership. Deloitte Consulting, with approximately 7,000 U.S. employees, describes a list of desired business results on their Web site (www.deloitte.com):

> Our Performance Improvement service line is a collection of market offerings designed to help clients in their efforts to: [a bulleted list] increase profitability, simplify business processes, reduce operating costs, increase strategic flexibility, improve productivity, improve capabilities to sustain high performance, improve service quality, develop structured execution plans and disciplines (Performance improvement, n.d).

The behavior-focused OBM approach, still mimicking ABA methodology, often lacks a clear appreciation of *performance* issues and of the larger organizational context. It is indeed ironic that the behavioral approach, typically thought of as examining behavior in context (Hayes, Hayes, & Reese, 1988), too often ignores critical aspects of context when applied to organizational settings. That need not be the case. An alternative is a systems-oriented, results-focused OBM.

THE PERFORMANCE PROPOSITION

OBM's mission is to improve performance in organizations. On that there is much agreement. Widely used texts such as Daniels and Daniels (2004) say as much in their titles. But there is less agreement about the definition of performance itself. In colloquial English, performance is sometimes used as a synonym for behavior. In most of OBM, performance is often defined as a combination of behavior and results. Daniels and Daniels (2004, pp. 34–35) defined performance as "a unit that consists of situation, behaviors, tasks, and results, which are combined to produce a specific accomplishment." And later, "performance is a summary term for behaviors and their effects on the environment." This definition can be read as a linear equation specifying that:

$$\text{performance} = \text{behavior} + \text{results}.$$

Gilbert (1978/1996, pp. 88–89) did not define performance as the linear sum of behavior and results, but rather as a benefit/cost ratio in which accomplishments (the benefits) were divided by a combination of costs that included behavior and the managed environment necessary to produce employee behavior. In equation terms, this specified that:

$$\text{performance} = \text{accomplishments} / \text{efforts}(\text{behavior} + \text{environmental supports} + \text{management system}).$$

This was not an accidental or trivial difference. In Gilbert's analysis, behavior was a *cost* and as such not to be increased unless the value of the accomplishments produced exceeded the effort associated with behavior.

Gilbert's (1978/1996) focus was on maximizing the results, not simply on maximizing the behavior involved. Conversely, OBM definitions of performance (e.g., Daniels & Daniels, 2004) emphasize that increasing behavior will lead to more performance. I believe the different definitions of performance reflect fundamentally different approaches to OBM: the difference between behavior-focused approaches and results-focused approaches.

Taking Gilbert's performance proposition seriously means that the balance of OBM's analytic, measurement, and evaluation efforts should be shifted toward results. Employee behavior, so often considered the dependent variable in behavior-focused approaches, is treated by Gilbert as more an independent variable affecting results-focused dependent variables. To this end, Gilbert suggested that a new technology or even science of accomplishments (at some points called "teleonomics" or "performance engineering") was needed. A science of behavior would be *involved* in this discipline, but the discipline would not be *about* behavior; it would be about results and all of the variables that affect results.

> Note first that I am not saying that behavior modification, as the behaviorists speak of it, is an unimportant and useless discipline in achieving more competent performance. Because it is in its infancy *as a discipline*, it has a lot of unrealized potential . . . But performance engineering—or teleonomics—is also in its infancy *as a discipline*; and those interested in it should not narrow their views to behavior modification as the sole, or even principal, technique for achieving their goals (Gilbert, 1978/1996, p. 99).

Systems-Oriented OBM

The results focus evident in Gilbert's definition of performance is a critical component of systems models of organizational functioning. Organizational systems models focus on results centered on customers and shareholders. These results can then be a source of information to management and employees to adjust practices so that gaps between actual performance levels and goal levels are reduced.

Traditional systems theory is not behavior theory, though their parallels have been noted by behavior analysts and OBM writers suggesting their philosophical and practical compatibility (see Brethower, 1999; Harshbarger & Maley, 1974; Hyten, 2002; Krapfl & Gasparatto, 1982; Malott, 2003). Both approaches include a version of inputs (similar to antecedents in behavior theory), processes (similar to behavior), and outputs that feed back to "upstream" components (similar to operant consequences at the level of individual behavior). But systems models are not simply scaled-up behavior models; if anything, behavior theory can be seen as a derivative of general systems theory, not the other way around.

Performance systems models provide at least three distinct benefits to OBM beyond behavior-focused approaches:

1. Context: a comprehensive view of the organization in its dynamic context. This is the "big picture" often missing from behavior-focused approaches. It helps us understand where to intervene and why that intervention is important to the survival of the organization. The context provided by performance systems models can help prevent targeting behaviors of minor importance.
2. Interaction: an understanding of how each subsystem affects others within the larger system. An understanding of subsystem interaction can predict likely side effects of change efforts, enabling us to prevent unintended adverse effects of intervening. A behavior-focused approach that does not consider subsystem interaction may get employees to do more of something that ultimately causes problems (e.g., bottlenecking) somewhere else in the organization.
3. Leverage: identification of additional variables that can be altered to improve performance. By "additional variables" I mean those beyond the antecedents and consequences of any particular behavior of interest. For example, cross-functional processes may require redesign to yield a more efficient workflow.

Systems Models

General systems theory is applicable to a wide variety of disciplines (see von Bertalanffy, 1968). It would seem to be a natural fit to complex multi-component entities such as corporations because it emphasizes interactions between parts and the whole. Indeed, Senge (1990) argued that systems thinking is one of the essential disciplines for business management. Brethower began adapting systems concepts to organizations in the 1960s. He developed a generic systems model that could be applied to any level within any organization (i.e., to the organization as a whole, to a department within the organization, and even to an individual) called the Total Performance System (Brethower, 1972; see Figure 2). This model illustrated how a goal-oriented entity receives inputs and processes them to outputs, and how those outputs are received by a downstream system (such as another business unit or a marketplace of consumers). System interactions are regulated by feedback from processing system operations as well as feedback from the receiving system.

In a series of articles spanning many years, Dale Brethower (1982, 1995, 2001; Brethower & Dams, 1999) showed how this model can be applied to understanding of critical performance issues and constraints that face organizations of any size (an application to a lemonade stand was particularly

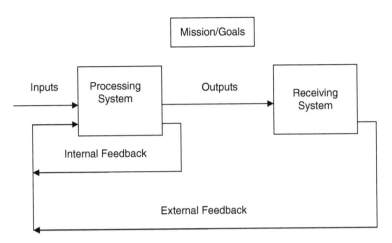

FIGURE 2 The total performance system model developed by Brethower.

amusing and instructive; 1995). Brethower (2008) even gave an account of historical influences on the development of systems approach to explain how it came to be a foundational part of the standards of practice for the Certified Performance Technologist (CPT) credential.

Geary Rummler (Rummler & Brache, 1995; Rummler, 1999, 2004) developed a similar systems model, adapted to show more detail of variables affecting a business (variously called the supersystems model, the relationship map, the adaptive systems model, or the anatomy of performance model in different writings; see Figure 3). This model described the greater organizational context that involves competitors and shareholders, and governmental, economic, and cultural influences. It also considered management as a subsystem within the organization. Rummler and Brache also described three levels of variables that drive performance within and across the processing system: *organization-level* variables such as company goals or strategy, *process-level* variables such as workflow across departments throughout the organization, and *job/performer-level* variables affecting the job-related behavior of individual employees. Each of these levels was, in turn, a function of its own goals, design, and management.

Rummler's systems model incorporated the behavioral variables Gilbert (1978/1996) discussed in his Behavior Engineering Model, but placed those variables in the context of other important variables affecting overall performance. In fact, the process level proved to be a rich source of deficiencies in many organizations. Thus, process mapping and process improvement efforts became commonplace performance improvement tools in the 1990s. Today they are still common tools in widespread organizational improvement approaches such as Lean/Six Sigma (Wedgwood, 2007).

There are other kinds of performance systems models as well. Abernathy (2000) described a model he also called the "Total Performance System,"

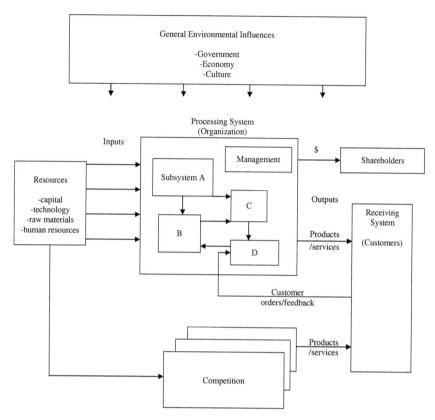

FIGURE 3 The supersystem model developed by Rummler and Brache.

including cascading measurement scorecards through all levels in the organization, performance-based pay, management practices emphasizing positive reinforcement, and data-based troubleshooting. The measures in the scorecards were designed to be results based. Performance pay was designed to be a joint function of those scorecard results and overall company profitability. Employee behavior was given more degrees of freedom than in behavior-focused approaches; that is, forms of behavior were left freer to vary so that employees may discover optimal ways to produce results. In Abernathy's system, behaviors of individual employees were ultimately strengthened through their relationship to successful results and associated earnings. This approach took behavior into account, but it did not emphasize direct behavior measurement of critical behavior topographies often used in behavior-focused approaches.

The Performance Value Chain

Hyten (2002) suggested that behavior analysts might be resistant to systems approaches because behavior seems to be downplayed. The behavior of line employees and managers needs to be appreciated for its role in producing results, but also needs to be understood in the larger organizational context. A way to illustrate this relationship is through the Performance Value Chain (Figure 4), which can be thought of as a representation of the center and right side of Rummler's Supersystem model (Figure 3) at a slightly different level of analysis. The level of analysis in the Performance Value Chain (PVC) emphasizes the nexus of behavior, processes, and results in the context of an adaptive, managed system.

Every part of the PVC should add value to the product or services offered by the organization. Costs are concentrated in elements to the left and middle of the PVC; benefits are derived on the right side.

The left side of the PVC depicts work-related behavior of employees as a part of a behavior subsystem. In this subsystem, productive employee behavior is influenced by the key factors first suggested by Gilbert's (1978/1996) Behavior Engineering Model (BEM). It is common for users of the BEM to group factors into categories different than in Gilbert's original model, or to relabel the categories (e.g., Binder, 1998), but there is general agreement on the main factors: task descriptions, prompts, goals, resources, equipment, consequences, feedback, and training, interacting with the employee's repertoire, capacity, and personal motives. In fact, although Gilbert

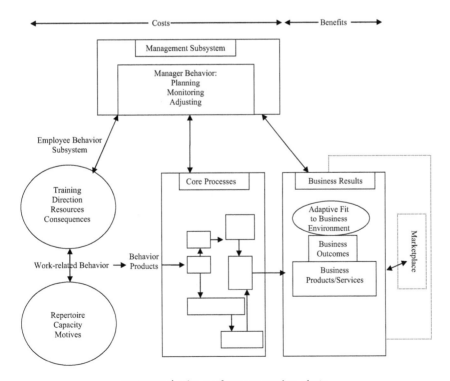

FIGURE 4 The performance value chain.

never used the term "systems" in his description of the BEM, he clearly described systems properties when he pointed out that changes to one of the cells often required changes in other cells. "So, if I improve the incentives for performance, people may learn more, even though I have made no effort to teach them better" (p. 94).

Employee behavior occurs in the context of business processes. In turn, the outputs of behavior flow through business units and across the "white space" depicted commonly in process maps. Process design is the principal factor governing efficiency and effectiveness of these transformative steps (Rummler & Brache, 1995). If each step in a process does not add some value exceeding the costs involved, the process will be deficient. Management has the task of designing and revising processes to prevent or remove deficiencies and optimize throughput, quality, or benefit/cost ratios.

Defective processes can result in poor business results for the organization even if job-level variables are optimally configured to promote desirable behaviors by the incumbent. For example, a quality-assurance process involving employees in several departments may be done correctly but have steps that add no value to the business result. If each department is supposed to "sign off" on a document to indicate that it is acceptable, but the review criteria are inadequate or key departments are omitted, the process will yield poor results. At each step, each employee may know what to do (in the sense of following a standard operating procedure), have the capacity to do it, and have the motive to do it well, but the result is still poor quality. The solution is to redesign the process, not tweak existing employee training, direction, resources, or contingencies. The behavior of employees is embedded within, and operates through, these processes. Thus, the design of processes can dramatically affect critical business results in the areas of quality, productivity, timeliness, costs, and customer satisfaction but is seldom addressed directly in the behavior-focused approach. OBM writers could do more to include process analysis in their design of interventions.

The right side of the PVC shows the business results that emerge from business processes. Business results, as a category, include three things: (a) business products/services sold or delivered to customers. These transactions produce business outcomes; (b) business outcomes include operational outcomes (e.g., quantity sold, percent returned as defective by customers, percent shipped on time), financial outcomes (e.g., sales revenue or profits), customer reactions, and impact on larger groups such as competitors, the marketplace as a whole, and society; (c) business outcomes in turn determine the success of the organization and whether it survives in the overall business environment. The ultimate result of the PVC is this adaptive fit of the organization with its business environment reflected in business growth.

Management systems play a critical role in the PVC. These systems include structural elements such as reporting relationships and internal processes such as channels of communication. At this level of analysis the behavior of managers must be taken into account because they: (a) plan business operations and strategy; (b) monitor business outcomes and the overall business environment; and (c) make adjustments to organizational structure, policies, processes, and behavior systems. This "manager-as-performer" has been described in various forms by Rummler (Rummler, 2001; Rummler & Brache, 1995), Redmon and Mason (2001), and Mawhinney (2001). Mawhinney referred to these managerial behaviors as "minding the meta-contingencies." Hyten (2002) suggested that more attention be placed on understanding how and why managers behave in analyzing business environments, make decisions that change the functioning of the organization, or plan for future organizational events.

Management behavior is a relatively untapped area for OBM research. Most OBM publications have focused on performance of non-management personnel (Nolan, Jarema, & Austin, 1999). Consulting firms often intervene in organizations through changing management behavior (often through training), but that typically doesn't lead to an understanding of the complex contingencies under which managers operate. Understanding the controlling variables affecting the strategic and tactical choices made by managers as they attempt to improve performance would fill a large knowledge gap in OBM.

Performance Driver System: A Case Study

Figure 5 depicts major management systems that most directly affect performance, hence the descriptor "performance driver system." These are things managers can change if business results, monitored as part of the PVC, are below expectations. Some of these elements are visible in the models discussed above while others have been less apparent (e.g., hiring practices). The functioning of each driver affects other drivers in this system, demonstrating the interaction effects that help to define systems properties.

Such interactive systems effects were evident in an accounting firm whose chief financial officer (CFO) had designed a performance pay system loosely based on Abernathy's plan described above (Morales & Hyten, 2006). The performance pay plan was evaluated across various job levels and time frames (Porter, 2002; Shelton, 2005; McDaniel, 2007). Additionally, other performance improvement projects were conducted over the course of the plan's implementation (Hyten, Chhabra, & Porter, 2003). Process changes were rapidly adopted because they enhanced department profitability, an integral part of the performance pay plan affecting bonus payouts (Chhabra, 2000).

As the pay plan went into effect at all levels (excluding equity partners) many organizational adjustments occurred, some desirable and some undesirable. For example, the pay plan prompted a number of questions about the metrics involved. What was interesting was that employees had been

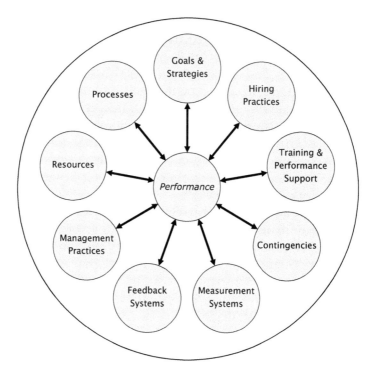

FIGURE 5 The performance driver system.

given these same data during meetings for years prior to the implementation of the pay plan with no such questions.

The performance pay system altered hiring practices in several ways. New hires could, in the performance pay plan, reduce productivity and bonuses if the work projected never materialized. Because of this contingency, the CFO developed a hiring plan to control hiring practices. Further, a review of employee performance data showed new hires who performed very poorly in their first year were not retained, either because they left voluntarily or because they were perhaps encouraged to leave by managers (Porter, 2002).

During senior management meetings an increasing emphasis was put on hunting for high-profit-margin work because of the pay contingencies associated with it. Managers began being more selective in taking on clients that could supply high-margin work. Because their pay was affected by senior manager decisions, midlevel accountants even began asking questions about the profitability of the work brought into the firm.

Training practices changed. At the beginning of the plan, the firm had a trainer whose approach centered on finding out what kinds of training people wanted, rather than looking at business and performance needs to decide what training people needed (see Brethower & Smalley, 1998). She continued her training practices and, because of the pay implications, upper managers released her. A new trainer was hired to address scorecard data that indicated some managers were chronically deficient in growing their own book of business. The new trainer worked with them on a one-to-one coaching basis. Because managers did not make appointments with this trainer, this area of poor performance was never fully remedied. Thus, the scorecard pay system did not provide adequate consequences to influence managers to seek out this coaching. Eventually, the scorecard itself was changed so that low performance in this one area could not harm the individual's scores, a less than optimal solution.

In fact, the behavior of the senior management team in maintaining the performance pay plan suggested that behavior history and social contingencies truncated the impact of the system. Senior management struggled with maintaining consistent contingencies associated with the measures chosen for the scorecards because of employee complaints. No student of behavior should be surprised that senior management would be more influenced by proximal sources of negative reinforcement than by the distal contingencies associated with delayed business results. It also seemed difficult to change old habits of promoting people based on politics instead of performance. This could have further undermined the performance pay plan for some employees, prompting more complaints or efforts to change the system in their favor (see Goltz, 2003 for a discussion of political behavior). Understanding the complex network of contingencies affecting management decisions proved to be a challenge.

Despite the few adverse systems effects noted above, the performance pay plan was viewed as successful and maintained for 5 years. Morales and Hyten (2006) presented data showing that the firm's net income doubled across these years (see Figure 6). Even while the number of full-time equivalent (FTE) employees decreased, the profit per FTE increased. Bottom-line financial data will always be a result of many variables, but data supported the conclusion that the performance pay plan contributed substantially to the results improvement.

The Performance Driver System (Figure 5) enables managers or consultants to see the leverage they have at their disposal to improve performance. A comprehensive systems analysis would enable managers to anticipate or react to the effects of changes to performance drivers on other drivers in the system. As evidenced by some of the stories above, controlling such complex system drivers as they interact is a challenge for managers even if they have a good understanding of systems models.

Systems models like the PVC include behavior as a critical subsystem, so the role of behavior and its controlling variables does not get lost amid all of the other features of the system. Indeed, behavior analytic expertise in understanding and managing behavioral contingencies is certainly very relevant in systems approaches (Malott, 2003). OBM practitioners can utilize concepts and tools from behavior analysis in the context of system tools

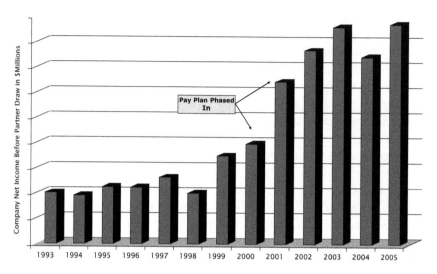

FIGURE 6 Company net income before and after introduction of a performance pay plan that took effect in the years 2000–2005. Exact dollar amounts are not shown on the y-axis for confidentiality reasons. Tick marks represent increments of one half million dollars.

and should demonstrate even more effectiveness in helping client organizations achieve their operational or financial goals.

Changing OBM Practice and Research

Many performance-oriented writers and consultants (e.g., Brethower & Smalley, 1998; LaFleur, Smalley, & Austin, 2005; Malott, 2003; Robinson & Robinson, 1995; Stolovitch & Keeps, 1999) have described this results-focused methodology. It does stand in contrast to the behavior-focused approach concentrating primarily on the left side of the PVC. In practice, a systems-oriented, results-focused approach would begin at the right side of the PVC (Figure 4), identifying business results to improve in order to enhance organizational success or adaptation. Such results, referred to as "Critical Business Issues" (CBI) by Rummler and Brache (1995), may be readily identified by management personnel who are in regular contact with business results data (if they are asked the right questions).

The importance of establishing the business case for a performance improvement effort cannot be overemphasized. Examples of business results that might be the anchor for performance improvement include revenues, costs, profitability, product quality, productivity, timeliness, market share, and customer satisfaction. These are not the kinds of targets that supervisors might generate when asked about their problems, which can lead OBM practitioners to jump leftward in the PVC to pinpoint behavior before establishing a business case in the right column to justify further analysis.

OBM writers have always urged practitioners to identify performance gaps in the organization (e.g., Bailey & Austin, 2001; Daniels & Daniels, 2004), but tools are needed to aid in this method. The OBM practitioner should interview managers regarding their CBIs in initial client meetings. Surprisingly, some clients may have difficulty identifying the business case for intervening. A Supersystem map (Rummler & Brache, 1995) would be helpful at this point to gain an understanding of the organization in context of its customers and competitors and show potential CBIs in the context of the organization's products or services. This information would also be helpful in anticipating possible interactions that may result from improvement efforts. For example, intervening to improve quality might cause problems in production or labor costs. Data on the CBI should be collected to show if there is a gap between current performance and the desired level. The gap analysis helps establish the importance of the CBI, and it serves as a benchmark for later evaluating performance-improvement efforts.

The next phase involves an analysis of the causes of poor business results. Processes and behavior systems should be examined for possible deficiencies. This analysis should be "solution-neutral," where there is no assumption at the outset that processes must be redesigned, that training is needed, or that reinforcement be amplified unless there is evidence that those particular interventions will contribute to the targeted performance issues.

Interventions are then designed to address the causes identified in this analysis and implemented. These interventions could go beyond simple supervision-related feedback. Elements of the Performance Driver System could be manipulated so that the need for direct supervision would be reduced. This is a pressing issue with companies trying to trim management levels to save costs, with increased telecommuting, or where employees are spread around the globe. Identifying the controlling variables over management decision-making is a particularly ripe opportunity because of their effect on systems interaction.

OBM practitioners can bring their unique expertise in behavior analysis and behavior change technology to bear in root cause analysis and intervention design. While it is true that some OBM practitioners have neglected to take systems fully into account in their work, it is certainly true that it is a rare systems practitioner who understands behavioral contingencies in all their complexity and how to alter them to promote behaviors leading to value-added results. The most effective systems-oriented, results-focused performance improvement approach must apply behavior analytic concepts. That does not mean contingency modification will always be the main focus of intervention; it does mean that prevailing behavioral contingencies must always be taken into account. Indeed, redesigned processes often require performers to behave differently than old processes, training systems should be linked with contingencies to maximize transfer of learning, management systems require manager behaviors to work, and sometimes interventions require changes in customer behavior. Thus, the tools of behavior analysis, given a proper systems context, can be focused with precision to make a meaningful impact on business results.

Intervention effectiveness can be evaluated at multiple levels, but business results data should be included. Business results data also enables return on investment (ROI) calculations, a very important cost-benefit metric in the business world and increasingly in the world of performance improvement (Phillips, 1997; Phillips & Phillips, 2007). It is not sufficient to show that behavior changed as a result of some intervention without showing impact on business results data. Ideally, one would have a "chain of evidence" showing that changes in employee behavior led to improvements in business results. But behavioral data based on direct observation are rarely taken in most organizations and would be expensive and impractical to introduce as routine practice. However, with the advent of technology, behavioral data are becoming more available for organizational research (Ludwig & Goomas, 2007).

Research questions stimulated by a systems approach might address topics other than the influence of antecedent or supervisor-mediated consequence variables on the behavior of line employees. For example, how can two sets of organizational practices be integrated to maintain high performance in a corporate merger or acquisition? What does it take to save a failing retail chain? What performance systems are necessary to ensure that a startup company succeeds? How can management practices be changed to increase innovation? Questions such as these might be of considerable interest to business leaders, and they would appear to require an approach that understands human behavior as it participates in complex systems. Such an approach might be a systems-oriented, results-focused OBM.

REFERENCES

Abernathy, W. B. (2000). *Managing without supervising: Creating an organization-wide performance system.* Memphis, TN: PerfSys.

Abernathy, W. B., & Harshbarger, D. (n.d.). A proposed new program perspective and curriculum for organizational behavior management. Retrieved October 28, 2008, from http://www.behavior.org/performanceMgmt_new/abernathy&harshbarger.cfm

Ayllon, T., & Roberts, M. D. (1974). Eliminating discipline problems by strengthening academic performance. *Journal of Applied Behavior Analysis, 7,* 71–76.

Baer, D. M., Wolf, M. M., & Risley, T. R. (1968). Some current dimensions of applied behavior analysis. *Journal of Applied Behavior Analysis, 1,* 91–97.

Bailey, J. S., & Austin, J. (2001). Deconstructing performance management processes. In L. J. Hayes, J. Austin, R. Houmanfar, & M. Clayton (Eds.), *Organizational change* (pp. 67–88). Reno, NV: Context.

Berger, S. M., & Ludwig, T. D. (2007). Reducing warehouse employee errors using voice-assisted technology that provided immediate feedback. *Journal of Organizational Behavior Management, 27*(1), 1–31.

Binder, C. (1998). The six boxes: A descendant of Gilbert's Behavior Engineering Model. *Performance Improvement, 37*, 48–52.

Brethower, D. M. (1972). *Behavioral analysis in business and industry.* Kalamazoo, MI: Behaviordelia.

Brethower, D. M. (1982). The total performance system. In R. O'Brien, A. Dickinson, & M. Rosow (Eds.), *Industrial behavior modification* (pp. 250–369). New York: Pergamon.

Brethower, D. M. (1995). Specifying a human performance technology knowledgebase. *Performance Improvement Quarterly, 8*(2), 17–39.

Brethower, D. M. (1999). General systems theory and behavioral psychology. In H.D. Stolovitch & E. J. Keeps (Eds.), *Handbook of human performance technology: Improving individual and organizational performance worldwide* (pp. 67–81). San Francisco: Jossey-Bass.

Brethower, D. M. (2001). Managing a person as a system. In L. J. Hayes, J. Austin, R. Houmanfar, & M. C. Clayton (Eds.), *Organizational change* (pp. 89–105). Reno, NV: Context.

Brethower, D. M. (2008). Historical background for HPT certification standard 2, take a systems view, Part 1. *Performance Improvement, 47*(2), 16–22.

Brethower, D. M., & Dams, P. (1999) Systems thinking (and systems doing). *Performance Improvement, 38*(1), 37–51.

Brethower, D. M., & Smalley, K. A. (1998). *Performance-based instruction: Linking training to business results.* San Francisco: Jossey-Bass.

Chhabra, M. K. (2000). *Performance improvement in an accounting firm: Comparing operational and financial data before and after process redesign.* Unpublished master's thesis, University of North Texas.

Daniels, A. C. (1977). Editorial. *Journal of Organizational Behavior Management, 1*, v–vii.

Daniels, A. C., & Daniels, J. E. (2004). *Performance management: Changing behavior that drives organizational effectiveness.* Atlanta: Aubrey Daniels International.

Dickinson, A. M. (2000). The historical roots of organizational behavior management in the private sector: The 1950s–1980s. *Journal of Organizational Behavior Management, 20*(3/4), 9–58.

Gilbert, T. (1978/1996). *Human competence: Engineering worthy performance.* Washington, DC: International Society for Performance Improvement.

Goltz, S. M. (2003). Considering political behavior in organizations. *The Behavior Analyst Today, 4*(3).

Goomas, D. T., & Ludwig, T. D. (2007). Enhancing incentive programs with proximal goals and immediate feedback: Engineered labor standards and technology enhancements in stocker replenishment. *Journal of Organizational Behavior Management, 27*(1), 33–68.

Harshbarger, D., & Maley, R. F. (1974) *Behavior analysis and systems analysis: An integrative approach to mental health programs.* Kalamazoo, MI: Behaviordelia.

Hayes, S. C., Hayes, L. J., & Reese, H. W. (1988). Finding the philosophical core: A review of Stephen C. Pepper's *World Hypotheses: A Study in Evidence. Journal of the Experimental Analysis of Behavior, 50*, 97–111.

Hyten, C. (2002). On the identity crisis in OBM. *Behavior Analyst Today, 3*(3), 301–310.

Hyten, C., Chhabra, M., & Porter, M. (2003, May). *Firm-wide analysis of performance barriers and the follow-up projects.* In B. Cole (Chair), Building performance systems in an accounting firm: Five years of strategy and projects. Symposium conducted at the annual meeting of the Association for Behavior Analysis, San Francisco.

Kangas, B. D., & Vaidya, M. (2007). Trends in presentations at the annual conference of the Association for Behavior Analysis. *The Behavior Analyst, 30*(2), 117–131.

Krapfl, J., & Gasparatto, G. (1982). Behavioral systems analysis. In L. W. Frederiksen (Ed.), *Handbook of organizational behavior management* (pp. 21–38). New York: Wiley.

Krause, T. R. (2005). *Leading with safety.* Hoboken, NJ: Wiley.

LaFleur, T., & Hyten, C. (1995). Improving the quality of hotel banquet performance. *Journal of Organizational Behavior Management, 15*(1/2), 69–93.

LaFleur, D., Smalley, K., & Austin, J. (2005). Improving performance in a nuclear cardiology department. *Performance Improvement Quarterly, 18*(1), 83–109.

Ludwig, T. D., & Goomas, D. T. (2007). Performance, accuracy, data delivery, and feedback methods in order selection: A comparison of voice, handheld, and paper technologies. *Journal of Organizational Behavior Management, 27*(1), 69–107.

Malott, M. E. (2003). *Paradox of organizational change: Engineering organizations with behavioral systems analysis.* Reno, NV: Context.

Maurice, C. (1993). *Let me hear your voice: A family's triumph over autism.* New York: Ballantine.

Mawhinney, T. C. (2000). OBM today and tomorrow: Then and now. *Journal of Organizational Behavior Management, 20*(3/4), 73–137.

Mawhinney, T. C. (2001). Organization-environment systems as OBM intervention context: Minding your metacontingencies. In L. J. Hayes, J. Austin, R. Houmanfar, & M. C. Clayton (Eds.), *Organizational change* (pp. 137–165). Reno, NV: Context.

McDaniel, S. C. (2007). *Analyzing the effects of a performance pay plan on manager performance in an accounting firm.* Unpublished master's thesis, University of North Texas.

McDougall, P. (2006, December 21). Accenture posts strong quarterly growth, raises 2007 outlook. *InformationWeek.* Retrieved March 17, 2008, from http://www.informationweek.com/shared/printableArticleSrc.jhtml?articleID=196701465

McSween, T. E. (1995). *The values-based safety process: Improving your safety culture with a behavioral approach.* New York: Van Nostrand Reinhold.

McSween, T. E. (2003). *The values-based safety process: Improving your safety culture with behavior-based safety.* Hoboken, NJ: Wiley.

Morales, B., & Hyten, C. (2006, April). *Scorecard-based, profit-indexed performance pay in a professional service firm.* Address at the annual conference of the International Society for Performance Improvement, Dallas, TX.

Nolan, T., Jarema, K., & Austin, J. (1999). An objective review and comparison of the *Journal of Organizational Behavior Management: 1987–1997. Journal of Organizational Behavior Management, 19*(3), 83–114.

Performance improvement. (n.d.) Retrieved March 19, 2008, from http://www.deloitte.com/dtt/section_node/0,1042,sid%253D153775%2526fd%253DY,00.html.

Phillips, J. J. (1997). *Return on investment in training and performance improvement programs*. Houston, TX: Gulf.

Phillips, J. J., & Phillips, P. P. (2007). *Show me the money: How to determine ROI in people, projects, and programs*. San Francisco: Berrett-Koehler.

Porter, M. D. (2002). *An evaluation of the effects of a performance pay plan on productivity of employees in a professional service firm*. Unpublished master's thesis, University of North Texas.

Pyzdek, T. (2003). *The Six Sigma handbook: A complete guide for green belts, black belts, and managers at all levels*. New York: McGraw-Hill.

Redmon, W. K., & Mason, M. A. (2001). Organizational culture and behavioral systems analysis. In Johnson, C. M., Redmon, W. K., & Mawhinney, T. C. (Eds.) *Handbook of organizational performance: Behavior analysis and management* (pp. 437–456). New York: Haworth.

Robinson, D. G., & Robinson, J. C. (1995). *Performance consulting: Moving beyond training*. San Francisco: Berrett-Koehler.

Rummler, G. A. (1999) Transforming organizations through human performance technology. In H. D. Stolovitch & E. J. Keeps (Eds.), *Handbook of human performance technology: Improving individual and organizational performance worldwide* (pp. 47–66). San Francisco: Jossey-Bass.

Rummler, G. A. (2001). Performance logic: The organization performance Rosetta stone. In L. J. Hayes, J. Austin, R. Houmanfar, & M. C. Clayton (Eds.), *Organizational change* (pp. 111–132). Reno, NV: Context.

Rummler, G. A. (2004). *Serious performance consulting according to Rummler*. Washington, DC: International Society for Performance Improvement.

Rummler, G. A., & Brache, A. P. (1995). *Improving performance: How to manage the white space on the organizational chart* (2nd ed.). San Francisco: Jossey-Bass.

Senge, P. M. (1990). *The fifth discipline: The art and practice of the learning organization*. New York: Doubleday.

Shelton, B. (2005). *An evaluation of two performance pay systems on the productivity of employees in a certified public accounting firm*. Unpublished master's thesis. University of North Texas.

Slowiak, J. (2007). Membership update. *OBM Network Newsletter, 21*(2). Retrieved August 27, 2008, from http://www.obmnetwork.com/resources/newsletter/2102/report.html

Stolovitch, H. D., & Keeps, E. J. (eds.) (1999). *Handbook of human performance technology: Improving individual and organizational performance worldwide*. San Francisco: Jossey-Bass.

Twyman, J. S. (2007a, May). *How do we get there?* Address at the annual conference of the Association for Behavior Analysis, San Diego, CA.

Twyman, J. S. (2007b, Fall). ABAI launches national public relations campaign. *ABA Newsletter, 30*, 3.

Von Bertalannfy, L. (1968). *General systems theory*. New York: Braziller.

Wedgwood, I. D. (2007). *Lean sigma: A practitioner's guide*. Upper Saddle River, NJ: Prentice-Hall.

Winett, R. A., & Winkler, R. C. (1972). Current behavior modification in the classroom: Be still, be quiet, be docile. *Journal of Applied Behavior Analysis, 5*, 499–504.

Walden Two Revisited: Optimizing Behavioral Systems

WILLIAM B. ABERNATHY

Southeastern Louisiana University, Hammond, Louisiana, USA

There has been little recent discussion about Skinner's utopian vision as presented in Walden Two. *Organizational Behavior Management could revitalize interest in this topic through its discussion of Behavioral Systems Analysis. A brief review of utopian thought and* Walden Two *is provided. Four recommendations are offered to improve the viability and effectiveness of Skinner's original utopian concepts: (a) experiment with utopian ideas in existing organizations rather than create new independent communities; (b) apply advances in performance measurement and performance pay to refine* Walden Two's *work "credit" system; (c) address the problem of poor performing members by implementing performance management; and (d) refine* Walden Two's *self-management "code" and general administration.*

UTOPIAN THOUGHT

The word *utopia* translates from the Latin as "no place land" and was coined by Sir Thomas More in 1515. A utopian community is defined in the New Lexicon Webster's Dictionary as: "Any imaginary political and social system in which relationships between individuals and the state are perfectly adjusted"; and a utopian thinker as: "Someone who believes in the immediate perfectibility of human society by the application of some idealistic scheme." Notable historical examples of utopian proposals were Plato's *Republic* (Bloom, 1991), Augustine Hippo's *The City of God* (Betternson, 1972), Thomas More's *Utopia* (1964), Francis Bacon's *The New Atlantis*

(1909–14), William Morris's *News from Nowhere* (1891), and Edward Bellamy's *Looking Backward* (2000). The utopian vision is also expressed in mythology such as in the epics *Arcadia* and *Shangri-La*.

Utopian communities have been organized on political principles (Greece's Sparta), religious principles (the Shaker movement), and scientific and technological principles (Buckminster Fuller's vision). They have most often been organized around economic principles as, for example, Edward Bellamy's *Looking Backward*. The Soviet Union was, in this sense, an economic utopian community. Generally, the goal of economic utopias is a more equitable distribution of goods with an increase in free time in which to pursue the arts and other personal interests. Consequently, the majority of these communities adopted some variation of socialism. As a reaction to the expansion of capitalism, almost 100 utopian communities were founded in the United States between 1805 and 1855 (Jacoby, 2005).

There are, however, exceptions in which economic utopias are built on free market principles. "Local Exchange Trading Systems" (LETS) are local nonprofit exchange networks in which goods and services are traded without the need for printed currency. In this arrangement, capitalism is eliminated (i.e., making money from interest or property), while free enterprise is encouraged (Feallock & Miller, 1976).

In many ways, applied behavior analysis employs utopian thinking in that its practitioners believe in the "perfectibility of human society" and attempt to change the relationships (contingencies) between the individual and the state (environment). This utopian parallel is especially evident in the area of Organizational Behavior Management (OBM). OBM uniquely focuses on changing organizational variables as well as an individual's local work context in order to optimize performance and reduce aversive control.

The perspective most related to general utopian thinking, however, is an offshoot of OBM variously termed *behavior systems analysis* or *performance systems analysis*. This view was formulated some 30 years ago in the Western Michigan University psychology department. Two seminal works were Dale M. Brethower's *A Total Performance System* (1972) and Dwight Harshbarger and Roger F. Maley's (eds.) *Behavior Analysis and Systems Analysis: An Integrative Approach to Mental Health Programs* (1974).

Behavior systems analysis is, in part, a reaction to the emphasis in OBM on the interactions between the supervisor and the subordinate in the workplace. Skinner, in *Walden Two*, did not mention supervisors preferring to rely on system contingencies to manage member behavior. Examples of organizational system contingencies include job definitions; employee recruiting and selection methods and criteria; employee orientations and job training; organizational policies, procedures, and communications; performance assessment methods; grievance and disciplinary procedures; promotion procedures; compensation and benefits; employee ownership; job assignments; staffing; scheduling and work distribution; bureaucratic

structure; job resources and tools; job methods; and workflow as well as what
Malott (2003) terms external *metacontingencies* such as vendor, customer,
competitor, governmental, and general economic contingencies. Behavior
systems analysis argues that these contingencies, and especially the organizational contingencies, must be reengineered to produce optimal and sustainable behavior changes and to reduce aversive control.

WALDEN TWO

In 1948, B. F. Skinner published *Walden Two* (Skinner, 1948). *Walden Two*
was a utopian novel that described a community designed around Skinner's
"experimental analysis of behavior." He later expanded his ideas on
designing cultures in *Science and Human Behavior* (1953), *Contingencies
of Reinforcement: A Theoretical Analysis* (1969), and *Beyond Freedom and
Dignity* (1971). In the 1960s and early 1970s there were a number of
attempts to apply the Walden Two concepts including Walden House (1969),
Lake Village (1971), Los Horcones (1971), and the Twin Oaks Community
(1974). Some of these applications failed, while others moved to modified
versions of Walden Two. I will argue that Skinner's objectives in 1948 were
laudable, but improvements could be made to Walden Two and applied to
the workplace in which most of us spend a large part of our adult lives.

Recommendations are provided that might improve the implementation
and sustainability of a "behaviorist utopia" within the context of existing
organizational structures. These are (a) experiment with utopian ideas in
existing organizations rather than create new independent communities;
(b) apply advances in performance measurement and performance pay to
refine Walden Two's work "credit" system; (c) address the utopian nemesis of
poor performing members by implementing performance management; and
(d) refine Walden Two's self-management "code" and general administration.

Recommendation 1: Refine Skinner's Utopian Concepts within Existing Organizational Systems

The historical failure rate of communes like Walden Two has been severe.
In some cases these were due to failures of leadership in which the leader's
personal interests outweighed community interests, or due to conflicts
among various factions within the community. However, one of the greatest
reasons for failure was due to communes that simply could not sustain
themselves economically. As a teenager in Arkansas, I witnessed first hand
the influx of California "hippies" who failed at communal farming in the
Ozark Mountains. In the business world this would be analogous to the failure
of new companies. According to the Small Business Association Web site
(sba.gov), 50% of small businesses fail in the first 5 years.

The solution to this critical problem for the utopian vision is to engage in more modest and practical experimentation. Existing organizations are an exciting alternative. Most organizations are already economically viable and have an identity and a political structure based on private, public, or employee ownership. If these organizations operated on sound behavioral principles, a more limited form of utopia would be achieved for working people. As these practices thrived, it is possible they would then spread to the society at large. OBM is in a unique position to lead this effort.

Skinner argued for developing utopian principles and techniques in smaller settings. Unlike Bellamy's (2000) and Marx's (1867) utopias, the community in *Walden Two* had a population similar to that of a medium-sized company of around 1,000 members. In his introduction to the 1976 printing of *Walden Two*, Skinner further stressed, "If we want to find out how people can live together without quarreling, can produce the goods they need without working too hard, or can raise and educate their children more efficiently, let us start with units of manageable size before moving on to larger units." (p. ix).

There was little mention in Skinner's writing of interactions of Walden Two members with the outside world other than selling produce and furniture to local businesses. Walden Two was a closed society. Many utopian communities have failed to meet their objectives because they were "closed" systems. As a result, aversive and dysfunctional practices evolve. Extreme examples of closed communes that went awry are the Jim Jones commune in which there were mass suicides and the Branch Davidians who were raided by the Bureau of Alcohol, Tobacco and Firearms in Texas. Though their odd behavior was typically ascribed to their religions, it is also a characteristic of closed social systems. These problems can be largely avoided by experimenting in mainstream businesses.

Business organizations are a more fertile alternative than independent communes for a number of reasons.

1. They have already proved economically viable and thus are more immune to economic failure than startup communes.
2. Existing business organizations typically have a more achievable vision of their objectives and strategies than the economic, social, or religious visions of communes.
3. The political structure in existing businesses is established, whereas new communes must develop it.
4. The work procedures and assignments are mostly developed in an existing business but not so in a new commune.
5. For-profit organizations (except monopolies) are less likely to become closed systems than communes, because to survive they must interact with customers, vendors, competitors, and the government.

A drawback to the application of behavior systems analysis to existing organizations is that we are not "engineering" the behavior system but rather "reengineering" it. Consequently, we must analyze the existing system before we can begin to reengineer. An example of behavior systems process analysis and reengineering is Rummler and Brache's *Improving Performance: How to Manage the White Space on the Organizational Chart* (1995). The authors describe a method for describing work inputs and outputs as well as work processes within the organization.

Recommendation 2: Implement "Profit-Indexed Performance Pay" to Refine the Walden Two Credit System

ISSUES WITH SOCIALISM, PROFIT SHARING, AND WAGES AND SALARIES

In socialist utopias, the community's goods and services are distributed equally among the members without regard to individual contributions to the society. This proves to be a fatal design flaw and should not surprise behavior analysts since the distributions are noncontingent. A serious flaw in socialist income distribution schemes is what economists term the *free rider effect* (Tuomela, 2000) and social psychologists call *social loafing* (Karau & Williams, 1993; Latane, Williams, & Harkins, 1979). Some people simply do not contribute their fair share of goods and services to the community or organization. Government welfare programs that distribute money on a noncontingent basis further illustrate these problems.

The business parallel to socialist communities is the profit-sharing program in which each employee receives an equal share of annual excess profits (Binder, 1990). More common and troublesome than profit sharing, however, is the wage-and-salary system. Because the concept of contingent reinforcement is poorly understood in the business community, the assumption is that wages and salaries are examples of pay for performance. Generally, people in the same job are paid about the same as determined by job market surveys. The wage and salary payments, however, are based on time on the job during the pay period rather than performance during the pay period. I have described this problem in the maxim, "When you pay for time, you get time. When you pay for results, you get results." Skinner (1996) himself pointed out that most wage and salary systems are not contingent on performance and, as a result, some other form of control is required. Unfortunately, this alternate form is typically aversive control. People work to avoid criticism, suspension, or termination. They do not work for their wage or salary but rather to avoid losing it. "Society isn't likely to convert to positive reinforcement in the control of its sheep. It couldn't convert because it's not raising sheep for the good of the sheep. It has no net positive reinforcement to offer. Nothing short of an

insurmountable fence or frequent punishment will control the exploited."
(Skinner, 1948, p. 302).

This reliance on aversive control has serious consequences for organizations. These include lax performance, escape and avoidance, and excessive bureaucracy. Performance is not optimal when the worker produces
only enough to meet the minimum work standards to avoid criticism.
There is no reinforcement for exceeding the standard. Aubrey Daniels
describes this as a failure to tap the employee's "discretionary effort."
(Daniels & Rosen, 1983). Compounding this problem, some organizations
increase standards when employees consistently exceed those standards
(Goomas & Ludwig, 2007).

In an aversive work environment, escape and avoidance behaviors
(tardiness, absenteeism) are likely. Skinner also noted (1953) that counter
control might also occur to undermine the goals for the aversive consequences (Ludwig, 2002; Ludwig & Geller 1999, 2000).

Aversive control also requires high levels of expensive supervision to
function effectively. The ratio of supervisors and managers to workers is
termed the "span of control." An organization with 100 workers and 10
managers and supervisors would have a span of control of 10. For example,
Entwisle and Walton (1961) surveyed three sets of organizations: 20 small
businesses (100 to 1,000 employees), 20 colleges or universities, and 20
automobile dealers. The median of spans of control in colleges extends
from 5 to 7 inclusive, while the span of control for companies extends from
4 to 7. Changes in the span of control increase the number of managers and
organizational levels geometrically, since the addition of more supervisors
necessitates the addition of more middle managers who then require additional senior managers. These layers of bureaucracy create an organization
that is unresponsive to both external and internal changes.

As Skinner points out in *Walden Two*, an alternative is to put employees in direct contact with contingencies rather than institute a bureaucracy
that serves as an intermediary between organizational contingencies and the
employee. "You can't foresee all future circumstances. You don't know
what will be required. Instead, you have to set up certain behavioral processes which will lead the individual to design his own 'good conduct'
when the time comes." (Skinner, 1948, p. 105).

The economist Martin Weitzman (1984) argued that the wage-and-salary
system is inferior to profit sharing since it is a risky fixed cost for the organization. When revenues decline, the organization has no alternative but to
lay off employees. When revenues increase, employees typically don't share
in the success. Partially or completely replacing fixed wages and salaries
with profit shares would enable employees to share in the success of the
organization. However, profit sharing in which each member or employee
receives the same allocation regardless of personal contribution is bad
behavioral technology.

THE SOLUTION: INDEX PROFIT SHARES TO PERFORMANCE

In *Managing Without Supervising: Creating an Organization-Wide Performance System* (Abernathy, 2000), an alternative pay system was described
that corrects many of the deficiencies in general profit sharing as well as with
wages and salaries. This system has been applied successfully in many organizations (Abernathy, 2001). Excess profits are allocated to employees. The
amount of the allocation employees receive is based on personal and/or
small team performance on a "performance matrix." Thus, the dollar value of
a performance score is "indexed" to the profit of the company. These allocations are distributed monthly rather than annually. Monthly allocations allow
the organization to substitute profit shares for some portion of base pay, thus
moving pay from a fixed to a variable expense (Weitzman, 1984).

Excess profits are defined as profits above the amount required to pay
a reasonable return on investment to owners, pay down debt, invest in new
business lines or technology, and build a cash reserve. Profit allocations are
defined as a percentage of an individual's base pay sufficient to keep potential
compensation in line with the job market. For example, employees might
be assigned a maximum profit share allocation of 20% of their base pay.
These allocations are adjusted for each individual member's performance as
computed on a "performance matrix." A member who fails to contribute
will receive none of his or her allocation for the month. See Table 1 for an
example of a computation of monthly performance pay.

In Walden Two, work "credits" were earned by members. A credit
value was assigned to each task, and when the task was completed the
credits were awarded to the member. The goal was to earn 4 hours of credit
each day. It is not clear in the text whether Skinner defined credits in terms
of the average time required to complete the task or on the value of the task
to the community. The latter approach is how prices are set in a free market.
The following quote illustrates the Walden Two credit process. ". . . we
reported to the work desk. What have you to offer my friends? She referred
to a small box of cards. I can give them work at 1.2 which doesn't call for
any particular experience." (Skinner, 1948, p. 71). Did Skinner mean
that the assigned task would be credited with 1.2 hours or did he mean that
when the work was completed 1.2 credits would be awarded based on
the value of the work to the community? If the former, Skinner was

TABLE 1 Example Computation of Monthly Performance Pay Based on an Employee with a
$2,000 Base Salary, an Assigned 5% of Base Pay Basis or Opportunity, and a Profit Sufficient
to Multiply the 5% Basis by 2 to Provide a 10% of Base Pay Performance Pay Opportunity

Salary	Basis%	Profit multiplier	Allocation	Matrix score	Perf. pay
$2,000	5%	2*	$200	80%	$160.00

*Multiplier increases as organizational profit increases. Unprofitable months produce a multiplier of zero
and no performance pay is awarded.

recommending what industrial engineers refer to as a *standard time* system. If the latter, he was suggesting a value-based credit system.

Standard time systems determine the time required to complete a task by a well-motivated worker. The standard times are multiplied by work volumes and are summed to compute the day's earned hours. The earned hours are then divided by the time on the job to determine a productivity ratio for each employee (Goomas & Ludwig, 2007). If an employee earns 8 hours and works 8 hours, the ratio is 100%, and the worker is considered a good performer.

There are two problems with standard time. First, standard time is typically defined for activities or behaviors rather than results. Consequently, a worker could produce a 100% productivity ratio based on various activities but never actually produce a result of value to the organization. Put another way, the ingredients for a cake are still not a cake. Second, standard time alone is a one-dimensional productivity measurement and does not consider quality, safety, and other critical performance dimensions. If Skinner's credit system was a standard time system, additional measurements would be required beyond the credits themselves.

An alternative to standard time is a value-based credit system. At a regional bank we rated job *outcomes* with respect to average time to complete, task constraints, task difficulty, and task desirability. The results of this approach, like previous standard time approaches, revealed common flaws (see Abernathy, 1980). In addition to the problems of one-dimensionality mentioned earlier, there was no effective means for assigning priorities to job tasks or ensuring any sort of balance among job tasks. The average time it takes to complete an activity says nothing about the importance of the task. Without priorities, employees' performance can become unbalanced since they may work only on low-priority tasks.

We attempted to solve these deficiencies by adding a priority dimension to the credit rating plan based on the value to the organization (how this is determined is outlined below). High-priority standard time values were multiplied by 3, average priority 2, and low priority 1. (This may have been what Skinner had in mind with his 1.2 credits for an hour's work.) Though this helped, it was still possible for employees to choose tasks they preferred and ignore critical tasks they did not wish to perform. Further, the meaning of a "standard hour" was corrupted by these priority adjustments because some low-priority task may have taken many hours to complete but end up earning low amounts of credits.

The performance matrix developed by Felix and Riggs at the University of Oregon Productivity Center (1986) corrects two problems with time- or value-based credits: prioritization and balance. The matrix converts raw data to a common measurement scale using a "percent gain" formula (actual − base / goal − base). Over several applications we have come to realize that *minimum* and *maximum* are more descriptive terms than *base* and *goal*. For example, for a measure of typing speed a base (minimum performance allowable) of 50 words per minute and an ultimate goal of 90 words per minute may be set. If actual performance is 60 words per minute then the percent gain is (60 – 50 / 90 – 50) = 25%.

Felix and Riggs's original matrix lowest percent gain was capped at –30%. Given the above typing example with a base of 50 and a goal of 90, this would represent a typing rate of 38 words per minute (38–50) / (50–90) = –30%. The original matrix base was 0% gain, or a typing rate of 50 (50–50) / (50–90) and the matrix goal of 100% gain (90–50) / 90–50). Capping (not allowing the percent gain to exceed –30% or 100%) the lowest and highest performance scores ensures balance since the performer cannot simply increase one measure's score to say 200%, ignore another measure, and still receive a high score and payout. Including negative scores (up to –30%) ensures the performer attends to all critical performances because allowing some measures to go negative subtracts from the overall performance matrix index. For example, a matrix might have two equally weighted measures: quantity of work and quality of work. If the quantity measure were at 100% with a 50% weight, but the quality measure was at –30%, the overall performance index would be 100% × 50% = 50% + –30% × 50% = –15%. An equation of 50% – 15% yields an overall index of 35% because 15% is subtracted from the quantity measure's 50%.

Figure 1 shows a sample matrix for a salesperson. The measures are gross revenue sold in the month, the gross profit percentage of the revenue sold, milestone completion on a sales project, and the salesperson's average

Performance Matrix

Performance Scales

Measures	–20	–10	0	10	20	30	40	50	60	80	100	WGT	WGT SCR
Gross Revenue	10K	15K	20K	25K	30K	35K	40K	45K	50K	55K	60K	.20	–4
GP Margin %	9.0	9.5	10	10.5	11.0	11.5	12.0	12.5	13.0	13.5	14.0	.20	0
%Project Milestone	50	55	60	65	70	75	80	85	90	95	100	.40	20
Customer Survey	4.0	4.5	5.0	5.5	6.0	6.5	7.0	7.5	8.0	8.5	9.0	.20	20

BASE   GOAL   36

Performance index

FIGURE 1 Sample performance matrix.

customer satisfaction survey rating. In this matrix the highest priority measure is meeting the project milestone deadlines with a priority weight of 40%. Though the performer's survey rating was high and the company was fairly successful on the project, the salesperson fell below personal minimum gross revenue expectations (base) and only met the base on the profit margin. Consequently, the total weighted score or performance index is 35% out a possible 100%. This is an example of how the matrix ensures balanced performance across multiple performance measures.

Each matrix measure's priority weight is determined by the priority weightings on the organization's "strategic matrix." The executive group meets to define the year's strategic goals and priority weightings for these goals. The strategic matrix defines what will be measured in each individual performer's matrix throughout the organization and the measure's strategic priority weighting. Ultimately, the strategic matrix is used to evaluate the effectiveness of the system at each year end. If the cascaded lower-level performance measures are valid, they should drive improvements in the strategic matrix.

After the strategic matrix is developed, all other scorecards are developed beginning with the executives, then the middle managers, line managers, and finally workers. This top-down method has been termed the *method of cascading objectives* (Kaplan & Norton, 1996; see Figure 2). The method of cascading objectives aligns priorities vertically across the organization. Each manager designs the matrices for direct reports. These individuals then design the matrices for their direct reports and so on to the worker level. This process ensures alignment since each "designer" wants to ensure the direct reports' measures and priorities drive success on his or her own matrix.

In summary, to address the performance measurement and performance pay issues, it is recommended that Skinner's Walden Two credit system be replaced by Felix & Riggs's (1986) Performance Matrix and Abernathy's (2000) Profit-Indexed Performance Pay. The performance matrix ensures the organization and employee work priorities are aligned by weighting each measure based on an organizational strategic scorecard. Profit-indexed performance pay ensures that payments to employees are affordable and that employees share ownership's concern about overall profits.

Recommendation 3: Address Poor Performers by Implementing a Performance Management System Concurrent with Performance Pay

A serious flaw in utopian socialist income distribution schemes is what economists term the *free rider effect* (Tuomela, 2000) and social psychologists call *social loafing* (Karau & Williams, 1993; Latane, Williams, & Harkins, 1979). Some people simply do not contribute their share of goods and services to the community or organization. Adjusting profit shares based on

Performance Constraint Analysis

Cascade Measures Down to Individuals & Small Teams

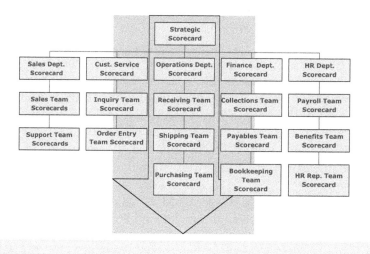

FIGURE 2 Method of cascading objectives.

each employee's performance index helps solve this problem. Even so, it is still likely that some employees will consistently have low scores and fail to contribute. This is particularly the case where performance pay accounts for only a small percentage of an employee's total earnings.

If an employee's pay is at market, he or she can economically ignore the performance pay plan. No "establishing" or "motivating" operation (Agnew, 1998; Agnew & Redmon, 1992) has been implemented. Skinner talked about motivation in terms of three types of variables: deprivation, satiation, and preexisting or antecedent aversive stimulation. For example, you cannot reinforce your dog to sit with food if the dog has not been deprived of food and isn't hungry. An organization that introduces performance pay as an addition to market comparable base pay has not created a "deprivation" state. An employee who fails to perform and earns no performance pay cannot move to another organization and increase his earnings since the current organization pays a market-comparable base.

Those of us who have been self-employed know well this motivating factor. As a self-employed person, there was no ceiling on my earnings but also no floor. To ensure consistent motivation across an employee group, performance pay must replace rather than simply augment base pay. Since performance pay isn't guaranteed, it is suggested that every leveraged dollar of base pay be replaced with a $3 performance pay opportunity. Organizations have had success when base pay was allowed to fall to 85% of market with a 145% of market pay earnings opportunity (Dierks & McNally, 1987). This compensation mix was achieved by substituting annual increases in performance pay for annual increases in base pay. In production areas, several organizations implemented 100% performance pay programs with good success.

H. G. Wells, in *A Modern Utopia* (2005), proposed a tongue-in-cheek solution to the problem of poor performers: "And you see the big convict steamship standing in to the Island of Incurable Cheats. The crew are respectfully at their quarters, ready to lend a hand overboard, but wide awake, and the captain is hospitably on the bridge to bid his guests good-bye and keep an eye on the movables." The organizational equivalent to Wells's proposal is to implement a leveraged pay system that makes it financially untenable for "incurable cheats" to remain with the organization.

Skinner, in *Walden Two*, addressed the problem of poor performance in these ways: "We don't condemn a man for poor work. After all, if we don't praise him, it would be unfair to blame him." (Skinner, 1948, p. 172). Skinner's first point is quite valid. Simply condemning people who perform poorly deflects us from identifying the genetic, experiential, or environmental constraints that are at the root of poor performance. Even if such condemnation improved the employee's performance, it is once again simply an example of a reliance on aversive control.

Skinner would send incorrigible poor performers to "psychologists." "But what if a man did poor work, or none at all, in every job you put him on? . . . The disease would be quite serious, and the man would be sent to one of our psychologists." (Skinner, 1948, p. 173). At first glance this solution seems ominous and almost humorous. However, if we substitute "behavior analyst" for "psychologist," the proposed solution becomes more palatable and tenable. I have argued elsewhere (Abernathy, in press) that such a behavior analyst would need an expanded repertoire of techniques. Figure 3 describes the range of performance constraints the behavior analyst should be able to address.

The performance analysis considers three key performance constraints: opportunity, capability, and context. The analysis moves left to right. That is, does the employee have the opportunity to perform is first addressed. If there is no opportunity, then capability and context are irrelevant. The behavior analyst would propose improving opportunity through more consistent work input and proper scheduling. If the opportunity to perform is present, the employee's capability to perform is considered by the behavior analyst next. Capability is improved through improving employee competence, work resources, and processes. Finally, if the opportunity and capability are present, the work context is analyzed. The key components in this analysis are prompts, feedback, and reinforcement. Other performance analysis

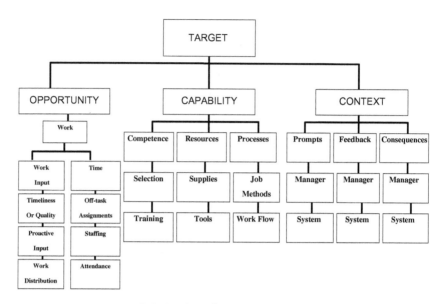

FIGURE 3 Performance analyses.

methods have been proposed as, for example, those of Tom Gilbert (1978) and Maria Malott (2003).

Consistently poor performers are a problem for any utopian vision. It is recommended that behavior analysts be employed to assist poor performers to improve. Further, it is recommended that base pay be set below market to ensure that acceptable performance levels are required for employee pay to achieve market levels or higher.

Recommendation 4: Refine Walden Two's Code and Administration

Skinner refers to the "code" throughout *Walden Two*. For example: "The main thing is, we encourage our people to view every habit and custom with an eye to possible improvement. A constantly experimental attitude toward everything—that's all we need." (Skinner, 1948, p. 29). There is often no one best means to produce a good or service, and these methods must change as the environment changes. An operant is a class of behaviors that produce a common result. Measuring and paying for results frees employees to continuously seek out the best production solutions (the most effective behaviors within an operant class) for them and their unique circumstances.

The contingencies that control an operant may be "rule governed" or "contingency shaped." Rule-governed behavior is behavior guided by instructions, while contingency-shaped behavior is developed through experiencing the consequences of behaviors. For example, you can learn to play tennis by hiring a coach who instructs you or by simply playing the game and responding to consequences. Skinner reiterates this point in a later book (1969, p. 170):

> Rule-governed behavior is usually designed to satisfy contingencies, not to duplicate other features of the behavior shaped by them. Contingency-shaped behavior is therefore likely to have a greater variety or richness. As Francis Bacon said, a painter or musician excels 'by a kind of felicity and not by rule,' where felicity seems to refer to the happy conse-quences which guide the artist in lieu of rules in the production of art. Contingencies contain reasons which rules can never specify.

CREATE AND REINFORCE SELF-MANAGEMENT

Skinner's position on supervisor praise seems diametrically opposed to current performance management practices that rely on manager praise to reinforce employee behaviors. ". . . I was conscious of the fact that no one thanked her or expressed gratitude in any other way . . . in accordance with the Walden Two code." (Skinner, 1948, p. 82). But is there anything wrong with admiring exceptional achievements or receiving recognition? Yes, if it points up the unexceptional achievements of others, it's wrong. We are opposed to personal competition." (Skinner, 1948, p. 169).

Walden Two makes no mention of conventional managers and supervi-sors. Instead, Skinner repeatedly refers to behavioral engineering and behavior engineers. One can interpret Skinner as arguing that organizations should eliminate the management and supervisor functions rather than try to improve them. "Governments which use force are based upon bad princi-ples of government. . . . Governments must always be right—they can't exper-iment because they can't admit doubt or question."

(Skinner, 1948, p. 194). Similar to governments, managers who rely on aversive control must also "always be right" or they lose their ability to coerce. This is why managers may be a bad choice as behavior analysts.

Bureaucratic management may naturally devolve over time. "Our way of thinking and our logical systems have hierarchical structures. If a system is too complex to be manageable—for example, a central nervous system in evolution—then it breaks apart into subsystems and thereby reduces its complexity" (Cramer, 1993). These subsystems are the various departments in an organization. In a self-managed workplace they are further refined into self-managed employee teams.

In place of military-style bureaucracies, organizations should work toward self-managed employee teams that are in direct contact with financial contingencies. These teams would voluntarily request the service of in-house behavior system analysts to assist them in removing performance constraints inherent in an organization's behavior system. The teams would operate in accordance with something similar to the *Walden Two* code.

WALDEN TWO'S PLANNERS

Skinner also refers to "planners" throughout *Walden Two*. "There are six Planners . . . they may serve for ten years but no longer." (Skinner, 1948, p. 54). Skinner limited the terms of planners to 10 years because he recommended they should not be democratically elected. In a business organization, the CEO or executive group serves as the planners. The planners should not be the sole owners in the company. Employee-owned companies or employee stock options would do much to defuse potential abuses of power by planners.

Presumably the planners determine the credit values of various tasks and perform other administrative duties. In our revised Walden Two, planners would be needed to connect the employee teams to the outside environment (Malott's metacontingencies; 2003). Planners would be surrogate customers who analyze consumer preferences, the market, resources, governmental regulations, competition, and changes in technology. Based on these analyses, they would change performance matrix measure priority weights and in some cases add or remove measures. They would not serve as managers nor have direct command and control powers.

Once the plan was communicated through the redesigned matrices, the day-to-day management would be performed by the self-managed employee teams that share in the company's profits based on team and personal performance. Behavior system engineers would provide technical staff functions and on-call assistance to the teams. Unlike conventional human resources, the engineers would integrate job descriptions, employee selection, training, and compensation with the performance matrix system. The functions of performance evaluation and promotion would no longer be relevant.

FREE TIME

Throughout *Walden Two*, Skinner makes the case for creating more free time for employees rather than continuously increasing pay. In Skinner's Walden Two people work only 4 hours a day. Those readers who are university professors are well aware of the tradeoff between higher pay and free time to pursue personal interests. In many organizations, there may be limits on how much revenue can be generated. In these cases improvements in efficiency would enable employees to work shorter hours or fewer days rather than receive pay increases. For job positions that require full-time staffing of 8 hours (e.g. customer service, nursing, etc.), job sharing could be used to distribute free time. "The difference is, we get rid of the work, not the worker." (Skinner, 1948, p. 76).

CONCLUSIONS

There is a long history of utopian thought and experimentation with utopian communities. Many of these communities failed, and the term *utopian* has taken on a pejorative connotation of unrealistic or impractical for many social planners. These failures were due to various reasons, including a lack of resources and leadership issues. However, a fundamental issue was a lack of understanding of behavioral principles and techniques. B. F. Skinner's Walden Two was an attempt to apply the behavioral techniques available in 1948 to the design and maintenance of a utopian community.

Traditionally, Organizational Behavior Management has focused many of its efforts on improving the interaction between the supervisor and the subordinate through better prompting, feedback, and reinforcement. It is argued that this was not Skinner's ultimate vision of how to improve society. "In general, by allowing natural consequences to take control whenever possible we generate behavior that is more likely to be appropriate to any occasion upon which it may occur again, and in doing so we promote the survival of the individual, the culture, and the species" (Skinner, 1987, p. 177).

Skinner favored placing employees (or communal members) in direct contact with the natural business contingencies. The supervisor was to shape behaviors and remove constraints for poor performers, and then get out of the way. "The contrived reinforcers of both education and therapy must eventually be terminated. Teacher or therapist must withdraw from the life of the student or client before teaching or therapy can said to be complete" (Skinner, 1987, p. 175). In his final address to the Association for Behavior Analysis, Skinner stated that he never liked the term *behavior management* and preferred *contingency management*.

Behavior Systems Analysis is a promising expansion of the traditional OBM perspective and techniques. Theorists and practitioners in this exciting field must first agree on what a behavior system is. This article argues that it is made up of *all* the contingencies that impact employee behavior. In addition to work processes, we must consider job definitions and organizational structure, employee recruiting and selection, training, performance assessment, promotions, compensation, and other variables. All of these variables are subject to improvement through a behavioral analysis. Further, these improvements should be made in an integrated fashion that considers systemic interactions.

Four recommendations were presented. First, existing business organizations are proposed as the ideal site for utopian experimentation. Second, an effective behavior system must begin with an organization-wide performance measurement and performance pay system. The performance matrix, implemented through the method of cascading objectives, is one possibility. Profit-indexed Performance Pay is an alternative pay system that conforms to behavioral principles. The author has implemented these two methods in more than 170 organizations. Third, we should address the utopian nemesis of poor performing members (free riders) through leveraged pay and performance management. Performance management should have an expanded repertoire of techniques delivered by internal consultants rather than managers. Fourth, Behavior Systems Analysis should adopt *Walden Two*'s self-management "code" by applying the "free operant" concept to the design and management of a behavior system.

REFERENCES

Abernathy, W. B. (1980). A bank-wide performance system. In R. O'Brien, A. Dickenson, & M. Rosow (Eds.), *Case studies in organizational behavior management*. New York: Prentice-Hall.

Abernathy, W. B. (1996). *The sin of wages*. Atlanta, GA: Aubrey Daniels International.

Abernathy, W. B. (2000). An analysis of the results and structure of twelve organizations' performance scorecard and incentive pay systems. In L. Hayes, J. Austin, R. Houmanfar, & M. Clayton (Eds.), *Organizational change* (pp. 240–272). Reno, NV: Context Press.

Abernathy, W. B. (2000). *Managing without supervising: Creating an organization-wide performance system*. Atlanta, GA: Aubrey Daniels International.

Abernathy, W. B. (2001). An analysis of the results and structure of twelve organizations' performanced scorecard and incentive pay systems. In L. Hayes, J. Austin, R. Houmanfar, & M. Clayton (Eds.), *Organizational change* (pp. 240–272). Reno, NV: Context Press.

Abernathy, W. B. (in press). Implications and applications of a behavior systems perspective. *Journal of Organizational Behavior Management*.

Agnew, J. L. (1998). The establishing operation in organizational behavior management. *Journal of Organizational Behavior Management, 18*(1), 7–19.

Agnew, J. L., & Redmon, W. K. (1992). Contingency specifying stimuli: The role of "rules" in organizational behavior management. *Journal of Organizational Behavior Management, 12*, 67–76.

Bacon, F. (1909–14/2001). *The new Atlantis*. New York: P. F. Collier & Son. Retrieved October 14, 2008 from www.bartleby.com

Bellamy, E. (2000). *Looking backward*. New York: Signet Classic.

Betternson, H. (1972). *The City of God by Augustine of Hippo*. London: Penguin Books.

Binder, A. S. (Ed.) (1990). *Paying for productivity: A look at the evidence*. Washington, DC: The Brookings Institution.

Bloom, A. (1991). *The Republic of Plato*. New York: Basic Books.

Cramer, F. (1993). *Chaos and order*. New York: VCH.

Daniels, A. C., & Rosen, T. A. (1983). *Performance management: Improving quality and productivity through positive reinforcement*. Tucker, GA: Performance Management.

Brethower, Dale M. (1972). *A total performance system*. Kalamazoo, MI: Behaviordelia.

Dierks, W., & McNally, K. (1987). Incentives you can bank on. *Personnel Administrator, 32*, 61–65.

Entwisle, D. R., & Walton, J. (1961). Observations on the span of control. *Administrative Science Quarterly, 5*(4), 522–533.

Feallock, R., & Miller, L. K. (1976). The design and evaluation of a worksharing system for experimental group living. *Journal of Applied Behavior Analysis, 9*(3), 277–288.

Felix, G. H., & Riggs, J. L. (1986). *Productivity by the objectives matrix.* Corvallis, OR: Oregon Productivity Center.

Gilbert, T. F. (1978). *Human competence: Engineering worthy performance.* New York: McGraw-Hill.

Goomas, D. T., & Ludwig, T. D. (2007). Enhancing incentive programs with proximal goals and immediate feedback: Engineering labor standards and technology enhancements in stocker replenishment. *Journal of Organizational Behavior Management, 27*(1), 33–68.

Harshbarger, D., & Maley, R. F. (Eds). (1974). *Behavior analysis and systems analysis: An integrative approach to mental health programs.* Kalamazoo, MI: Behaviordelia.

Jacoby, R. (2005). *Picture imperfect: Utopian thought for an anti-utopian age.* New York: Columbia University Press.

Kaplan, R. S., & Norton, D. P. (1996). *The balanced scorecard: Translating strategy into action.* Boston: Harvard Business School Press.

Karau, S. J., & Williams, K. D. (1993). Social loafing: A meta-analytic review and theoretical integration. *Journal of Personality and Social Psychology, 65,* 681–706.

Latane, B., Williams, K., & Harkins, S. (1979). Many hands make light the work: The causes and consequences of social loafing. *Journal of Personality and Social Psychology, 37,* 822–832.

Los Harcones: *Comunidad Walden Dos.* (1971). http://www.loshorcones.org.

Ludwig, T. D. (2002). On the necessity of structure in an arbitrary world: Using concurrent schedules of reinforcement to describe response generalization. *Journal of Organizational Behavior Management, 21*(4), 13–38.

Ludwig, T. D., & Geller, E. S. (1999). Behavioral impact of a corporate driving policy: Undesirable side-effects reflect countercontrol. *Journal of Organizational Behavior Management, 19*(2), 25–34.

Ludwig, T. D., & Geller, E. S. (2000). Intervening to improve the safety of delivery drivers: A systematic behavioral approach. *Journal of Organizational Behavior Management, 19,* 1–124.

Malott, M. E. (2003). *Paradox of organizational change.* Reno, NV: Context Press.

Marx, K. (1867). *Das Kapital.* New York: L.W. Schmidt.

More, T. (1515, 1964). *Utopia.* Cumberland, RI: Yale University Press.

Morris, W. (1891). *News from nowhere or an epoch of rest.* Boston: Roberts Brothers.

Rummler, G. A., & Brache, A. P. (1995). *Improving performance: How to manage the white space on the organizational chart.* San Francisco: Jossey-Bass.

Skinner, B. F. *Walden Two.* (1948, 1976, 2005). Indianapolis, IN: Hackett.

Skinner, B. F. *Science and human behavior.* (1953). New York: The Free Press.

Skinner, B. F. (1969). *Contingencies of reinforcement: A theoretical analysis.* New York: Meredith.

Skinner, B. F. (1971). *Beyond freedom and dignity.* New York: Bantam Vintage.

Skinner, B. F. (1987). *Upon further reflection.* New York: Prentice Hall.

Tuomela, R. (2000). *Cooperation: A philosophical study,* p. 264. Dordrecht, The Netherlands: Kluwer.

Weitzman, M. L. (1984). *The share economy: Conquering stagflation.* Boston: Harvard University Press.

Wells, H. G. (2005). *A modern utopia.* New York: Penguin Classics.

Use of a Cooperative to Interlock Contingencies and Balance the Commonwealth

MARK ALAVOSIUS

University of Nevada, Reno, Reno, Nevada, USA

JIM GETTING

Auburn University, Auburn, Alabama, USA

JOSEPH DAGEN and WILLIAM NEWSOME

University of Nevada, Reno, Reno, Nevada, USA

BILL HOPKINS

Auburn University, Auburn, Alabama, USA

Cooperatives are systems organized along key principles to balance the distribution of wealth across organizational members. The cooperative movement has an extensive history and has contributed to the design and operation of a large variety of endeavors that seek to maximize returns to a maximum number of stakeholders. While cooperatives are ubiquitous in commerce and community organizations, the designs of the contingencies that define a cooperative have rarely been subject to behavioral analyses. We report a large-scale examination of a safety incentive program enabled by cooperatives of small businesses that applied some of their financial resources to an incentive system organized to sustain active safety management within co-op members. The evaluation indicated that the frequency, severity, and cost of work-related injuries were reduced when safety incentives were applied. High return on investment indicates that the program was cost effective. User satisfaction with the procedures was also high, and the program became an enduring feature of the operation of the safety cooperatives.

The owners, executives, managers, and employees of the Abacus Management Group, Inc., offered considerable expertise, time, and effort in the project described here. The owners, managers, and employees of 248 Rhode Island companies supported this project in more ways than we can list. Cooperation was key to the outcomes achieved.

USE OF A COOPERATIVE TO INTERLOCK CONTINGENCIES AND BALANCE THE COMMONWEALTH

Business enterprises focus on the ultimate goal of making a profit for owners and stakeholders. Any commercial organization is effective to the extent that it generates a desired good or service and delivers it to the market at a price that at least matches the competition's and is below the organization's production and related costs. Thus profit is made. Behavioral systems analyses consider the marketplace context of a given industry and map the inputs and outputs of an individual organization in context of the prevailing market contingencies. An individual company or business unit is typically analyzed in light of its performance against competitors. Organizational behavior management delves more locally into the internal workings of a given organization and seeks to optimize human performance within a company or business unit. Thus broad behavioral systems analyses set the stage for localized assessment and management of human capital, and both might combine to maximize organizations' performance. A well-planned, integrated organization can prove to be a highly efficient profit center, and indeed that is the goal of most system analyses and organizational behavior management initiatives.

What is good for a business is not necessarily good for the community or culture that houses the production or consumes the product or service. We need not look far to see the damage done by highly effective organizations. Textile companies produce fashionable apparel but pollute the environment; energy companies produce fuel but warm the globe; the food industry produces volumes of inexpensive food as obesity skyrockets. The list of unintended consequences of industrial might is extensive and remarkable for revealing the commonality that highly effective business organizations that generate profit for the few may by their success harm the well-being of many. The unintended consequences of highly effective businesses are termed *externalities* and include all the undesired costs of business outside of the direct costs of doing business. Businesses actively seek to offload externalities and focus on the more manageable costs of providing a good or service. The tobacco industry, for a stark example, sought for decades to avoid paying for the enormous costs of illness caused by smoking their product. Only under extreme pressure from litigation have the tobacco companies come to admit their efforts to squash awareness of the dangers of their product and begun to contribute to efforts to treat those harmed by smoking (Biglan, in press).

The *commonwealth* is a somewhat quaint term referring to the collective well-being of a culture or community. When defining the commonwealth for any particular group, you must consider the boundaries of that group and qualitative aspects of a good life. Skinner (1948) provided a picturesque illustration of his concept of commonwealth in *Walden Two*. His utopian community was based on a small enclave of individuals who savored a life of efficient production, communal child-rearing, and boatloads of leisure. Interestingly, this was a small community, thus the boundaries where relatively easy to demark. Skinner's description of life within the community is notable for his molecular analyses of interlocking behavioral contingencies that sustain cooperation within the compound. His description of food preparation and window cleaning are organizational behavior management projects that, with data and a sound evaluation design, could today be possibly published in *JOBM*. The Walden Two members sought self-sufficiency but were open to commerce with other communities. Skinner provides less detail on a systems analysis of Walden Two in context of other communities but at least posits the benefit of interlocking Walden Two with Walden Three, which interlocks with Walden Four and so on. Skinner's description of the quality of life within Walden is accomplished through systematic development of the internal workings. In a very real sense, the residents experimentally create the contingencies that shape their lives. Cooperation is a hallmark of the behavioral repertoires of Walden members who migrate to chosen paths within the options available to them.

Cooperation is necessarily a community endeavor wherein multiple agents work for a common goal. Contingencies operating on one individual interplay with contingencies for others such that their combined efforts yield benefit to all. Throughout history there have been cooperatives designed for the commonwealth of some tribe or grouping. A history of cooperatives is well beyond the scope of this paper but a few examples are enlightening. In 1844, 28 impoverished weavers in Rochdale, England, formed a cooperative that they famously named the Rochdale Society of Equitable Pioneers (Rochdale Pioneers, 1844). Suffering under an economy that provided less than a living wage for the fruits of their looms, they pooled their resources to open a store to sell affordable goods themselves. Perhaps from their familiarity with warp and woof, the Rochdale Pioneers wove interlocking behavioral contingencies that defined ownership and management of their store. They also wrote these down as a contract (the Rochdale Principles). Together they succeeded and were soon imitated. By 1854 there were a thousand cooperatives in England. Their principles are considered the foundation of modern cooperatives and have global impact. Today it is estimated that 800 million people on Earth participate in cooperatives, and these cooperatives employ about 100 million workers (International Co-operative Alliance, 2008).

Apart from Skinner (1948) and Los Horcones (1989), little work has been done by behavior analysts to articulate and experimentally evaluate cooperatives. *Walden Two* provided the blueprint for living arrangements that led one group of behavioral researchers in Kansas to establish a functional housing cooperative in 1969. Named "Sunflower House," it was designed by behavior analysts as a living cooperative. Sunflower House consisted of two houses joined by a common living area and held a maximum of 30 students. Students applied for residence in Sunflower House and agreed to provide 5–7 hours of work each week. Members remained in the house for an average of 1 year and ranged in age from 17–50.

This egalitarian cooperative required profound management to function: advertising, home repairs, household chores, shopping, meetings, etc., all required programmed contingencies. Member behaviors were managed by providing contingent rent credits or fines, and money accumulated via fines was added to the cooperative general fund. Much like Walden Two, all residents engaged in a variety of necessary activities and roles for the survival of the cooperative. For example, members acted as financial officers, cooks, shoppers, and cleaners. Additionally, all residents both cleaned and performed managerial duties with positions rotated often such that no student held one position indefinitely. Embedded feedback loops and weekly household meetings provided democratic control of all management and systematic modifications. The original resident-coordinator, a behavior analyst, coordinated all activities and experiments but faded until all duties were transitioned to members of the cooperative.

Multiple studies emerged from Sunflower House across such areas as increasing household task performance, decreasing fines and complaints, and increasing meeting productivity (Altus, Welsh, & Miller, 1991; Altus, Welsh, Miller, & Merrill, 1993; Feallock & Miller, 1976; Johnson, Welsh, Miller, & Altus, 1991; Miller & Altus, 1994). All interventions and measures were selected by member vote; thus members were intimately involved with all aspects of the experimental procedures—a feature that provides a strong case for the use of cooperatives and a democratic structure to both guide program development and promote long-term adoption of behavioral solutions.

Cooperatives inherently function differently than other organizations, and the democratic leadership requires members be informed about the nature, structure, and function of cooperatives. Longevity rests in the design of the contingencies that perpetuate cooperative interactions even as individual members come and go. Mr. Castle says of *Walden Two*, "Ventures of this sort have often run along very well for awhile. What we want to know is whether the thing carries the potentialities of permanence. I want to see more of this wonderful second generation" (Skinner, 1948, p. 122). The average student spent 1 year at Sunshine House, but their experimental procedures endured 5 to 9 generations. Thus a renewable membership sustained their commonwealth.

The Sunshine House project is rather unusual in that research publications describe its refinements as a housing co-op. It is a small-scale community and provides an interesting example of a research program exploring cooperatives. There exist multiple forms of cooperatives such as purchasing co-ops, worker co-ops, housing co-ops, utility co-ops, and so on. Elaboration of their functional and structural characteristics is well beyond the scope of this paper. Basic principles, dating back to the Rochdale Pioneers, provide a foundation for sharing wealth, democratic control, education of members, and dissemination through cooperative relations with other cooperatives. Behavior analysts might view the many variations of cooperatives as research sites and construct experimental analyses to explore the contingencies that sustain cooperative endeavors. Cooperatives create natural laboratories to examine the interaction of behavioral systems analyses that explore community or marketplace contingencies, with organizational behavior management that explores individual behavioral contingencies. To illustrate the potential advances that might be made by applied research in cooperatives we analyze the outcomes achieved by a multisite safety incentive system funded by the surplus accrued to members of an insurance cooperative created to manage the high cost of work-related injuries and illnesses.

METHOD

Context

In the early 1990s, a crisis occurred in the Rhode Island business community. Traditional insurers declined to write workers' compensation insurance for many of the state's employers. By federal law, employers are required to have workers' compensation coverage in order to be in business. The crisis was caused by the high and inflating costs of medical care, unacceptable incidence rates, fraudulent claims, and other factors that created an unprofitable venue for the insurance companies. With a state economy in peril, the legislature amended regulations and permitted the formation of novel insurance models, including the formation of self-insured groups. The parameters of these are provided elsewhere (Alavosius, Adams, Ahern, & Follick, 2000) but will be summarized here. Basically, self-insurance in workers' compensation is where an employer sets aside sufficient funds to cover the likely expenses to be incurred by injuries, illness, and fatalities to the workers. Typically, self-insurance is an expensive proposition in which only wealthy and larger companies with excellent safety records are likely to bear the financial risks associated with this liability. Contrast this with a traditional insurance model where an insurer bears the employer's risk. The insurer is able to underwrite risk by writing policies for many employers such that a financial reserve sufficient to cover the likely losses is generated by the pooled premiums. With many policies, the insurer thereby disperses risk across many companies.

The Rhode Island economic base is predominantly small employers clustered in relatively few sectors. At the time of the workers' compensation crisis, jewelry design and manufacturing was the largest segment of the industrial workforce. This industry includes a large variety of potentially hazardous operations (e.g., plating, fabrication, finishing, and packaging) and generates a complex range of work-related injuries and illnesses (Alavosius, 1994). The rest of the economic base included boat builders, machine shops, fabricated products, and related industries. The very continuation of these businesses was in jeopardy given their inability to obtain workers' compensation or to individually self-insure. As small businesses, few of these employers could afford self-insurance and could not remain in business unless a solution emerged.

Participants and Settings

Three self-insured groups (SIGs) were formed by a management group (third-party administrator [TPA]) that bound multiple employers into cooperative associations that financed and managed their workers' compensation risks. These associations were notable for this discussion in that the members (employers) were competitors in the marketplace but cooperatives in terms of working together to manage an externality of doing business (worker injuries, illness, and fatalities). The self-insured group (SIG hereafter) was an association whose principles defined shared liability for losses, democratic control, distribution of surplus (if any), membership responsibilities, performance measures, and its own perpetuation. These principles can be linked back to those written by the Rochdale weavers in 1844. Three associations were formed with a combined membership of approximately 350 companies employing approximately 15,000 workers. Each employer contributed to a risk pool commensurate with their loss history and risk exposure. This contribution is equivalent to a premium to an insurer except that the pool was owned by the members. Any surplus after all claims were paid reverted to the members proportional to their contributions and losses. In traditional insurance such leftovers are profits to the carriers and lost as business expenses to employers.

The role of the TPA was contingency manager. The TPA was a centralized management group through which flowed all data pertinent to the SIG's workers' compensation needs (e.g., risk management, risk financing, SIG membership services, etc.). Thus the TPA had ready and timely access to an enormous amount of data relevant to the member companies and their health and safety risk exposures.

The SIGs were systems composed of many independent but cooperating companies and designed to interlock the risk financing and risk management elements of a comprehensive cost-containment model that yielded savings to the members. The drivers of workers' compensation costs were defined essentially as high rates of injuries (claims) that required prolonged, expensive, and not always effective treatment. Safety services were developed to help companies' management identify and control hazards and at-risk practices; case management services supported injured workers as they progressed through medical and rehabilitative care and returned to work. The SIGs provided a coordinated solution to a crisis that was unsolvable by solitary companies. Much like the Rochdale Pioneers, the SIG members joined forces to combat economic ruin. A common cause voiced by employers for forming an association was to gain control of forces that threatened their livelihood. The members found cause to engage actively with safety management, when formerly many had downplayed this feature of their company since that risk was borne by insurers. Now that the employers were their own insurers, the potential cost and benefit of effective management was contingent on their actions. In this cooperative model, investment in loss control (safety services and case management) could create sizable returns.

The SIG operations included materials (data collection systems, relational databases, reports, policies, manuals, etc.) and skilled managers and technicians to service the membership and coordinate their interaction with community services (providers like medical centers and rehabilitation centers, regulators such as OSHA [Occupational Safety and Health Administration]). A network of integrated financial and social contingencies was built around the foundation principles of shared liability for losses. The data allowed these contingencies to be tuned with precision. Thus competitors in the market cooperated on health and safety and shared jointly and severally in the liabilities of work-related injuries and illness. The incentives were structured such that employers shared best practices and supported each other in preventing injuries and seeking optimal care for injured workers. These associations were in existence for over 7 years and were quite effective in meeting their goals, namely controlling the growing costs of work-related injury and illness.

As noted, the SIGs were effective and the associations soon enjoyed lower workers' compensation costs than might have been available if insurers were willing to write policies. At the start of the associations, employers were paying approximately 6% of payroll for workers' compensation coverage; by year 7 this was cut in half. Additionally, surpluses accrued as the annual contributions of each exceeded the actual losses. With the surplus, members had the luxury of investing in risk management technologies beyond those typically affordable to small companies. After several years of operation, all member companies had sent managers through training in basic safety procedures for their operations and case management activities to support injured workers' return to work. These trainings provided instruction and materials (e.g., manuals describing audit systems, accident investigation protocols, safety committee operations, lock-out/tag-out procedures, light-duty procedures, work modifications, etc.) geared to their industry. The SIGs were formed around a general trade group, but considerable variability was found among the structure and operation of individual businesses. Specialized needs were identified through epidemiologic analyses of years of injury/illness reports from the member companies, and workshops were provided by the TPA to control risks unique to their work (Alavosius, Adams, & Follick, 1993). Those companies with persistent safety problems completed an intensive training/consultation series to remediate management. These companies achieved accident rates below industry averages (Alavosius et al., 2000). The safety training, consultation, field work, case management, and performance reports had established low injury rates, financial stability for the SIGs, and a surplus to now fund efforts tuned to maintaining success. A decision was made by two associations to use some of their surplus to fund safety incentive systems to sustain active safety management within their member companies. The incentives began with one group (SIG A—141 companies), and the second group (SIG B—107 companies) replicated the procedures 16 months later. Thus a multiple baseline across associations was used to evaluate the effects of the incentives.

Personnel

The incentive systems required the contributions of multiple people. The first author was Director of Loss Control for the third-party administrator (TPA) who managed the SIG's programs. He was responsible for design, direction, and analysis of the safety services to member companies. An incentive coordinator (the second author) was responsible for design, evaluation, and ongoing incentive operations. The leadership of the TPA was actively involved in all aspects of the program and instrumental in coordinating SIG operations with the incentives. An incentive steering committee was formed, composed of owners of member companies. Lastly, each participating company designated at least one safety/incentive manager to manage operations within the local member company and liaison with the incentive team. Thus several hundred people (executives, managers, supervisors) managed a system that coordinated contingencies deployed across 248 separate companies that collectively employed about 7,800 workers.

Dependent Variables

Frequency of injuries, reported as an incidence rate, was a key metric. Incidence rates are the number of reported injuries recorded per 100 employees. Any unit of time, such as a week, month, or year, can be used to calculate a rate. In its simplest calculation, the number of injuries is divided by the number of employees in the workforce, then multiplied by 100. Incidence rates were calculated for 4 levels of severity of an event in order to depict a stratified measure of outcomes. Four mutually exclusive categories were used: information only, treatment only, lost time 1–3 days, and lost time greater than 3 days. Information-only reports are close calls and minor injuries that do not require any professional medical care. These have no incurred costs borne by the SIG. Treatment-only reports are injuries that have some medical cost, typically a physician's fee, but less than 1 full day of missed work. Lost time 1–3 days are injuries with incurred costs and lost work time of more than 1 but no more than 3 full days. Lastly, lost-time greater than 3 days events are injuries with incurred costs and more than 3 full lost workdays.

Lost days per 100 employees were examined as a second metric of intervention effectiveness. A lost day is counted if the employee misses an entire scheduled day of work; partial days are not counted. A lost-day incidence rate is calculated similarly to the incidence rate for injury frequency.

Incurred costs were also estimated. These costs include costs of physician's services, hospital fees, cost of wage replacement to employees, legal costs to litigate disputes, indemnity costs (i.e., settlement for disabilities or disfigurements), and any other miscellaneous costs associated with treatment of the injury. Incurred costs do not include any costs to the employers such as lost productivity, replacement costs, and other indirect costs of injuries. To standardize estimates of incurred costs, costs were fixed by claims adjusters at 3 months post incident date. The "true" costs of an injury are not known until the claim is closed and all expenses are paid. Some claims are open for many months or even years as rehabilitation and return-to-work is quite lengthy following some injuries. We used a 3-month development period for cost estimates, as this was found to reasonably estimate the final costs given the TPA's reserving practices.

Independent Variables

Incentive procedures were developed to distribute monetary rewards, funded by the surplus, to employees who met various qualifying criteria. The SIG Board of Directors designated an Incentive Steering Committee to oversee operations. Several guiding principles were set to define the actual incentive contingencies. Since the surplus was commonwealth accrued by all members, the SIG leaders required that all member companies have the option to participate in the incentives. All participating members' employees were to be eligible for awards; company owners and executives were excluded. Given the large number of participating workers (approximately 5,500 in group A; 2,300 in group B), a lottery system was used to deliver routinely a manageable number of meaningful awards to a randomly chosen subset of eligible workers. Frequent incentives were delivered publicly, and all SIG members were informed of awards. Given the paucity of published reports on incentive systems of this scale (McAfee & Winn, 1989), outcome data (e.g., the frequency, severity, and costs of injuries) and assessment of logistical details were used to guide refinements in a continuously improving system that ran for multiple years. A full description of all the adjustments in the incentive system is well beyond the scope of a journal article, but key ingredients are summarized below.

ANTECEDENTS

Training for safety coordinators in all participating companies was provided at the beginning of the incentive program both for SIGs and when significant modifications were made. Initial training was a 1-hour workshop during the month prior to the launch of the incentives. During this training, safety coordinators were taught the key rules of the incentive system and their administrative procedures. Brief refresher training was included to review material taught in previous safety workshops. This reviewed general safety management operations, such as how to perform safety audits, how to set up and lead safety teams, and how to develop a safety improvement plan. Upon conclusion of the training, safety coordinators returned to their companies and held a meeting with their employees to announce the safety incentive system and describe the rules for participating. A safety incentive system manual was disseminated to all safety coordinators. It described the rules for determining incentive eligibility, the purpose of the system, and strategies for making the program effective in sustaining safety operations. Manuals included schedules, forms, and handouts to standardize rollout of the system. Handouts to employees were provided in both English and Spanish to assist safety coordinators in communicating with their employees.

Various prompts were provided to all companies. These included small yellow pins and magnets inscribed with safety slogans including "Safety Pays," later changed to "Play It Safe and Win." Safety coordinators were instructed to give them to all employees and ask them to wear the pins and place the magnets in prominent locations in their work areas or near major work hazards. Paycheck stuffers were provided so that all employees would receive prompts to work safely. These included descriptions of the safety incentives. Large color posters (36 in. by 24 in.) bearing the safety slogans were provided to each company. The posters were provided as a means to announce and describe the safety incentives to workers, as well as a place to post updates such as names of incentive recipients, feedback on workplace safety, and safety inspection results.

CONSEQUENCES

The crux of the safety incentive system was a lottery-style reward system. The process of selecting winners, qualifying them, and distributing incentives remained constant throughout the intervention. Variations in the amounts of awards were made as effects were demonstrated and efficiencies were explored.

Individual employees who had not had serious work-related injuries (i.e., requiring more than 3 days away from work) for a period of time became eligible for a monthly drawing for cash incentives. This criterion was set to minimize the chance that eligibility for an incentive might restrict reporting of injuries. A relatively minor injury (i.e., resulting in less than 3 days of lost work) did not disqualify an employee. Each month, safety coordinators faxed a list of employees who met the eligibility criteria for the prior month to the workers' compensation management firm. From the lists, winners were randomly selected. Potential winners were then checked against the claims database of the workers' compensation management firm to confirm that they had not had an injury that would result in ineligibility. Some incentives were delivered monthly. Larger awards were made for maintaining safety for longer periods (e.g., 2-month awards, 4-month awards, 6-month awards). The details of the award amounts and schedules were modified routinely. We began with a 4-month demonstration project, then designed 12-month programs for the subsequent years with SIG A. When replicating with SIG B we began with 12-month programs as that SIG's directors were convinced of the system's effectiveness after viewing the performance of SIG A. The details of all the incentives are beyond the scope of this report. To illustrate the complexity of the system, the following structure was used for 4 months in 1993 to pilot test the system with SIG A:

- A total of $45,000 was awarded to employees; $10,000 to companies

  - Each month 100 workers shared $4,000 with awards from $25 to $100
  - 2-month pool for 118 workers sharing $8,500 from $25 to $1,000
  - 4-month pool for 11 workers sharing $12,000 from $250 to $5,000
  - $10,000 was awarded to companies for demonstration of exemplary safety processes

- Total of $55,000 was dispensed in 4 months

Thus there were 687 financial awards ranging in value from $25 to $5,000 with odds of any eligible employee winning being approximately 1 in 9.5. The data indicated this system had promise, and the SIG directors provided $80,000 for employee financial awards and $20,000 for company awards in 1994. A revised and more tiered system was developed and delivered in that year with the grand prize reduced to $2,500 and 1,634 individual awards ranging from $25 to $2,500. Subsequent years saw additional refinements.

Each employee in a SIG had an equal chance of earning an incentive. In order to receive an incentive, a winning employee had to work in a company that provided the TPA with evidence of active safety management. Evidence included submission of safety committee minutes, inspection reports, and accident investigation reports if any lost-time incidents were reported. Thus the individual incentives were interlocked with measures of company management. For each SIG, a winner's list was faxed back to all safety coordinators in all companies for each month by the 17th of the month following the month for which the drawing was held. Each month the safety coordinators posted the first names and initial of last name of all winners, the amounts each won, and the name of each winner's employer.

Checks to winners were enclosed in a congratulations card that again stated they had won by avoiding injury and reminding employees to work safely and to help others do the same. Checks and cards were sent to the safety coordinators along with directions for arranging a small celebration. Specifically, they were asked to gather their workers together, discuss briefly the importance of safety, and deliver the check(s) with a round of applause. Personnel from the TPA's Loss Control Department attended these celebrations.

Additional incentives were awarded for company efforts to promote worker safety. Incentives were provided for safety innovations (e.g., better guarding of equipment), exemplary safety committee operations and reporting, safety observation systems, and specialized safety training programs. Safety coordinators submitted written documentation to the TPA, and a panel of experts including the regional director of OSHA evaluated the merits of submissions and determined awards. Throughout the incentive period modifications were made to the incentives. These are too numerous to list, but the process was to observe the outcome data and participants' reactions and tailor the awards to maintain enthusiasm and engagement with active safety management. As years progressed, the number of individual awards increased, the probability of any individual employee receiving an award increased, and the amounts of the awards were reduced. Thus, following a relatively costly and extensive launch, the system sought economies and deeper penetration into the collective's workforce.

Formal written feedback ("report cards") was provided to each safety coordinator from the TPA routinely (initially every 6 months, then quarterly) to apprise them of their company's performance in terms of safety management. The report cards listed for each company their loss ratio (% of contribution to the cooperative's loss pool used to pay for losses), frequency of injuries, incidence rate of injuries, tally of safety committee minutes, safety self-inspection results, comparison with their previous reports, comparison with other co-op members, and ranking as gold, silver, bronze, or other status in their cooperative. These reports helped each company gauge its performance against themselves and against similar companies.

Integrity of Interventions

One measure of integrity with which the interventions were applied in each individual company was receipt of lists of employees eligible for rewards from the safety coordinators. Every month of the intervention, greater than

90% of the lists were received on time, with the remaining lists received after a phone call prompt. This suggests that the safety coordinators understood the administrative procedures and consistently followed them.

Loss-control professionals from the TPA made regular visits to companies to check on parameters of the system. These professionals looked to see if posters, pins, magnets, and winner's lists were deployed and asked questions about the safety system. With one exception that was quickly corrected, the professionals reported consistent application of the safety incentive system within desired parameters, and employees regularly commented that they liked the system.

In a third measure, the TPA's claims/case managers reported any complaints or confusion that came up in communications with both SIGs' members during their interactions. Over the course of the intervention with both SIGs, fewer than five occasions were reported to the safety incentive coordinator and all were resolved with a phone call.

Data Analysis

As noted earlier, a wealth of data from the co-op members, medical providers, and others flowed through the TPA. Data were promptly entered into a relational database enabling nearly real-time evaluation of the SIGs' performance. For evaluation of the safety incentive program, queries of the database yielded metrics such as incidence rates per individual company, incidence rates for entire SIGs, cost of injuries and illnesses (e.g., medical, rehab, other), characteristics of injuries and illnesses (e.g., diagnosis, body part injured, characteristics of accidents [location, job title of injured, accident type, etc.]), characteristics of company (e.g., nature of business, size of workforce, etc.), and other data pertinent to intervention planning and assessment. Data were plotted and reviewed frequently. Monthly, the leadership of the TPA and SIG directors reviewed summary reports.

Experimental Design

A multiple baseline across SIGs was used to evaluate the effects of data-driven safety incentives on critical outcomes achieved through co-op members' safety management. Sixteen months after roll-out of the incentives with SIG A, SIG B launched their program. Following 1 year of baseline, at least 3 years of data under the incentives were examined to evaluate effects of the incentives.

RESULTS

Cumulative records presenting the incidence rates of lost-time reports of 1–3 days and lost-time reports with greater than 3 days are shown in Figures 1 and 2 respectively for SIG A and in Figures 4 and 5 for SIG B. Figures 3 and 6 show the cumulative incurred costs (3 months developed) for SIG A and SIG B. In all records, 1 year of baseline data is presented for comparison with multiple months under the incentive system (40 months for SIG A, 36 months for SIG B). These data present compelling evidence that the rates of work-related injuries were reduced significantly when safety incentives were administered within the cooperatives. The financial metrics indicate substantial savings in workers' compensation costs as a function of the reduced injury rates. Measures of return on investment (ROI) were calculated by cost-to-benefit analyses. Costs were calculated for the administrative fees

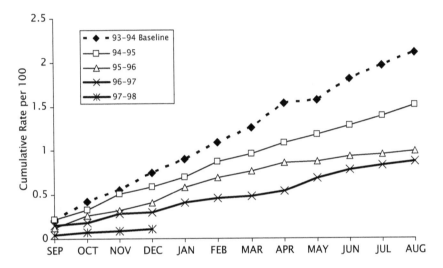

FIGURE 1 SIG A: Cumulative rate of lost-time injuries 1–3 days per month.

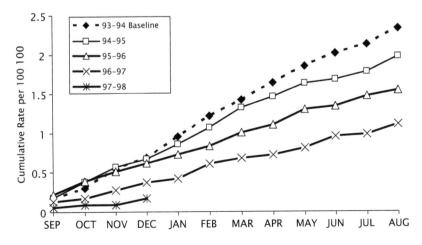

FIGURE 2 SIG A: Cumulative rate of lost-time injuries greater than 3 days per month.

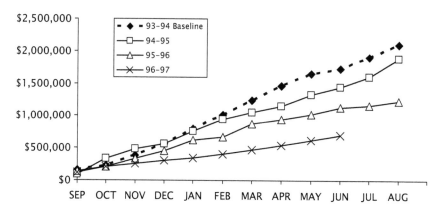

FIGURE 3 SIG A: Cumulative incurred costs (3 months developed) per month.

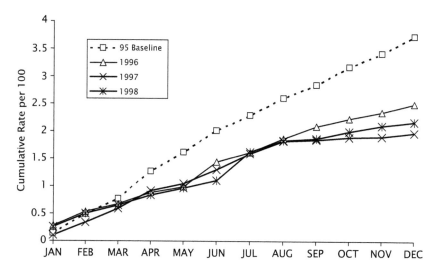

FIGURE 4 SIG B: Cumulative rate of lost time injuries 1–3 days per month.

of the incentive systems by the TPA plus the costs of the incentives. Benefits were calculated as the change in incurred costs of injuries during interventions relative to 12-month baselines. The estimates of savings are no doubt very conservative as they do not include the substantial indirect costs of accidents or inflation in medical costs during the years this study was conducted (estimated at 10% per year). For SIG A, the ROI was 1:4.08; for SIG B the ROI was 1:5.15.

DISCUSSION

The data of Figures 1–6 indicate that the safety incentive system resulted in meaningful reductions of injury cost, lost workdays, injury frequency, and

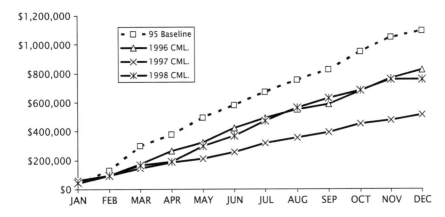

FIGURE 5 SIG B: Cumulative rate of lost time injuries greater than 3 days per month.

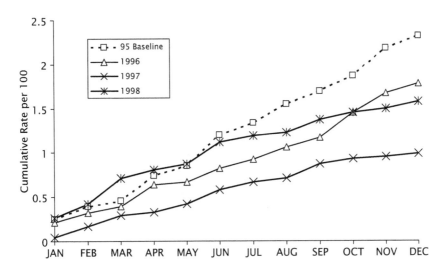

FIGURE 6 SIG B: Cumulative incurred costs (3 months developed) per month.

human suffering in both cooperatives. The intervention in the second cooperative (SIG B) began 16 months after SIG A launched their program. This created a multiple baseline design (Cook & Campbell, 1979) allowing for rigorous evaluation of the results. The changes in data following the beginnings of the safety incentive system for both cooperatives, coupled with the control elements of the multiple baseline design, provide considerable evidence that safety incentive systems can be effective when applied on a large scale.

Interlocking organizational contingencies define the foundation of cooperatives and offer a technology for managing benevolent organizations. In these SIGs, the comprehensive loss control program integrated management of injured workers as they navigated the healthcare system and returned to work with data-driven prevention programs that developed active safety management in member companies. The TPA had access to extensive data sources to continuously refine its management of the cooperatives. As a result of the TPA's methods, the member companies realized substantial savings that otherwise would have been paid to traditional insurers. The potential for investing effectively some of that surplus in incentives to all employees of the member companies was made possible by the data that flowed through the TPA. A balanced distribution of incentives, contingent on important behaviors and outcomes, required rapid measurement and analyses of data from many individual companies. Perhaps the greatest technology enabling continuous refinement of the incentive systems was a coherent database and control systems to provide many managers with timely measures of their efforts. The design of the interlocking contingencies was possible by data to direct delivery of financial rewards and objective feedback.

Our presentation in this paper of the incentive system operations, procedural refinements, and analyses summarizes complex applications occurring over 5 years. Many details are omitted to clarify the presentation. Excessive details can obscure the foundational elements that serve as the skeleton of a novel solution to many organizations facing economic crises. Future dissemination will explore more fine-grained analyses of how the incentives affected other important processes and outcomes in the cooperatives. This report illustrates that behavioral systems analyses coupled with organizational behavior management can produce lasting and significant benefit to large collectives of organizations. Additionally, by addressing the problem of maintenance of effective interventions in many companies at a system level, contingencies can be designed that bridge across many thousands of individuals in hundreds of independent companies. It is difficult to imagine how attacking the problem at a company level could have possibly achieved similar outcomes within any reasonable timelines unless huge amounts of labor and technology were used to replicate interventions company by company.

The incentives were embedded within the context of many other systematic interventions, and no efforts were made to isolate them from other powerful interventions (e.g., safety training, consultation, performance feedback). Our goal was to share the commonwealth (surplus) accruing in the SIGs with all employees in the member companies. Thus not only the owners but the employees of these companies benefited financially from coordinated safety management. Promotion efforts were designed to maximize discussion of safety management by all members of the companies. Certainly the verbal behavior of many was changed by introduction of the promotional materials, incentives, and celebrations. The incentives set the occasion for communications from the shop floor upward through work organizations that solicited and supported active safety management and maintenance of the many structures and procedures that were established by the TPA's safety training and consultation efforts.

Today, economies are in recession. Food and fuel costs are soaring. Wages do not keep pace with the cost of living. Foreclosures are at record levels, and millions face unemployment. The gap between rich and poor widens as profit-driven organizations protect their stakeholders. The drivers of change are building and activism is on the rise. A look ahead is informed by a look back to 1844 when 28 impoverished weavers created interwoven contingencies to manage their plight. Much needs to be learned about the design and spread of organizations that foster cooperation and concern for the commonwealth. The project presented here can be replicated systematically in other contexts (e.g., education, healthcare, consumer energy, etc.) where crises set the stage for remaking business models. We speculate that cooperatives will be one important venue for the continued development of behavioral applications for the benefit of very large numbers of people. Cooperatives provide a complex set of interlocking relations that will allow examination of dimensions of these contingencies and how technologies can balance the greatest good for the greatest number. Future studies will provide substantial direction for investigating the processes and organizations best suited to cooperative functions and development. For example, the democratic nature of cooperatives stands as one institutional variable worth exploring further. At interest is the greatest good for the greatest number of cooperative members while avoiding costly externalities. These sustained communities may currently offer the best counter-control to the goals of corporations seeking maximum profit for elite stakeholders and set a new direction for organizational behavior management research.

REFERENCES

Alavosius, M. P. (1994). Safety: The key to lower workers' comp costs. *American Jewelry Manufacturer*, March, 63–66.

Alavosius, M. P., Adams, A. E., Ahern, D. K., & Follick, M. J. (2000). Behavioral approaches to organizational safety. In Austin, J., & Carr, J. (Eds.), *Handbook of applied behavior analysis*. Reno, NV: Context Press.

Alavosius, M. P., Adams, A. E., & Follick, M. (1993). An epidemiologic analysis of occupational accidents within a large sample of jewelry manufacturers. Address at the Annual Meeting of the Association for Behavior Analysis, Chicago, IL.

Altus, D. E., Welsh, T. M., & Miller, K. L. (1991). A technology for program maintenance: Programming key researcher behaviors in a student housing cooperative. *Journal of Applied Behavior Analysis, 24,* 667–675.

Altus, D. E., Welsh, T. M., Miller, K., & Merrill, M. H. (1993). Efficacy and maintenance of an education program for a consumer cooperative. *Journal of Applied Behavior Analysis, 26*, 403–404.

Biglan, A. (in press). Reducing corporate externalities. *Journal of Organizational Behavior Management.*

Cook, T. D., & Campbell, D. T. (1979). *Quasi-experimentation: Design and analysis issues for field settings.* Boston: Houghton Mifflin.

Feallock, R., & Miller, K. L. (1976). The design and implementation of a work sharing system for experimental group living. *Journal of Applied Behavior Analysis, 9*, 277–288.

International Co-operative Alliance. *History of the cooperative movement.* Retrieved November 8, 2008, from http://www.ica.coop/al-ica/

Los Horcones. (1989). Walden Two and social change: The application of behavior analysis to cultural design. *Behavior Analysis and Social Action, 7*, 35–41.

McAfee, R. B., & Winn, A. R. (1989). The use of incentives/feedback to enhance work place safety: A critique of the literature. *Journal of Safety Research, 20*, 7–19.

Miller, K. L., & Altus, D. E. (1994). Programming for survival: A meeting system that survives 8 years later. *Journal of Applied Behavior Analysis, 27*, 423–433.

Rochdale Pioneers (1844). *Laws and objects of the Rochdale Society of Equitable Pioneers.* Rochdale, England: Jesse Hall.

Skinner, B. F. (1948). *Walden Two.* New York: MacMillan.

The Role of Advocacy Organizations in Reducing Negative Externalities

ANTHONY BIGLAN

Oregon Research Institute, Eugene, Oregon, USA

An externality is a cost that a corporation's actions impose on society. For example, a power plant may emit mercury but might not pay for the cost of that pollution to the people living near the plant. It is possible to analyze a diverse range of problems of society in these terms, including the health effects of corporate practices, the unsustainability of manufacturing processes, and the marketing of products contributing to environmental damage, and economic policies that maintain high levels of poverty due to effective lobbying by the business community. This article examines the problem of externalities in terms of metacontingencies. Externalities continue precisely because there is no cost to the organizations for practices that impose these costs on third parties. The article describes the cultural practices needed to motivate governments to make corporations bear the true costs of their practices—costs that are currently imposed on others.

THE ROLE OF ADVOCACY ORGANIZATIONS IN REDUCING NEGATIVE EXTERNALITIES

One of the central problems in societies' efforts to ensure wellbeing is the presence of negative externalities of corporate practices. A negative

The National Cancer Institute (CA38273) and the National Institute on Drug Abuse (DA018760) provided financial support for the completion of the work on this manuscript. The author wishes to thank Christine Cody for her editorial assistance.

externality is a cost imposed on society by the production or marketing of a good or service that the price charged for that good or service does not reflect (Organisation for Economic Cooperation & Development, 1993). For example, a power plant may emit mercury, but may not pay for the cost of that pollution to the people living near the plant. Tobacco companies market an addictive product that leads to cancer, heart disease, and more than 400,000 deaths in the U.S. (Centers for Disease Control & Prevention, 2006), but healthcare providers, employers, governments, smokers, and their families bear most of these costs. Food manufacturers market unhealthy foods that contribute to obesity and cardiovascular disease (Brownell & Horgen, 2004; Pollan, 2006; 2007) but do not pay for the treatment of these problems. A real estate developer builds a housing development, but a local government, and ultimately a city's taxpayers, bear the true costs of roads and sewage systems. We can analyze a diverse range of society's problems in terms of negative externalities, including health effects of corporate practices, the unsustainability of manufacturing processes, the marketing of products that contribute to environmental damage, and economic policies that maintain high levels of poverty due to effective lobbying by the business community.

At the outset, I want to state that this article is not an attack on capitalism per se. The benefits of capitalism are extensive. They include all of the technologies available in the 21st century, including the computer on which I write this article. It is only through the competitive processes of the marketplace that individuals and organizations have the incentives to innovate to produce better, more efficient, and less expensive goods and services. However, if the justification and support for capitalism is its contribution to human wellbeing, then wellbeing should be our ultimate goal. In that context, it is appropriate to see if societies can evolve cultural practices that retain the beneficial aspects of capitalism while reducing its negative externalities.

The problem with externalities is that companies have little incentive to prevent them. Any cost a company incurs affects its profits. Thus, in a market system, corporations tend to select practices that detect and reduce such costs. However, they have no incentive to reduce costs that others bear. Indeed, companies may find it profitable to engage in activities that avoid the imposition of such costs upon themselves. They may litigate or lobby governments to prevent having the costs of externalities imposed on them; they may engage in public relations to obscure or counter the public perception that their actions impose costs on others, as ExxonMobil did regarding global warming, until recently (msnbc.com, 2005).

Economists have argued that a straightforward way to deal with the problem of externalities is to impose a tax on practices that impose external costs, so that companies will have an incentive to reduce them (Gwartney & Stroup, 1987). The larger problem, however, is the imbalance between the power of corporations to avoid paying for externalities and the power of the individuals those externalities harm. Perhaps the most striking example involves the consequences of cigarette smoking over the past 50 years. Research in the 1950s showed that cigarette smoking caused lung cancer (Wynder & Graham, 1950); subsequent research showed that it caused heart disease (U.S. Department of Health & Human Services, 1983). In recent years, about 450,000 U.S. deaths have occurred annually due to smoking (Centers for Disease Control and Prevention, 2006).

In *U.S. vs. Philip Morris et al.* (2006), the federal district court in Washington, DC, found that the tobacco industry had been aware of the harmful effects of cigarettes since the 1950s but had conspired to convince the public that smoking's harmfulness was unproven (*U.S. v. Phillip Morris et al.*, 2006). It was not until the 1990s that individual smokers and governments that had borne the cost of smoking's side effects began to recoup any of those costs (National Association of Attorneys General, 1998). Moreover, smoking continues to kill more than 400,000 Americans each year, while the cigarette industry continues to be quite profitable (Centers for Disease Control & Prevention, 2006; Parker-Pope, 2001). From one perspective, this problem continues because the tobacco companies are better organized and more effective in influencing public policies that might have curbed their practices than were the victims of cigarette marketing in influencing policy to prevent these harms.

The problem of cigarette smoking is only an example of a more generic problem. In general, societies need ways that are more effective at detecting and ameliorating externalities. With this article, I present a framework for dealing with the problem of externalities. The framework is derived from behavior analysis of human behavior and cultural practices (e.g., Glenn, 1988, 2004; Glenn & Malott, 2004), which is one branch of evolutionary analysis (Wilson, 2007). It first presents a method for identifying externalities that merit societal efforts to counteract them. It then analyzes the forces that maintain externalities. That analysis suggests that corporations have evolved practices to prevent society from imposing the costs of externalities on the companies. What seems needed, therefore, is strengthening of the practices of advocacy groups to influence policies to ameliorate the most costly externalities. The last section of the article outlines strategies for strengthening advocacy organizations.

CRITERIA FOR TARGETING EXTERNALITIES

Which externalities need targeting? Accepted principles of public health provide a framework for answering that question. In general, public health targets the most common and costly problems (Biglan, 1995). Infectious diseases have long been a high priority because, if they are not controlled, they have the potential to kill many people. Reducing disease depends on reducing the factors that contribute to the disease. Thus, public health has evolved practices such as sanitation and quarantine to prevent infectious diseases. As health experts have identified smoking, obesity, alcohol abuse, and risky sexual behavior as risk factors for disease, they too become targets for public health. Experts then develop practices to reduce the prevalence of these behaviors. In short, the generic features of public health involve identifying any disease, behavior, or cultural practice that contributes to the prevalence of common and costly diseases and developing practices that reduce the prevalence of that risk factor.

The framework extends to the practices of organizations. Manufacturing processes that lead to worker injury have substantially decreased in the last century. More recently, experts have identified the marketing practices of tobacco companies as a risk factor for smoking and thereby death and have mounted efforts to restrict those practices (National Cancer Institute, 2008; *U.S. v. Philip Morris et al.*, 2006). Indeed, tobacco-marketing practices are prototypical examples of corporate practices that produce externalities requiring restrictions.

Although these examples involve physical diseases and the factors that contribute to disease, the principles are generally applicable. It is possible to evaluate any practice in terms of the proportion of the population it affects and the extent of harm it causes. We might evaluate a company's decision to reduce or eliminate healthcare costs or to reduce retirement benefits in terms of the number of people that decision affects and the extent of harm done to them. The marketing of fuel inefficient cars may contribute to the emission of greenhouse gases; it is then possible to estimate the impact of that marketing on the environment.

From this standpoint, corporate externalities that currently affect the most people in the most harmful ways should receive top priority. How far should this process go? Societies have slowly evolved increasingly higher standards for the wellbeing of their populations. Child abuse was once commonplace and accepted (deMause, 1990), as was child labor. At a minimum, I would argue that practices shown to have a direct effect on the economic wellbeing, physical illness, or psychological wellbeing of a significant proportion of the population should be the first ones we target. What proportion should we consider significant? Fortunately, for most aspects of wellbeing, there are increasingly accurate estimates of the proportion of the population in developed countries who are not doing well. For example, data exist on the rates of child poverty, major physical illnesses, and, to a lesser extent, psychological disorders (National Research Council & Institute of Medicine, 2009). The criteria for determining what proportion of the population a problem must affect before a nation targets that problem reflect its national aspirations. For example, are U.S. citizens satisfied that this country is last out of 25 developed nations in reducing its rate of child poverty?

Of course, the prevalence of a problem in a population is due to multiple influences; corporate externalities may be a minor influence on a problem. Epidemiologists have a procedure for determining the extent to which a risk factor contributes to a problem. It is population-attributable risk, an estimate of the proportion of cases one can attribute to a risk factor. For example, Pierce, Gilpin, and Choi (1999) estimated that advertising for Camel cigarettes influenced 2.1 million young people to become smokers between 1988 and 1998 and that 520,000 of them would eventually die of smoking-related illness.

Evidence of this sort is not currently available for most corporate externalities, which points to the need for research to estimate the precise degree to which corporate practices contribute to problematic outcomes. Requiring such evidence will be a counterweight to the risk of imposing unjustified costs on corporations.

Some externalities are difficult to analyze in terms of significant harm to those alive today. A manufacturing or marketing practice (e.g., sale of fuel inefficient cars) that contributes to greenhouse gas accumulation is making no one sick at present. However, its long-term impact on human wellbeing could be very substantial (World Health Organization, 2002; 2008). The present framework nonetheless applies. We would target a manufacturing process if current scientific evidence finds that it contributes significantly to greenhouse gases because greenhouse gas accumulation threatens a large proportion of the people on the planet.

GENERAL PRINCIPLES FOR REDUCING EXTERNALITIES

The economic analysis of externalities is very much in keeping with functional contextualist analyses of human behavior (e.g., Biglan & Hayes, 1996) and analyses of the metacontingencies influencing organizations' actions (Biglan, 1995; Glenn, 1986; 1988). Overwhelming evidence points to the effects consequences have on human behavior (Biglan, 1995). We know that consequences shape most aspects of human behavior, from toilet training (Azrin & Foxx, 1974) to the cooperative behavior in small groups (Bay-Hintz, Peterson, & Quilitch, 1994). Moreover, evidence is growing that material consequences shape and maintain the practices of groups and organizations (Glenn & Malott, 2004). The evolution of group or organizational practices in areas as diverse as agriculture and war making have been analyzed in these terms (Biglan, 1995).

When applied to the problem of externalities, this framework suggests that companies have no incentive to reduce externalities, since they receive no negative consequences for producing them but likely will experience negative ones by reducing or eliminating them. Reducing pollution may increase the cost of a manufacturing process and thereby reduce profits.

Eliminating marketing of cigarettes to youth will reduce market share and profits (Biglan, 2004; National Cancer Institute, 2008). In fact, most methods for reducing externalities involve imposing costs on the company that produces them.

Governments can impose taxes that increase the costs of a practice such as polluting the air (Gwartney & Stroup, 1987). In essence, the society charges a company for the costs it has been imposing on society. Society can then use the tax revenues to ameliorate the problem. Market systems, in which companies can buy and sell the right to engage in a costly practice (e.g., polluting), have proven an efficient way to motivate companies to reduce these costs (Congressional Budget Office, 2001). For example, a cap-and-trade system that set limits on sulfur dioxide and allowed low-emission companies to sell their rights to emit sulfur dioxide to higher emitting companies was instrumental in reducing these emissions (Congressional Budget Office, 2001). However, the benefits of such systems are limited to situations where the cost tends to be widely dispersed. For example, there is a widespread benefit to reducing carbon emissions, because they contribute to worldwide reductions in global warming. However, mercury emissions tend to fall near power plants. A cap-and-trade system for these emissions may result only in some areas having reduced harm while others continue in peril.

Governments can also simply prohibit a practice, as they have done with child labor, chlorofluorocarbons, and some forms of deceptive advertising. This involves increasing the cost of the practice; there are criminal penalties for failure to comply.

The costs of externalities could also increase when public perceptions are changed. For example, if the harmful impact of a company's failure to protect its workers' safety is widely publicized, it may affect people's willingness to buy its products. The company may no longer be able to afford to scrimp on worker safety.

The remedies mentioned thus far involve negative consequences for practices that produce externalities. However, this overlooks the possible value of positive consequences for companies that adopt less harmful practices. Research on the *matching law* (McDowell, 1988) has shown that the behavior of individual organisms is a function of the relative rate of consequences for different behaviors. Analogously, it seems likely that one could reduce a corporate practice not only by increasing the cost of the harmful practice but also by increasing the profitability of a more desirable alternative practice. For example, pollution might decrease through incentives for installing pollution control equipment. Providing positive consequences for alternative practices may have the additional advantage of reducing resistance to efforts to bring about change in corporate practices.

There are additional possibilities. A corporation might decide to abandon a profitable practice simply because it concludes it is wrong or harmful. In this case, the leadership might come to value reducing a harmful practice more than it values profits, so that it becomes willing to achieve a reduced level of profit. The economics literature seldom countenances such a possibility. However, in a sense, any of the just-described strategies for reducing externalities ultimately involves changing the psychological value of practices and outcomes for the involved parties. Recent work on relational frame theory (Hayes, Barnes-Holmes, & Roche, 2001) provides a framework for understanding how the value of a particular consequence is a function of the relations an individual has with that consequence and other stimuli. For example, a CEO who meets a person with an illness or disability caused by a company practice may come to value that practice in a new light. Similarly, taxing a polluting practice changes the value of the practice for corporate leaders. It is not different in kind from changing the value of a practice, because corporate leadership makes psychological contact with the harm that a polluting practice inflicts on others.

However, the biggest problem society faces is not how to control externalities once identified but how to ensure that societies will take steps needed to control them. Companies have incentives to prevent the imposition of costs on their externalities and have created sophisticated methods to prevent government action. We need to understand these processes before we can understand how society might develop effective methods of ameliorating negative externalities.

THE EVOLUTION OF CORPORATE INFLUENCES ON POLICYMAKING

In a capitalist system, corporations adopt and retain or abandon practices because of their impact on profits (Biglan, 1995). Design, manufacturing, and marketing are obvious examples. Companies that design a better product, develop a more efficient method for manufacturing a product, or find the most effective ways to advertise a product are more likely to achieve profits; as a result, their practices will be more likely to continue (Glenn, 2004). Companies that fail to achieve profits because they fail to develop new and better products, manufacture products inefficiently, or fail to advertise them effectively may become bankrupt. On the other hand, they may abandon ineffective practices in light of their failure to contribute to profitability.

From one point of view, all of this is basic economics. However, we could also usefully view this within an evolutionary framework. Practices are selected by their consequences (Biglan, 2003; Glenn, 2004; Glenn & Malott, 2004; Wilson, 2003; 2007). From this standpoint, the evolution of corporate practices is one example of the tendency of human groups in general to retain practices that contribute to their survival as a group and to abandon those that do not.

Design, manufacturing, and marketing practices are not the only ones selected by market forces, however. Companies will develop and maintain *any* practice if it contributes to profitability. If lobbying the government for a contract is profitable, then the company will invest in lobbying. If supporting politicians who are likely to vote for policies favorable to the company improves the company's profits, the company may encourage its employees to donate to those politicians. If a public relations campaign can make the market more favorable for the company, the company will invest in public relations.

In addition, companies in the same industry typically have some common interests that motivate them to form industry associations to advocate and lobby for policies favorable to the industry. Trucking companies may lobby to keep fuel taxes low. The cigarette industry created the Tobacco Institute, which systematically obscured the effect of smoking on cancer and heart disease through a well-organized public relations campaign lasting over 40 years (*U.S. v. Philip Morris et al.*, 2006). In general, such industry associations will work to prevent the imposition of externalities' costs on the companies in their industry. These practices evolve because of their contribution to the profitability of the industry.

At an even higher level, the business community has evolved practices that ensure favorable conditions for business in general. Indeed, one can trace the conservative ascendancy of the past 30 years in the United States to the efforts by networks of business organizations and wealthy individuals to create a climate more favorable to business. Lew Lapham (2004) and Eric Alterman (2003) recount a 1971 seminal memo written by Lewis Powell before his appointment to the Supreme Court. Powell had received a request from his neighbor, Eugene B. Sydnor, Jr., who was Chairman of the U.S. Chamber of Commerce Education Committee, to provide ideas about how to improve public support for business. At the time, public trust of business was very low and there were growing concerns in the business community that government would adopt policies that would be increasingly harmful to business.

Powell recommended creating a network of effective advocates for business interests. The memo seems to have been an important impetus for sectors of the business community to support the creation or strengthening of think tanks and advocacy groups such as the Heritage Foundation and the American Enterprise Institute, which effectively make the case for minimizing taxes and regulation on business. Simultaneously, it stimulated conservative groups to support the education of youth favorable to business interests and to nurture the careers of those they viewed as effective advocates for favorable business policies. Lapham and Alterman document how advocacy for business interests has grown since 1971, how public support for business-friendly policies has increased, and, as a result, how public policy has become more favorable to business in the United States.

The financial consequences to the network of business interests have been enormous and have easily justified their investments. For example, according to Federal Reserve Board (Friedman, 2006), in 1989 the wealthiest 1% of Americans owned 30% of the total wealth of $25 trillion, or $7.775 trillion (in 2004 dollars), while the poorest 50% owned 3% of the wealth—$763 billion. By 2004, the total wealth had risen to $50.25 trillion and the top 1% of wealthiest people owned 33% of the wealth or $16.774 trillion, while the poorest 50% owned $1.278 trillion—only 2.5% of total wealth. The Congressional Budget Office analysis of the 2001 through 2003 tax cuts shows that they disproportionately favored the wealthy, continuing a trend that began in the 1970s (Kamin & Shapiro, 2004). For example, the top 1% of earners received a tax cut of about $41,000 in 2004, which was 40 times the amount received by those in the middle fifth of the income distribution.

The analysis describes the larger landscape within which efforts to reduce negative externalities must operate. The problem in controlling externalities is not one of identifying practices that are costly to others or even knowing how to reduce those externalities. It is a problem of gaining the influence to implement policies to affect them.

In a society with an elaborate, sophisticated, and well-funded network of organizations working to prevent any imposition of costs for the negative externalities of companies, we need a similar network of organizations to work for the wellbeing of those affected by externalities. Indeed, I would argue that the solution to the vast majority of society's problems requires a network of sophisticated and well-funded organizations working for the common good.

THE ROLE OF NONPROFIT AND ADVOCACY ORGANIZATIONS

Nonprofit and advocacy organizations seem to be the primary way to counter corporate externalities. To the extent that persons harmed by a practice can organize to support action in their interest, they may be able—directly or indirectly—to influence corporate practices. I write this, not as a statement of fact, but as a hypothesis that might guide research. In essence, I am arguing that understanding advocacy organizations, their current and potential role in society, and the factors that might improve their impact could contribute to the improvement of human wellbeing because it could lead to policies and practices to reduce negative externalities.

Advocacy organizations may be nonprofit or for profit. They include organizations that work to address a specific problem, such as heart disease or cancer, but they also include political advocacy organizations that receive no tax exemption for their efforts. In the United States, nonprofits may not advocate for candidates, but they may advocate for public policies and even for ballot measures. (See http://www.mapaidsline.org/publicpolicy/vote/Restrictions.htm.)

The Generic Features of Effective Advocacy

The practices involved in reducing tobacco use, which, increasingly, have involved efforts to constrain tobacco company practices, provide one of the most well-documented analyses of effective advocacy (Biglan & Taylor, 2000). The tobacco control movement includes four key features: (a) delivery of epidemiological evidence to the public and policymakers, (b) ongoing research to produce a growing body of evidence-based practices affecting smoking, (c) a network of organizations advocating for effective tobacco measures and/or doing research relevant to the problem, and (d) a surveillance system to track smoking and related practices, such as its marketing (Biglan, under review; Biglan & Taylor, 2000). Each practice involved in this effort contributed to strengthening other practices. As the movement enumerated—and communicated to a growing proportion of the population—the harmful consequences of smoking, support for control efforts and research on control efforts grew. Those efforts, in turn, strengthened the resources available to advocacy organizations.

A virtuous cycle formed in which information about the problem led to greater support for elaborating the extent of the problem and communicating that information to a wider and wider audience. These activities in turn led to policies that further supported the reduction in smoking. Examples of such policies include support for smoking cessation in healthcare settings and restrictions on tobacco advertising (National Association of Attorneys General, 1998). The success of these evolving practices is evident in the change in both the rate of smoking in the United States and the spread of policies and norms that constrain smoking (Biglan & Taylor, 2000). For example, between 1965 and 2002, the rate of males smoking in the United States dropped from 51.6% to 25.2% and for females went from 34% to 20% (Bonnie, Stratton, Wallace, & Committee on Reducing Tobacco Use, 2007).

A similar virtuous cycle appears in most successful efforts to address public health problems. Mothers Against Drunk Driving (MADD) publicized deaths due to drunk driving and pushed for stronger laws and greater enforcement to reduce the problem. Notably, a significant reduction in alcohol-related car crashes accompanied these efforts (Fell & Voas, 2006). Those efforts have included control of alcohol sales to minors. MADD has not addressed restrictions on alcohol marketing to the extent warranted, however (Biglan, under review).

The Consequences Shaping the Practices of Advocacy Organizations

Unlike traditional for-profit organizations, advocacy organizations do not derive their financial support directly from their success in accomplishing their mission. That is, what they achieve with respect to altering harmful corporate practices does not result directly in funds to sustain their activities. Whereas the success of a for-profit corporation in marketing a product or service at a profit provides the funds that shape and sustain the organization's practices, the success of an advocacy organization may or may not result in further funding. In essence, advocacy organizations must do two things: work for the targeted change and obtain funds to continue its activities. Such organizations may or may not be successful in the latter activity, and their success or failure in raising funds may have little to do with whether they are successful in advancing their advocacy agenda. For example, a health-promoting organization such as the American Cancer Society (ACS) may conduct a campaign to influence people to quit smoking. It is possible for the campaign to have little influence on people quitting but nonetheless to generate contributions to the organization because people perceive that the ACS is doing something useful. Conversely, the campaign could be very successful but be very costly and generate no contributions to the organization. Understanding these two different contingencies is critical in understanding how to strengthen the effectiveness of advocacy organizations in society.

Evolving Policies that Strengthen Advocacy Organizations

We are unlikely to have a significant effect upon a wide range of societal problems unless we strengthen the effectiveness of advocacy organizations. Typically, people concerned about a particular issue will seek to strengthen the resources and effectiveness of organizations working on that issue. However, a more generic analysis of the problem may point to policies that could improve the support and effectiveness of organizations working on the entire range of problems, which includes preventing harm resulting from externalities.

The fundamental problem in trying to evolve organizational practices to control corporate externalities effectively is to create a set of contingencies to shape and maintain effective practices among advocacy organizations. At the core, we must ensure that organizations working on negative corporate externalities have the resources necessary to advocate effectively. However, we also need to ensure that their advocacy practices are, in fact, effective. Here is a set of policies that could sharpen the contingencies that influence advocacy organizations to act effectively in the interest of public wellbeing.

JUSTIFICATION OF THE PUBLIC BENEFIT

If we are to have a class of organizations that receives increased societal support for working on externalities, we need societal agreement about what constitutes a sufficiently important externality. The public health principles enumerated above provide some guidance. Only externalities that affect the health of a significant proportion of the population would be targets, and therefore only organizational practices targeting these externalities would qualify for enhanced public support. Examples include manufacturing and marketing practices shown through rigorous empirical research—including experimental designs—to harm public health. Elsewhere, I have argued that, before a marketing practice could be targeted, there would need to be experimental evidence that the practice influences people to engage in an unhealthy behavior (Biglan, under review). That case is clear with respect to tobacco marketing, but the evidence is not yet clear regarding marketing of alcohol and unhealthy foods; experimental studies of the impact of current marketing practices for these products simply do not exist. For example, experimental analyses of the impact of exposure to advertising of these products might show that exposure significantly increases both the *intentions* of young people to use these products or their *actual use* of them. Other practices to target under this standard include those that have proven to contribute to global warming and those that increase the proportion of people living in poverty, such as payday loans (Federal Trade Commission, 2008).

TRANSPARENCY

If advocacy organizations had a mandate to publish their goals annually, and to report on their actions and on the success or failure in achieving those goals, contributors and the public could gauge more precisely the value of those efforts. Such transparency would sharpen the contingency between effective advocacy and funding, as money would tend to flow to the organizations showing the greatest success. Nonprofit organizations are currently required to disclose their activities in some detail, but the transparency I am suggesting would involve considerably more detail and precision.

GREATER TAX BENEFITS FOR CONTRIBUTIONS TO QUALIFYING ORGANIZATIONS

When organizations meet the above criteria, their contributors could receive increased tax benefits. Although money donated to any nonprofit organization is currently deductible from one's taxes, the amount deductible for giving to these organizations might increase. For example, people might be able to deduct from their taxes 150% of what they donate.

Advocating for Policies that Strengthen Advocacy Organizations

In essence, I propose creation of a special class of nonprofit advocacy organizations with the power and support to advocate for policies necessary to reduce corporate externalities. Any effort to create such a system will undoubtedly face opposition, not only from organizations with externality-producing practices but also by advocacy organizations that would not qualify for the proposed benefits. Thus, achieving policies that could strengthen advocacy organizations would require its own effective advocacy.

Above I argued that corporate practices to prevent curtailing of externalities exist at three levels—individual companies, entire industries, and the business community as a whole. A similar analysis fits the advocacy sector. Individual organizations work on controlling specific externalities. Networks of organizations work on problems such as pollution, unsustainable environmental practices, tobacco control, and so on. However, I have been unable to identify organizations that work generally for policies to reduce externalities. Having such organizations may be essential for achieving the kinds of policies I propose. The generic analysis provided here is the intellectual framework that justifies creating such overarching advocacy organizations.

It may seem unlikely that society would ever agree to the types of policies I suggest. Corporate lobbies against them will claim they are radically at variance with the traditions of Western capitalist democracies. However, the history of the evolution of other cultural practices that have expanded human wellbeing suggests a different view. Consider London in the 19th century, when it was the world's largest and wealthiest city: it was common for raw human sewage to run freely in the streets and empty into rivers that provided the city's drinking water. The city leaders at that time would have seen our modern sanitation practices as radical indeed.

Consider the more recent example of how the United States and other developed nations have evolved economic management practices to reduce significantly the boom-and-bust business cycles that were common until the mid-20th century (Moynihan, 1975). Most experts once considered it a radical idea to manage an economy to prevent inflation and unemployment. In each instance, practices emerged that improved human wellbeing. This happened because empirical evidence accumulated regarding the harm of the existing practices and sound evidence guided the implementation of more effective policies.

CONCLUSION

Scientists who study organizations are in a unique position to analyze externalities of corporations and the contingencies that influence both for-profit organizations and those working to counter negative corporate externalities. With this article, I hope I have provided a framework to stimulate further research on these important problems. As evidence mounts that global warming is occurring much faster than earlier predicted (Lean, 2007), it becomes imperative for scientists to analyze how we can alter corporate contributions to this and other problems.

In 50 years, people may look back on this era and see it as a time when the scientific and public health communities failed to conduct the bold analyses needed to influence corporate practices and, as a result, societal systems that ensured human wellbeing collapsed (Diamond, 2004). On the other hand, they may say that, thankfully, science conducted effective contextual analyses that brought the practices of for-profit corporations in line with the long-term needs of human beings. Behavior analysis has the tools to specify the necessary actions of advocacy and for-profit organizations and to analyze the impact of changing the consequences of those actions. Their use on this problem could prove to be one the field's greatest contributions to human wellbeing.

REFERENCES

Alterman, E. (2003). *What liberal media?* New York: Basic Books.

Azrin, N. H., & Foxx, R. (1974). *Toilet training in less than a day.* NY: Simon & Schuster.

Bay-Hintz, A. K., Peterson, R. F., & Quilitch, H. R. (1994). Cooperative games: A way to modify aggressive and cooperative behaviors in young children. *Journal of Applied Behavior Analysis, 27,* 435–446.

Biglan, A. (1995). *Changing cultural practices: A contextualist framework for intervention research.* Reno, NV: Context Press.

Biglan, A. (2003). Selection by consequences: One unifying principle for a transdisciplinary science of prevention. *Prevention Science, 4,* 213–232.

Biglan, A. (2004). *Direct written testimony in the case of the U.S.A. vs. Phillip Morris et al.* Washington, DC: U.S. Department of Justice. Retrieved April 30, 2008, from http://www.ori.org/oht/testimony.html

Biglan, A. (under review). *Challenges to the further success of prevention science.*

Biglan, A., & Hayes, S. C. (1996). Should the behavioral sciences become more pragmatic? The case for functional contextualism in research on human behavior. *Applied and Preventive Psychology, 5,* 47–57.

Biglan, A., & Taylor, T. K. (2000). Why have we been more successful in reducing tobacco use than violent crime? *American Journal of Community Psychology, 28,* 269–302.

Bonnie, R. J., Stratton, K., Wallace, R. B., & Committee on Reducing Tobacco Use (2007). *Ending the tobacco problem: A blueprint for the nation.* Washington, DC: Institute of Medicine.

Brownell, K. D., & Horgen, K. B. (2004). *Food fight: The inside story of the food industry, America's obesity crisis, and what we can do about it.* New York: McGraw-Hill.

Centers for Disease Control and Prevention (2006). *Fact sheet: Cigarette smoking-related mortality.* U.S. Department of Health and Human Services. Retrieved May 2, 2008, from http://www.cdc.gov/tobacco/data_statistics/factsheets/cig_smoking_mort.htm

Congressional Budget Office (2001, June). *An evaluation of cap-and-trade programs for reducing U.S. carbon emissions.* Washington, DC: Congress of the

United States. Retrieved May 1, 2008, from http://www.cbo.gov/ftpdocs/28xx/doc2876/CapTrade.pdf

deMause, L. (1990). The history of child assault. *The Journal of Psychohistory, 18,* 1–29.

Diamond, J. (2004). *Collapse: How societies choose to fail or succeed.* New York: Viking Adult.

Federal Trade Commission (2008, March). *Payday loans equal very costly cash: Consumers urged to consider the alternatives* (FTC Consumer Alert). Retrieved May 2, 2008, from http://www.ftc.gov/bcp/edu/pubs/consumer/alerts/alt060.shtm

Fell, J. C., & Voas, R. B. (2006). Mothers Against Drunk Driving (MADD): The first 25 years. *Traffic Injury Prevention, 7,* 195–212.

Friedman, L. (2006). Inequality counts. *The Nation.* Retrieved May 2, 2008, from http://www.thenation.com/doc/20060529/friedman

Glenn, S. S. (1986). Metacontingencies in Walden Two. *Behavior Analysis and Social Action, 5,* 2–12.

Glenn, S. S. (1988). Contingencies and metacontingencies: Toward a synthesis of behavior analysis and cultural materialism. *The Behavior Analyst, 11,* 161–179.

Glenn, S. S. (2004). Individual behavior, culture, and social change. *Behavior Analyst, 27,* 133–151.

Glenn, S. S., & Malott, M. E. (2004). Complexity and selection: Implications for organizational change. *Behavior and Social Issues, 13,* 89–106. Retrieved May 2, 2008, from http://www.bfsr.org/BSI_13_2/Contents.html

Gwartney, J. D., & Stroup, R. L. (1987). *Economics: Private and public choice.* San Diego: Harcourt Brace, Jovanovich.

Hayes, S. C., Barnes-Holmes, D., & Roche, B. (2001). *Relational frame theory: A post-Skinnerian account of human language and cognition.* New York: Kluwer Academic/Plenum Publishers.

Institute of Medicine. (In preparation). *IOM report on effective interventions.* Washington, DC: Institute of Medicine.

Kamin, D., & Shapiro, I. (2004). Studies shed new light on effects of Administration's tax cuts. *Center for Budget and Policy Priorities.* Retrieved May 2, 2008, from http://www.cbpp.org/8-25-04tax.htm

Lapham, L. (2004). Tentacles of rage. *Harper's Magazine.*

Lean, G. (2007). Global warming "is three times faster than worst predictions." *The Independent.* Retrieved May 2, 2008, from http://www.independent.co.uk/environment/climate-change/global-warming-is-three-times-faster-than-worst-predictions-451529.html

McDowell, J. J. (1988). Matching theory in natural human environments. *The Behavior Analyst, 11,* 95–109.

Moynihan, D. P. (1975). A brief narration. *American Psychologist, 30,* 939–940.

msnbc.com (2005, April 22). ExxonMobil spends millions funding global warming skeptics. Retrieved May 2, 2008, from http://www.msnbc.msn.com/id/16593606/

National Association of Attorneys General. (1998). *Master Settlement Agreement, November 1998.* Last accessed May 1, 2008, from http://www.naag.org/backpages/naag/tobacco/msa

144 *A. Biglan*

National Cancer Institute. (2008). *The use of the media to promote and discourage tobacco use. Tobacco Control Monograph No. 19*. Bethesda, MD: U.S. Department of Health and Human Services, National Institute of Health, National Cancer Institute.

National Research Council & Institute of Medicine. (2009). *Preventing mental, emotional, and behavioral disorders among young people: Progress and possibilities. Committee on Prevention of Mental Disorders and Substance Abuse Among Children, Youth, and Young Adults: Research Advances and Promising Inverventions*. Washington, DC: The National Academies Press.

Organisation for Economic Cooperation and Development. (1993). *Glossary of industrial organisation economics and competition law*, compiled by R. S. Khemani & D. M. Shapiro, commissioned by the Directorate for Financial, Fiscal and Enterprise Affairs, OECD. Retrieved July 24, 2008, from http://stats.oecd.org/glossary/detail.asp?ID=3215

Parker-Pope, T. (2001). *Cigarettes: Anatomy of an industry from seed to smoke*. New York: Norton.

Pierce, J. P., Gilpin, E. A., & Choi, W. S. (1999). Sharing the blame: Smoking experimentation and future smoking-attributable mortality due to Joe Camel and Marlboro advertising and promotions. *Tobacco Control, 8*(1), 37–44.

Pollan, M. (2006). *The omnivore's dilemma*. New York: Penguin USA.

Pollan, M. (2007, January 28). Unhappy meals. *The New York Times Magazine*. Retrieved September 10, 2007, from http://www.michaelpollan.com/article.php?id=87

U.S. Department of Health and Human Services (1983). *The health consequences of smoking: Cardiovascular disease. A report of the Surgeon General*. Rockville, MD: U.S. Department of Health and Human Services, Public Health Service, Office on Smoking and Health. DHHS Publication PHS 84-50204. Retrieved July 24, 2008, from http://profiles.nlm.nih.gov/NN/B/B/T/D/_/nnbbtd.pdf

United States v. Philip Morris et al., Civil No. 99-CV-02496GK (U.S. Dist. Ct., D.C., 2006).

Wilson, D. S. (2003). *Darwin's cathedral*. Chicago: University of Chicago Press.

Wilson, D. S. (2007). *Evolution for everyone: How Darwin's theory can change the way we think about our lives*. New York: Delacorte Press.

World Health Organization (2002). *World Health Report 2002: Reducing risks, promoting healthy life*. Geneva: WHO.

World Health Organization (2008). *Global climate change and health: An old story writ large*. Retrieved May 9, 2008, from http://www.who.int/globalchange/climate/summary/en/8

Wynder, E. L., & Graham, E. (1950). Tobacco smoking as a possible etiologic factor in bronchiogenic carcinoma: A study of 684 proven cases. *Journal of the American Medical Association, 143*, 329–336.

Identifying and Extinguishing Dysfunctional and Deadly Organizational Practices

THOMAS C. MAWHINNEY

University of Detroit Mercy, Detroit, Michigan, USA

It is possible to define an organization's culture in terms of its dominant behavioral practices and their molar consequences, from the shop floor to the executive suite (Redmon & Mason, 2001). Dysfunctional and potentially deadly practices (for the organization as a whole) can be "latent." They often go undetected until their dramatic consequences are overtly manifest. For example, leadership of Alaska Airlines appeared to have had no idea how dangerous their aircraft maintenance practices were prior to the notorious crash of Alaska Airlines' Flight 261 (Mawhinney, 2007, National Transportation Safety Board, 2002) in which 88 people perished. Similarly, the leadership of Barings Bank either had no idea that their high performing trader in Singapore, Nick Leeson, was about to kill the company until the deed was done (Leeson, 1996). This was in spite of the fact that some of the managers above Leeson were believed to have poorly fulfilled their responsibilities to limit the bank's financial risks (Lesson, 1996). The concepts of latent dysfunctional and latent deadly practices are developed in ways that can guide behavior systems analysts interested in identifying and replacing such practices with functional practices.

The author would like to thank Cloyd Hyten and several anonymous reviewers for helpful comments on earlier versions of this manuscript.

INTRODUCTION

In hindsight, Redmon and Mason (2001) correctly anticipated the need among formal organizations (FOs) in the private sector to adopt or develop "more effective methodologies for organizational culture change . . . needed to permit alteration of *large-scale practices* [emphasis added] and to facilitate *rapid* response to threats to survival" (p. 437). Then and now, globalization posed a challenge among domestic formal organizations in the private sector. Then and now, demands for greater efficiency required by tighter budgets pose a continuing challenge among public service organizations.

At the other end of the scale of organizational practices, however, are small-scale, neglected, idiosyncratic variations in compliance with seemingly mundane SOPs (standard operating procedures). Minor as they may seem, small-scale, neglected, idiosyncratic variations in compliance with seemingly mundane SOPs can, nevertheless, have life and death consequences for FOs, their members and customers. For example, who would have thought that a relatively small variation in the amount of grease applied to one of a passenger airliner's flight control mechanisms would result in the loss of 88 lives (National Transportation Safety Board, 2002) or that stowing out-of-date oxygen generators with tires in a freight compartment would cost the lives of 110 passengers and crew (Wikipedia, 2008)? The thesis advanced in this article is that apparently innocuous dysfunctional yet potentially deadly organizational practices exist in FOs and need to be conceptualized, identified (their consequences predicted when possible), and eliminated or supplanted with decidedly functional practices. By these means FOs can better fit themselves for survival, not to mention protecting the priceless lives of their members, their customers, and the general public.

In this article examples of practices that have proven deadly in terms of human and/or FO life are used to exemplify practices of interest and some tactics for identifying and removing them. First, a number of conceptual issues and some relevant terms and concepts are introduced. They provide a foundation for understanding the "nature" of FOs and to what the term *deadly* refers with respect to FOs per se and their stakeholders.

ORGANIZATIONS AS LIVING SYSTEMS

For present purposes FOs are conceived as living systems (Glenn, 2004; Lovelock, 1988; Mawhinney, 1992a, 2001; Miller, 1978; Skinner, 1972, 1981). Further, they are formally organized and managed adaptive systems guided by their missions and goals to go beyond mere survival (Brethower, 1972; 1982; 2000; 2001; Luthans & Kreitner, 1975; Malott, 2001; 2003; Redmon & Mason, 2001; Rummler, 2001). As such, neither millions nor billions of dollars worth of well-designed physical artifacts can bring an FO to life.

Only the human operant behavior observed in actions among organizational members (Baum, 2005; Hopkins, 1995, 1999; Poling & Braatz, 2001) can accomplish that feat.

Immutable Objective Survival Contingencies

An FO's metacontingencies (plural) refer to some identifiable number of FO practices and their molar consequences for organizational subunits and the organization as a whole. For example, when FO members use methods of statistical process control and total quality management practices within, respectively, production and service delivery processes, the consequences are likely to be reduced processing costs that support price reductions and market share gains from competitors (Deming, 1986/2000; Mawhinney, 1992b). For example, HR training and pay practices that result in lower absenteeism and turnover and higher quality job performances, which are reflected in lower production costs, lower output repair costs, higher customer satisfaction, and market share gains from competitors, are elements of functional metacontingencies. Metacontingencies typically differ from behavioral contingencies of reinforcement (Baum, 2005; Skinner, 1969) in that their consequences for the organization do not necessarily function as reinforcers of the behavioral practices the consequences of which have some effect on the FO's performance as a whole. Thus, implementing statistical process control or, more generally, quality control practices may require shop floor–level training and performance reinforcement contingencies (cf. Henry & Redmon, 1990). The upper echelon members of the FO's hierarchy often participate in employee stock option plans and receive bonuses contingent on their FO's quarterly or annual profitability. These are consequences over which they have some control by developing, implementing, and tweaking the FO's competitive strategy in ways that may improve organizational level performance (Thompson, Strickland, & Gamble, 2008). To the extent their efforts result in improved FO performance and increased market price of its stocks, these organizational members' behavior and practices might be reinforced by the performance of the organization as a whole.

When used in the singular, organizational metacontingency refers to an omnibus contingency among all organizational practices, whether functional or dysfunctional, and their molar consequences as reflected in survival-related financial criteria.

At least one criterion is universally applicable to FOs. That is to say, every living FO is subject to a universal survival-related environmental rule with respect to its unique metacontingency. That rule requires that all cash inflows (CI) and certain cash reserves of a given FO must be sufficient to pay for all of its financial obligations, cash outflows (CO), as they come due. Failure to satisfy this contingency, within temporal limits that may vary somewhat from one FO to another, exposes the FO to the prospects of bankruptcy

(Kremer, Rizzuto, & Case, 2000). This survival criterion can be stated as follows: CI + certain cash reserves ≥ CO, or cash inflows and certain cash reserves must be equal to or greater than cash outflows. Van Horne (1971) presented data from Beaver (1966) showing that the ratio of cash flow to total debt predicted business failures. He also noted that the five ratios Altman (1968) identified and used in a multiple discriminant analysis model was able to "forecast failure quite well up to two years before bankruptcy" (Van Horne, 1971, p. 621).

Although the amount of cash flows required will vary from one FO to another, the degree to which an FO is at risk of bankruptcy can be estimated using Altman's Z-score (Altman, 1968) and updates to it (Altman, 2000; Gritta, Adrangi, Sergio, & Bright, 2006). These criteria reflect the "general health" of each FO or its financial fitness for survival. A different criterion might be in order for some FOs in the financial services industry, including banks, brokerage houses, and savings and loan companies, in that they may be required to carry cash reserves in addition to cash used to pay for current obligations. (Cutting dividends and raising cash with new stock issues is one tactic used to remedy this sort of "problem," at least in the short run.) But the criterion above does apply to the case of Barings Bank described later in this article.

An Organization's Metacontingency Reflects Effects of Competitors' Practices

Whether the practices related to maintaining sufficient cash flows are functional or dysfunctional relative to an FO's survival depends in part on the practices of direct competitors, unless the FO enjoys a monopoly. A hypothetical example highlighting the role of competitors and economic competition among FOs within a common industry might help. Consider three FOs, A, B, and C, that are initially identical. Each holds a third of their common industry's market share. They all compete on the basis of product quality versus low prices and suffer from chronic absenteeism and turnover and a host of minor dysfunctional practices about which their leadership teams are unaware. Then, one of them, A, adopts a set of practices that reduces absenteeism and turnover, increases member efficiency, reduces production costs and *increases output capacity* whether output increases or not. Next, FO A leaves prices unchanged, shares the gains by increasing members' wages and salaries, purchases equipment that helps members improve output rate and quality, and reduces some of its long-term debt that further reduces future costs as interest expenses are reduced, while B and C *remain unchanged.* Coincidentally, aggregate demand for the industry's outputs increases and FO A's sales increase, using up its *excess capacity.* Formal organization A's only variable costs are additional materials increase. Sales of FOs B and C also increase, but their costs rise more than A's.

This occurs because increasing their outputs requires expenditures beyond additional materials expenses because of increased overtime pay and addition of full-time members. Market shares remain constant among the companies, but A is more profitable and its share prices rise to the benefit of its shareholders, some of whom are members of FO A (e.g., employees' 401K plans holding company stock). The practices that resulted in A's increased profitability were clearly functional practices that displaced dysfunctional practices, providing funds used for engaging in yet more functional practices. Thus, whether leaderships of FOs B and C know it or not, FO A is likely changing environmental rules of effective competition or what practices will make them better fit for survival than they are at the moment. But the story does not end here. All three FOs might still be harboring dysfunctional practices that might grow and at some point threaten their survival. But they might also enjoy small performance improvements across many tasks that can, in time, produce relatively large financial gains (Mawhinney, 1999). Thus, A, B, and C *should* allocate some resources to ferreting out and eliminating dysfunctional practices and identi- fying and promoting functional practices. For example, they could assess the effectiveness and efficiency of their human resources, calculating the ratio of sales revenue, cash flows, and profits to total membership of their FO and their competitors. Better ratios might be due to practices on the shop floor, substitution of technology for human resources, or some combina- tion. This sort of analysis would help pinpoint whether an advantage or deficit in performance relative to competitors was a result of human performance or technological differences among competitors.

Practices and Metacontingencies and Organizational Practices

Organizational practices are amalgams of *rule-governed* (Agnew & Redmon, 1992; Baum, 2005; Blakely & Schlinger, 1987; Cerutti, 1989; Hayes, Bond, Barnes-Holmes, & Austin, 2006; Malott, 1992; Rachlin, 2004, Schlinger, 1993; Schlinger & Blakely, 1987, 1994; Skinner, 1957; 1969; Zettle & Hayes, 1982) and *contingency-shaped behavior* (Skinner, 1969). Rule-governed and con- tingency-shaped behaviors are a function of interactions among individual and/or group behavior and objective three-term environmental contingen- cies, or the now-familiar A : B → C (Poling & Braatz, 2001) contingencies that may evolve into behavioral contingencies of reinforcement $S^D : B \rightarrow R+$ (Skinner, 1969). In the most general terms, *rules are contingency-specifying stimuli and/or statements* (CSS) such as role-specifying stimuli and/or state- ments (RSS) that, very importantly, *have function-altering effects on elements of objective environmental contingencies* (cf. Agnew & Redmon, 1992; Schlinger, 1993; Schlinger & Blakely, 1994; Hayes, Bunting, Herbst, Bond, & Barnes-Holmes, 2006). Function-altering effects are observed when the functions of antecedents, A, and consequences, C, are altered by a CSS or RSS. These effects are evident when the As or Cs so altered function as or as though they were S^Ds and R+s as elements of behavioral contingencies of reinforcement. The typical CSS or RSS is a verbal statement, but there is a host of CSSs and RSSs that are not verbal, for example, stop signs, street names, route markers (numbers), prices on products for sale, a position at a workbench and quality of tools on the wall, and a desk with a plush swivel chair, speaker phone, and client list—in other words, a "corner office."

What these stimuli have in common is that they "say" something about the contingencies to which they refer or within which they function as elements of objective environmental contingencies. For example, a slot machine in a casino is a physical but lifeless manifestation of an objective three-term environmental contingency, A : B → C. The contingency exists whether a slots player interacts (B) with the machine (A) or not. Yet, the one-armed bandit "beckons" the ardent and veteran slots player to interact with its programmed feedback function (Baum, 1973). That feedback function is a potentially addictive variable ratio or variable amount schedule of reinforcement. The one-armed bandit's feedback function is: $\sum R+ = \sum B/N$ X $A - \sum \$k$, where the sum of winnings, $\sum R+$, equals the sum of arm pulls, $\sum B$, divided by the mean ratio schedule requirement, N, times, X, the average amount won per winning pull, $A, minus the sum of the price paid for each arm pull, $\sum \$k$. But, the point made here is that there is a difference between fixed immutable objective environmental contingencies (Baum, 1973; Poling & Braatz, 2001) and the behavioral processes they might evoke and maintain if and when behavior interacts with them. If behavior does interact with them, the result is behavioral contingencies of reinforcement, $S^D : B → R+$ (Baum, 1973, 2005, Hantula, 2001; Skinner, 1969; Zeiler, 1977). In addition, slots players learn from other gamblers and/ or devise their own rules regarding how to "beat the house" by means of moving from one machine to another based on some criteria or criterion and rules regarding what to do with winnings, for example, plow them back into bets or put them aside and so forth (Rachlin, 2004). But for gamblers, the house "stacks the cards against them" while top-level corporate strategists participate in a "game" that permits them to develop and implement competitive strategies that can and do, with some frequency, result in winning market shares from their competitors.

The popular press repeats with some frequency the fact that Toyota Motors has, for decades, been taking market share from domestic auto makers. And their winning ways are largely a function of differences in their practices relative to those of their competitors, now called the "Detroit Three" instead of the "Big Three." But, Toyota and the domestic auto makers can change the rules of competition in their industry by what they do (Mawhinney, 1992a), while the gambler's one-armed bandit remains immune to the strategies of its players; in other words, its feedback function is fixed much as the supply of crude oil appears to be at the moment. The feedback functions of FOs, on the other hand, are dynamic and subject to change by top level leaders of FOs and their competitors (Mawhinney, 1992a; 2001). For the gambler, it matters little whether another gambler happens to have a heart attack while playing in the same casino. When one competitor perishes within an industry populated by competing FOs, on the other hand and other things equal, the surviving competitors will each take a share of the market abandoned by the departed competitor. Such are the differences between contingencies that are not altered by behavior of people that interact with them and dynamic social contingencies such as those among people and FOs that cooperate and compete among themselves as social entities (Baum, 2005; Mawhinney, 1992a; 2005; Mechner, 2008a, 2008b). (Look for changes such as these as GM [currently in Chapter 11 bankruptcy] and Chryster [potentially emerging from Chapter 11] strive to survive in the global auto industry.)

If behavioral contingencies of reinforcement evoked and maintained by a common environmental contingency were completely predictable, however, OBM practitioners could design or engineer (Gilbert, 1978) the FO's performance by creating an array of bureaucratic rules or SOPs that would reliably produce an FO metacontingency that would always result in the FO's CI + certain cash reserves exceeding its CO. While this is an unlikely event (cf. Mawhinney & Fellows-Kubert, 1999), OBM practitioners have demonstrated their ability to improve FOs' performances using knowledge of the ways in which members' performance-related behavior interacts with environmental contingencies, producing improved contingencies of performance reinforcement (Abernathy, 2001; Hantula, 2001; Stajkovic & Luthans, 1997), and in a safe manner (Geller, 2001; McSween, 2003; Sulzer-Azaroff, McCann, & Harris, 2001). In addition, they have actually identified "new" social contingencies of reinforcement that improve performance-related behavior. For example, Alvero and Austin (2004) found that when members of a work group function as observers and recorders of safety-related behavior of peers, the observers' levels of safety-related behavior improves.

Contingency-shaped rule following may arise during occasions of problem solving. During problem solving episodes a person is presented with a task such as "fixing something" that functions as a reinforcer if and when a "fix" is accomplished (Cerutti, 1989; Michael, 1993; Olson, Laraway, & Austin, 2001). The solution, once discovered, may be codified and written down in terms of what one should do to replicate a "fix" in the presence of the same type of objective environmental contingencies (problems) in the future. The written rules would be hard copy instructions that, if followed or complied with, would permit others having had no experience with the problem to fix that "something" without going through the same trial and error process again (Skinner, 1953, 1969). Formal organizations are replete with such rules and instructions conveyed orally or in writing and divined from observing effective behavior-environment interactions of others that serve as models. Not all, but many, bureaucratic rules and SOPs were once novel solutions to recurring problems.

But contingency-shaped rule following can also be dysfunctional. For example, a rule that in words would be "Punishment is a better performance motivator than rewards" can be shaped up by one's behavior interacting with environmental social contingencies. If a trainer of exceptionally high-performing individuals whose performance is "in statistical control" (varying randomly about a high mean performance level), administers "rewards" following occasions of high trainee performance and "punishments" following occasions of low trainee performance, "rewarding" and "punishing" will respectively and predictably be followed by lower and higher instances of trainee performance. Most readers will recognize that this would be due to the phenomenon called regression to the mean among instances of performances observed and rewards and punishments administered contingent on very high and very low performances.

Evidence regarding emergence of this sort of individual rule creation and following and a cogent discussion of its etiology is provided by Notz, Boschman, and Tax (1987); see also their references to work by Kahneman and Tversky (1973). In a similar manner FO members may learn from experience that FO rules can be broken or may learn from peers that deviations of behavior from SOPs are, in some cases, even functional, whereas compliance with the SOPs is dysfunctional. Those of us old enough to recall the "rule ins" by air traffic controllers know that there is some truth in that proposition; in other words, breaking or ignoring rules can be functional. Forbidden from going on strike, air traffic controllers who normally used their discretion when deciding which SOPs were sacrosanct and which were obsolete followed "every rule in the books" to put pressure on their employer to obtain better pay and working conditions. But, in other cases, deviations from SOPs can be deadly, as demonstrated when Japanese nuclear materials processing workers "broke the rules" and created a deadly nuclear reaction (Efron, 1999).

How organizational member behavior and system variables are supposed to interact with one another is typically introduced to members via CSS (Skinner, 1957) and RSS in the form of verbal rule specifications such as mands and/or tacts where the speaker is a real person (executive, manager, supervisor, or shop-floor worker; Skinner, 1969; Zettle & Hayes, 1982). But, they can also be conveyed by a *hypothetical* person or entity called "the system," "the maintenance manual," "the APA style manual," "management," "the union," "the contract," or simply the FO's name or "the company," for example, Association for Behavior Analysis (ABA), Florida Association for Behavior Analysis (FABA), Ford, General Motors (GM), International Business Machine (IBM), Apple, Microsoft, Bank of America, the Cambridge Center for Behavioral Studies, the Red Cross, Habitat for Humanity, the Internal Revenue Service (IRS), and the Fed. Each has its own "rule book" or literature created to convey to insiders and outsiders information regarding "who they are" and "what they do, stand for and promote" (Thompson et al., 2008). More often than not they are verbal descriptions of generic $A : B \rightarrow C$ contingencies such as rules, regulations, standard operating procedures, task and job descriptions or specifications, or roles within and/or between member behavior, the work environment, and the FO's external environment.

Rule following and rule complying behavior is observed when a person's or group's behavior interacts with three-term environmental contingencies, $A : B \rightarrow C$, resulting in three-term *behavioral contingencies of reinforcement*, $S^D : B \rightarrow R+$ (Agnew & Redmon, 1992; Baum, 2005; Blakely & Schlinger, 1987; Cerutti, 1989; Hayes, Bond, Barnes-Holmes, & Austin, 2006; Hopkins, 1999; Mechner, 2008a, 2008b; Schlinger, 1993; Schlinger & Blakely, 1987, 1994; Skinner, 1969). For example, suppose that workers, after a baseline is stabilized, are informed (CSS) that they will be paid a bonus for each unit of work completed beyond some quota (e.g., Thurkow, Bailey, & Stamper, 2000). Now, suppose that some workers increase their work rate and earn bonus pay as specified in the CSS while one of them never performs at a rate sufficient to "make quota" and receive a bonus payment during either baseline or intervention. The increased rate of performance among some workers would qualify as an exemplar of a contingency of reinforcement, while that of the worker whose work rate remained unchanged and below quota would not. This is a very important distinction. Objective three-term environmental contingencies and behavioral contingencies of reinforcement differ in that the former can exist even if behavior never makes contact with the contingency (Poling & Braatz, 2001), while the latter are defined by the fact they either change or maintain behavior at some level (Mawhinney, 1975).

It is worth noting that verbal humans are capable of developing individual and group norms of conduct or rules that may appear at odds with natural laws of behavior, such as reinforcement value matching (Herrnstein, 1970) and/or maximization (cf. Mawhinney, 1982; Mawhinney & Fellows-Kubert, 1999) and/or economic value optimization (Hursh, 1984; Hyten, 2001) or escalation of commitment (Hantula, 1992; Hantula & Crowell, 1994). An example of this sort of apparent anomaly is what Skinner (1953) called *countercontrol*. It may be observed when union members forego immediate income and force income losses on other stakeholders (e.g., owners) when they go on strike. They go on strike for higher wages and benefits and/or control of working conditions. They might, for example, strike to gain the right to refuse to do certain types of work by winning contractual limits on the scope of their job descriptions, in other words, official RSS. The objective of countercontrol tactics is typically a reduction in the power of a "controller" (e.g., employer) to demand and obtain certain types and/or rates of behavior among organized employees. Featherbedding is an extreme example of union gains by counter control, at least in "the old days."

A classic example of featherbedding was the preservation of the fireman's position in the cab of diesel locomotives when they took the place of coal-fired stream engines; the fireman would stay in the cab, while the fireman's function, feeding coal into the steam engine's firebox, was "long gone." It should be evident at this juncture that organizational members exposed to the same formal objective environmental three-term contingencies, for example, bureaucratic rules as CSS, RSS, and task related SOPs, may or may not spawn the same individual and/or group behavioral contingencies of reinforcement. And some behavioral deviations from official contingencies may be functional, some dysfunctional, and some potentially or actually deadly for the FO's members and stakeholders in the short or long run. The exemplars below focus attention on the fact that deviations of behavior from specifications of functional practices, even small deviations, can have huge negative consequences for the FOs in which they occur.

THE CRASH OF ALASKA AIRLINES' FLIGHT 261, JANUARY 31, 2002

During the accident airplane's flight from Puerto Vallarta, Mexico, to Seattle-Tacoma International Airport, Washington, the horizontal stabilizer necessary to control the aircraft's pitch failed, and the plane dove into the Pacific Ocean. The National Transportation Safety Board concluded that the probable cause of the crash of Alaska Airlines' Flight 261was "loss of airplane pitch control resulting from the in-flight failure of the horizontal stabilizer trim system jackscrew assembly's acme nut threads. The thread failure was caused by excessive wear resulting from Alaska Airlines' insufficient lubrication of the jackscrew assembly" (National Transportation Safety Board, 2002, p. 180). Pitch is the degree to which an airplane's nose moves upward as it climbs or moves downward as it dives or descends during flight.

Proper lubrication and safety of the acme nut is a function of the airline's maintenance practices and any associated training, supervision and/or inspection practices. The system of practices responsible for critical flight control components such as the acme nut and jackscrew assembly includes operant behavior of managers, supervisors, inspectors, lead mechanics, and maintenance mechanics, which constitutes a hierarchy of interlocking behavioral contingencies such as those described by Malott (2003). The CSS conveyed by rules for lubricating the vertical pitch control system were provided, in part, by the Alaska Airlines' maintenance task card (see Appendix A).

In addition, the manufacturer's maintenance manual indicated that when lubricating components by forcing grease into *vented* parts (i.e., new grease forced into a part is permitted to force old grease out), maintenance personnel should "force grease into fittings until all old grease is extruded [forced out of the part]" (National Transportation Safety Board, 2002, p. 30).

Interviews with mechanics who lubricated the accident aircraft's eleva-
tors and horizontal stabilizer (pitch control system) in 1997, and the last one
in 1999, were conducted to learn "how they [maintenance mechanics]
understood and practiced the lubrication procedures" (National Transportation
Safety Board, 2002, p. 30).

One mechanic stated that

> he would apply grease to acme nut grease fittings until "the grease starts
> to come out . . . the sides where you're greasing, where it starts to bulge
> out." The mechanic stated that he would also use a "paint brush" to
> apply grease to the acme screw threads. He added, "When I do it, I do
> the brush, too, but I don't feel it's enough. I always do an overkill.
> I always like to put more on . . . [to] put a big glob on my hand and
> make sure it's on. More's better. It's not going to hurt anything."
> (National Transportation Safety Board, 2002, p. 31)

The mechanic who completed the accident aircraft's last lubrication of ele-
vators and horizontal stabilizer stated that

> that he would know if the grease fitting for the acme nut was clogged
> "because you'd feel it in the [grease] gun as you try to put it [grease] in.
> If it wasn't going in, you could feel it." When asked how he determined
> whether the lubrication was being accomplished properly and when to
> stop pumping the grease gun, the mechanic responded, "I don't." When
> asked whether he would be able to see grease coming out of the top of
> the acme nut during lubrication, the mechanic responded, "You know, I
> can't remember looking to see if there was.'" [Visual inspection may not
> have been possible according to National Transportation Safety Board
> (NTSB) personnel (see below), who attempted to replicate procedures
> called for when greasing these components.] . . .
>
> The mechanic also stated that he applied grease to the acme screw with a
> brush, adding, "You basically take out a little bit of grease with you, or
> you pump it out of the grease gun onto a paint brush and just paint a real
> light coat on there." (National Transportation Safety Board, 2002, p. 31)

To put these interviews in context, it is helpful to consider what the NTSB
found when it had members of its own staff perform the lubrication tasks:

> Safety Board investigators who attempted to perform the lubrication
> procedure noted that, because of the access panel's size, it could be
> difficult to insert a hand into the access panel and that after a hand was
> inserted, it blocked their view of the jackscrew assembly, thereby requir-
> ing them to accomplish the task primarily by "feel" [This is how the
> procedure was described by the mechanic who performed the last
> lubrication]. (National Transportation Safety Board, 2002, p. 116)

The evidence above indicates that the practices of mechanics who accomplished lubrications of the acme nut and jackscrew assembly of the accident aircraft *differed somewhat* in spite of *common rules as SOPs regarding the task*. The NTSB's own attempts to effectively lubricate the assembly suggest there were physical impediments to performing that task, with the simple solution being enlargement of the access panel. But the differing practices among mechanics implicate a system issue involving efficacy of training and supervision or the lack thereof.

The manufacturer's initial lubrication interval of 600 to 900 flight hours was extended to 3,600 in 1996. Alaska Airlines then requested from the FAA and was granted permission to extend its lubrication interval to 2,250 flight hours (National Transportation Safety Board, 2002, p. 33). This meant that skipping a lubrication or insufficient lubrication became more critical, since there would be a longer time span of greater wear due to less lubrication over such intervals.

The early history (beginning in 1966) of the acme nut and jackscrew assembly system maintenance records kept by the manufacturer of the DC 9 (predecessor of the MD 80 series) showed that some assemblies exhibited more wear than others. Therefore, a means of checking for wear was developed by the manufacturer. Called an *end play check*, this procedure was devised to measure the distance between threads of the acme nut and jackscrew. The manufacturer "specified that acme nut thread wear periodically be measured using . . . [the] . . . end play check procedure [just described], and the *acme nut* [emphasis added] was to be replaced when the specified end play measurement (0.040 inch) was *exceeded* [emphasis added]" (National Transportation Safety Board, 2002, p. 22). Although the manufacturer provided a tool called a *restraining fixture* to be used in end play checks, Alaska Airlines and other operators made some of their own.

While a day-shift mechanic and an inspector were performing an initial end play check for the accident aircraft on September 27, 1997, they observed an end play reading of 0.040 inch and "...a nonroutine work card (MIG-4) was generated.... The MIG-4 noted the following discrepancy: 'Horizontal Stab-acme screw and nut has maximum allowable end play limit (.040 in.).' The 'planned action' box, which was filled out by the day-shift lead mechanic and inspector, stated, 'Replace nut and perform E.O. 8-55-10-01.' The swing-shift supervisor also signed off on the planned action." (National Transportation Safety Board, 2002, p. 51). "A different mechanic and inspector made an entry in the [paperwork's] 'corrective action' section, which stated, 'Rechecked acme screw and nut end play . . . Found end play to be within limits .033 for step 11 and .001 for step 12. Rechecked five times with same result'" (National Transportation Safety Board, 2002, p. 52). The accident aircraft departed the maintenance area on October 2, 1997.

The NTSB report provides important insight into the rules responsible for the differing decisions made by the day-shift supervisor and inspector and graveyard-shift lead mechanic in response to an array of contingencies. The acme nut and jackscrew assembly was, according the aircraft manufacturer, to be "replaced when the specified end play measurement (0.040 inch) was *exceeded* [emphasis added]" (National Transportation Safety Board, 2002, p. 22). In defense of the day-shift mechanic's call for the acme nut to be replaced, the day-shift inspector made the following remarks: "So 40 thousandths [0.04 inch] would be right on the edge. How much further do you have to go before you're out of limits, especially if you got another two years before you're going to check it again?" (National Transportation Safety Board, 2002, p. 53). This implicates a rule that took into account the dynamics of wear and the length of time over which it, wear, would work to increase end play beyond the limit. The mechanic who called for replacement of the assembly recalled that he had worked on virtually every MD-80 flown by Alaska Airlines and had never seen one with an assembly so worn for its age as the one on the accident aircraft. The graveyard-shift lead mechanic defended the decision not to replace the assembly by noting that "the [paperwork calling for acme nut and jackscrew assembly replacement] should *not* [emphasis added] have been generated to begin with. There shouldn't have been . . . [a replacement order] . . . at all for the problem because it [the end play check measurement result] was within the allowable limits on the work card" (National Transportation Safety Board, 2002, p. 53). The mechanic and inspector who conducted the recheck both concluded that the end play *was within limits*. Apparently, the rules to which they responded did not include dynamics of wear through time.

What neither of the two Alaska Airlines end play check teams could have known and *what was not known prior to the NTSB's investigation of the Flight 261 crash was that the on-wing end play check had low reliability compared to bench checks*, checks made with the acme nut and jackscrew assembly removed from the airplane and tested indoors where conditions could be better controlled. This was something discovered when Boeing provided NTSB investigators with a matched sample (on-wing and bench-checked measurements) of N = 64 acme nut and jackscrew assemblies. The NTSB estimated validity using the correlation between on-wing checks and bench checks. The following facts are well worth noting:

> In 45 of the 64 cases (70.3%), the on-wing end play measurements were higher than the bench-check measurements; in 6 of the 64 cases (9.4%), the on-wing and bench-check end play measurements were equal; and in 13 of the 64 cases (20.3%), the on-wing end play measurements were lower than the bench-check measurements. (National Transportation Safety Board, 2002, p. 109)

Had the data been a random sample of assemblies from the entire fleet of MD-80s in service, the on-wing results would appear to be a conservative estimate in that they erred on the side of greater "measured" wear in service compared to bench-based measures. This would be expected to result in replacements being made prior to what would occur if all measures were unbiased in either direction, higher or lower. The risk of an on wing measure underestimating wear would, nevertheless, remain. And readers may recall that any event with a probability greater than zero, if that probability is "real," will occur at some point in time. Readers may also be interested in the following facts: air transportation is the safest, at .01 deaths per 100 million miles traveled compared to trains, at .04 deaths per 100 million miles and, worst, automobiles at .94 deaths per 100 million miles (Wikipedia, 2007a). (Caveat: These statistics will change with time and readers may want to update these data from time to time.)

Identification and Detection in the Flight 261 Case

The omnibus or overarching problem uncovered in the NTSB's (National Transportation Safety Board, 2002) investigation of Flight 261 was identified as *unreliable measurement systems* and variability among practices relative to fixed rules in maintenance manuals and regulations. Since the sine qua non of measurement validity is reliability, important measures used by Alaska Airlines and the industry were questionable with respect to their validity. The existence of unreliable measures and practices related to maintenance of the Flight 261 type airplane existed for more than 30 years before they were uncovered by the NTSB following the loss of 88 lives. The presence of variance in both lubrication practices and in judgments made regarding what to do in response to end play readings on the "edge" of the accepted range were both due to variations in rules or practices among maintenance and inspection personnel. The NTSB's methods related to identifying whether maintenance mechanics understood their task responsibilities, rules followed in response to SOPs, involved interviews with the accident airplane's mechanics. Their rules or self-stated practices implicated absence of sufficient training and/or supervision among these FO members. Identification of problematic practices among all airlines and the FAA thus far has primarily been a function of lives lost due to them.

Remediation and Prevention in the Flight 261 Case

While it is tempting to assign fault to individuals under the circumstances described above, clearly, the problems revealed by the facts regarding maintenance at Alaska Airlines were ultimately rooted in the highly complex system of formal rules or SOPs and employee rules or practices likely spawned by them. In large complex FOs, responsibility for system configuration, for example, specialized departments, their size (as number of staff assigned to units), and proportion of the FO's dollars budgeted in support of them is the official responsibility of top level executives and managers (Mawhinney, 2001; Rummler, 2001). This is the case even given the fact that faults with their *system* may be physically and hierarchically distant from one another. The CEO or president and a mechanic with hands reaching into a panel on the vertical stabilizer of an MD-80 aircraft can be far removed from one another in physical and psychological terms. Nevertheless, from a systems vantage point, the actions of one can have much to do with those of the other and vice versa.

The following actions by Alaska Airlines' leadership provide evidence that the issues above were recognized by Alaska Airlines when faced with the prospect of losing its heavy maintenance authority [permission to perform its own aircraft maintenance], to which they promptly responded as one would predict based on behavior analytic theory (Agnew, 1998; Michael, 1993; Olson et al., 2001):

> . . . the action plan stated that Alaska Airlines had "created an executive level safety position, vice president of safety, that reports directly to our CEO." In addition, the plan stated that Alaska Airlines had created more than 130 new positions in its maintenance and engineering division, 28 new positions in its flight operations division, and 11 new positions in its safety division. (National Transportation Safety Board, 2002, p. 99)

How members in these positions are functionally related to one another and what that has to do with behavior on the shop floor, of course, depends on what sort of overarching safety "philosophy" was adopted up and down the hierarchy of interlocking behavioral contingencies at multiple management levels of the FO's safety system or "culture" (Malott, 2003; McSween, 2003; Sulzer-Azaroff, McCann, & Harris, 2001).

Specific recognition of the fact that variation among environmental contingencies and related rules followed by maintenance personnel were responsible for critical aircraft safety–related maintenance issues appeared in the airline's "action plan [that] stated that the Alaska Airlines maintenance training program had been reorganized to develop a 'training profile for all maintenance personnel by area' and that [on the job training] would be 'standardized and formalized'" (National Transportation Safety Board, 2002, p. 99). Both safety-related values (Hayes, Bunting, Herbst, Bond, & Barnes-Holmes, 2006) and specific practices are transmitted behaviorally via on the job training. On the job training might be made more effective if observer effects were strategic elements of that sort of training (Alvero & Austin, 2004; Sasson & Austin, 2004/2005).

Errors will surely go underdetected and underreported if there are aversive organizational contingencies that spawn individual member rules that help members avoid contact with aversive contingencies. Censoring reports of one's own errors or errors made by others (censoring data) prevents insights from errors being used to avoid them in the future (Deming, 1986/ 2000). In the area of medical care, what are called "blame-free" organizational reporting cultures are thought to reduce risks to patients and can be facilitated using Web-based reporting systems (Mekhjian, Bentley, Ahmad, & Marsh, 2004). This sort of reporting system should be applicable to a wide array of FO systems or cultures. It might also be used to collect information regarding potential precursors.

While couched in terms of aviation accident prevention, the concept of *precursor events* is readily applicable to virtually any practice found in any FO. "Precursor events can be any service information or experience, or test or inspection data that could be interpreted as a predictor that the event [behavioral error and/or mechanical failure] consequences [result of the event] could occur if the event conditions [context of the event] were present. Accident precursor data can be from any discipline (e.g., risk analysis, statistics, engineering, ergonomics, psychology, sociology, and organizational behavior)" (Federal Aviation Administration, 2008). Variations in practices among maintenance mechanics and conditions under which they performed their tasks, in the Alaska Airlines case, serve as exemplars of precursors. In the Alaska Airlines case, precursors were maintenance practices, in conjunction with aircraft conditions, that if continued after the crash of Flight 261 would have resulted in those practices functioning as precursors (predictors) responsible for additional crashes due to the same causes. Unfortunately for those who lost their lives on Flight 261, the precursors identified as a consequence of the NTSB investigation following that flight's crash were subsequently well known, but only after their victims paid the ultimate price for their discovery.

Evidence regarding precursors and how to identify and use them already exist in the OBM literature (see Sigurdsson & Austin, 2006). Put as simply as possible, Sigurdsson and Austin (2006) conducted regression analyses in an attempt to learn how well institutionalization variables in a number of OBM field experiments predicted intervention and postintervention maintenance effect sizes assessed by Cohen's *d* statistic (Cohen, 1969). Precursors can be identified with less sophisticated methods than the statistical methods used by Sigurdsson and Austin (2006). However, for both nonfatal and fatal air transportation incidents and accidents, archival data submitted to regression analyses are well suited to identifying precursors. First, however, members of the OBM community who exchange ideas and facts via *JOBM* must overcome the apparent bias against the use of quantitative analyses and preference for qualitative approaches when assessing cumulative data from the field (cf. Stajkovic & Luthans, 1997).

The description of the mechanics' lubrication tasks suggests that they may have, at times, worked in isolation from others. If so, then they would not always benefit from social interactions and shaping by team members (Hyten, 2001). Methods of increasing safe driving via an individual self-management system backed by monetary incentives was found effective among short-haul truck drivers working alone (Hickman & Geller, 2003). This system might work in an aviation maintenance environment. So might the self-monitoring package Olson and Austin (2001) used to produce cumulatively large improvements of safe driving practices among bus operators.

Both identification and prevention of potentially deadly practices appear to be significantly heightened by airplane crashes involving loss of life and associated threats to the FO's life (cf. Agnew, 1998; Michael, 1993; Olson et al., 2001). But, Alaska Airlines was insured against losses due to financial claims among relatives of crash victims as well as aircraft loss. This no doubt helped it through the years immediately following the crash.

THE DEATH OF BARINGS BANK AT THE HANDS OF ROGUE TRADER NICK LEESON AND INEPT MANAGEMENT

The primary function of this case is to insure that readers are not left with the impression that FOs always have time to adapt to or recover from latent deadly practices or dysfunctional practices the cumulative effects of which can result in an FO's demise.

Nick Leeson attracted the attention of his superiors at Barings Bank when he solved a problem involving stock certificates of their Jakarta operations worth £100 million to Barings if linked to their owners. He was subsequently appointed general manager of trading operations in Singapore, where Barings owned a seat on the Singapore National Monetary Exchange (SIMEX). There he was responsible for setting up operations: "I would recruit traders and back office staff and make money" (Leeson, 1996, p. 29).

When one of Leeson's hand-picked traders made a £20,000 error that Lesson discovered too late to immediately transmit to London, he used a dormant account to book a fictitious transaction that would hide the loss. Thereafter the dormant account was used more frequently to conceal growing losses in Singapore from Barings's management in London. A 1994 audit failed to detect his activities in the dormant account but called for creation of an independent "Risk Compliance Officer," a traditional defense against unauthorized trading and concealment. *Leeson's superiors rejected the recommendation.* Thus, Leeson's activities "would continue to go unsupervised" (Leeson, 1996, p. 94), and 1994 was characterized by his concealment of mounting losses.

A newspaper headline Leeson saw, after his scheme had been detected and while attempting to escape to England, read "BRITISH MERCHANT BANK COLLAPSE" (Leeson, 1996, p. 222). Barings Bank perished due to its trading losses at the hands of Leeson and the management that failed to properly supervise his activities, for example, letting him control paper- and computer-based records and accounts he could alter directly and/or indirectly via people whose behavior he supervised and manipulated.

The bank's losses amounted to $1.4 billion, ranking 6th highest among the 16 in a tally reported on Wikipedia (2007b). Virtually every Barings Bank stakeholder suffered from this *latent deadly practice* when it ultimately turned irrevocably *deadly* for its host FO. The loss occurred because Barings's leadership failed to adopt well-known, almost boilerplate, defenses against it.

Identification and Detection

Detecting attempts to hide real losses by using fictitious gains from trades of financial instruments is as simple as effectively auditing transaction records. The issue is whether the transactions do or don't "add up." In this day and age it is possible to run a continuous audit and for auditors to select and examine specific transactions using computer information technology (Razaee, 2002).

Remediation Challenge: The Baring Bank Case

The French bank Societé Generale's loss of about $7.4 or so billion to a rogue trader in January 2008 suggests that vulnerability to rogue traders remains even in this age of high technology. However, technology per se can do nothing, so whatever it does cannot pass the "dead man's test" (Daniels & Daniels, 2004). Here a specific remedy is not indicated. Rather, behavior analysts are encouraged to create, model, and assess disciplinary policy alternatives implicated by behavioral decision theories. The aim should be to identify rules that will make it unattractive for traders to violate not-so-mundane trading limits and to confess a large loss before it grows larger. The vantage points of framing effects (Kahneman & Tversky, 1982; Rachlin, 1989), relational frame theory (Hayes, Bunting, Herbst, Bond, & Barnes-Holmes, 2006), and immediate aversive or positive versus delayed aversive consequences (Baum, 2005; Rachlin, 1989; 2004) might provide guides for an innovative program of this sort. For example, evidence regarding framing effects suggests that people are risk seeking with respect to losses and risk averse with respect to gains.

So people, according to this theory (Kahneman & Tversky, 1982), are likely to choose riskier alternatives when dealing with potential losses. In addition, individuals with a history of variable reinforcement relative to a task such as options trading would be predicted to escalate commitment to a given strategy in the face of unusually high losses arising from a shift in trading activity in a market (Hantula, 1992; Hantula & Crowell, 1994). Effects of both of these phenomena could be mitigated by training traders regarding the human behavioral propensities in the context of tasks such as professional options trading. Specifically, they should be provided training regarding how to react in the face of unusual losses by reporting them rather than devising ways of hiding them. But, such training would not be predicted to work unless accompanied by a policy of progressive discipline: an escalating magnitude of negative consequences, rather than immediate demotion or termination of employment, should follow repeated excessive losses, and positive reinforcement should follow honest reporting of losses!

Had Leeson's subordinates known what constituted suspicious and improper activities on Leeson's part, they might have been in a position to "blow the whistle" on his unauthorized practices. Thus, training staff how and when to report suspicious activities among peers and superiors and what constitutes such activities, and promising job protection in the event they have to report such activities, might help guard against practices like Leeson's. And, simply knowing that support staff knew what constituted rule breaking might have been sufficient to prevent him from taking a chance in the first place. Leeson might have "thought twice" about his deviant behavior had he not been certain his office staff had no idea what he was doing.

CONCLUSIONS

The terms, concepts, and vantage points introduced in this article are intended to help behavior systems analysts talk about the interplay among environmental contingencies and behavioral contingencies in FOs. These contingencies involve contingencies among contingencies, e.g. individual and group practices and their consequences for the organization as a whole observed in FO's *fitness for survival*. Attention was focused particularly on conceptions of the interplay of practices within FOs and their consequences for life and death of not only FOs but their members and other stakeholders. It highlighted and focused attention on the fact that small deviations in seemingly mundane and routine practices can have catastrophic consequences for FOs' members and their other stakeholders. The Alaska Airlines case focused attention on small variations in practices among members that can have potentially deadly consequences for an FO and did have for both members and customers of Alaska Airlines. But undesired effects of this class of practices may be mitigated or amplified by variation among tools and methods or practices regarding their use (cf. Daniels & Daniels, 2004; Deming, 1986/2000; Mawhinney, 1987).

The terms and concepts introduced in this article are intended to permit behavior systems analysts to talk coherently, among one another at least, about the interplay of large FO systems' contingencies, including those linking individual and group behavior within FOs with their competitive and natural environments (e.g., de facto flight physics and practices that prevent members, and pilots, from violating them). Suggestions were made regarding how to detect what may appear to be inconsequential practices with their potentially dysfunctional and/or deadly consequences, for example, inadequate lubrication of flight control mechanisms and pilots' loss of flight control resulting in a crash. This included recognition of the fact that rather than reacting to deadly events, for both FOs' assets and humans, we should be developing systematic ways of identifying dysfunctional and deadly practices as *precursors* (Federal Aviation Administration, 2008), manifest in small deviations from proper practices that can produce dysfunctional and/or deadly consequences in spite of their resemblance to functional practices.

But there are few empirical studies in the pages of *JOBM* that have addressed this issue. At least one has. That is the study by Sigurdsson and Austin (2006), described above, that was aimed at identifying predictors of response maintenance based on attributes of interventions designed to improve practices in FOs. What should have been learned from the two cases above is that selection of practices upon which to focus attention and particularly seemingly minor variations in them are worthy of the same sort of attention, in other words, how to predict their occurrences and consequences. If predictions of deadly consequences of practices can be made by *precursors* (Federal Aviation Administration, 2008) then they may be identified and extinguished or replaced before their undesired consequences turn deadly.

Formal organizations that engage in this practice (precursor development), or avail themselves of the services of consultants that can help them develop such practices, are likely to be more fit for survival than their competitors in both the short and long run. They are also less likely to endanger the lives of members and their other stakeholders. For these reasons the behavior systems analytic practices, how we talk about and go about FO assessment and improvement, presented in this article are offered for the community's consideration, criticism, improvement, and, perhaps, adoption.

REFERENCES

Abernathy, W. B. (2001). An analysis of twelve organizations' total performance systems. In L. J. Hayes, J. Austin, R. Houmanfar & M. C. Clayton (Eds.), *Organizational change* (pp. 240–272). Reno Nevada: Context Press.

Agnew, J. L. (1998). The establishing operation in organizational behavior management. *Journal of Organizational Behavior Management, 18*(1), 7–19.

Agnew, J. L., & Redmon, W. K. (1992). Contingency specifying stimuli: The role of "rules" in organizational behavior management. *Journal of Organizational Behavior Management, 12*(2), 67–75.

Altman, E. I. (1968). Financial ratios, discriminant analysis and the prediction of corporate bankruptcy. *Journal of Finance, 23* (September), 589–609.

Altman, E. I. (2000). Predicting financial distress of companies: Revising the Z-Score and ZETA® models. Working Paper, New York University. Retrieved June 11, 2008, from http://pages.stern.nyu.edu/~ealtman/Zscores.pdf

Alvero, A. M., & Austin, J. (2004). The effects of conducting behavioral observations on the behavior of the observer. *Journal of Applied Behavior Analysis, 37*(4), 575–577.

Baum, W. M. (1973). The correlation based law of effect. *Journal of the Experimental Analysis of Behavior, 20,* 137–153.

Baum, W. M. (2005). *Understanding behaviorism: Behavior, culture and evolution.* Malden, MA: Blackwell Publishing.

Beaver, W. H. (1966). Empirical research in accounting: Selected studies. Supplement to *Journal of Accounting Research,* 71–111.

Blakely, E., & Schlinger, H. (1987). Rules: Function-altering contingency-specifying stimuli. *The Behavior Analyst, 10*(2), 183–187.

Brethower, D. M. (1972). *Behavior analysis in business and industry: A total performance system.* Kalamazoo, MI: Behaviordelia.

Brethower, D. M. (1982). The total performance system. In R. M. O'Brien, A. M. Dickinson & M. P. Rosow (Eds.) *Industrial behavior modification: A management handbook* (pp. 350–369). New York: Pergamon Press.

Brethower, D. M. (2000). A systemic view of enterprise: Adding value to performance. *Journal of Organizational Behavior Management, 20*(3/4), 165–190.

Brethower, D. M. (2001). Managing a person as a system. In L. Hayes, J. Austin, & R. Houmanfar (Eds.), *Organizational change* (pp. 89–105). Reno, NV: Context.

Cerutti, D. T. (1989). Discrimination theory of rule governed behavior. *Journal of the Experimental Analysis of Behavior, 20,* 259–276.

Cohen, J. (1969). *Statistical power analysis for the social sciences.* New York: Academic Press.

Daniels, A. C., & Daniels, J. E. (2004). *Performance management: Changing behavior that drives organizational effectiveness.* Atlanta, GA: Performance Management Publications.

Deming, W. E. (1986/2000). *Out of the crisis.* Cambridge, MA: MIT Press.

Efron, S. (1999, October 1). Dozens hurt in Japan's worst nuclear accident. *Los Angeles Times.* Retrieved April 16, 2006, from http://www.isop.ucla.edu/eas/newsfile/jpnnuclear/991001-lat1.htm

Federal Aviation Administration (2008). *Applying lessons learned from accidents.* Retrieved January 21, 2008, from http://lessons.air.mmac.faa.gov/ll/des8/

Geller, E. S. (2001). Actively caring for occupational safety: Extending the performance management paradigm. In C. M. Johnson, W. K. Redmon, & T. C. Mawhinney (Eds.), *Handbook of organizational performance: Behavior analysis and management* (pp. 303–326). New York: Haworth.

Gilbert, T. F. (1978). *Human competence: Engineering worthy performance.* New York: McGraw-Hill.

Glenn, S. S. (2004). Individual behavior, culture, and social change. *The Behavior Analyst, 27*(2), 133–151.

Gritta, R. D., Adrangi, B., Sergio, S., & Bright, D. (2006). *A review of the history of air carrier bankruptcy forecasting and the application of various models to the U.S. airline industry: 1980–2005.* Paper presented at the XIV International Economic History Congress, Helsinki, Session 45. Retrieved June 17, 2008, from http://www.helsinki.fi/iehc2006/papers2/Gritta.pdf

Hantula, D. A. (1992). The basic importance of escalation. *Journal of Applied Behavior Analysis, 25*(3), 579–583.

Hantula, D. A. (2001). Schedules of reinforcement in organizational performance, 1971–1994: Application, analysis and synthesis. In C. M. Johnson, W. K. Redmon, & T. C. Mawhinney (Eds.), *Handbook of organizational performance: Behavior analysis and management* (pp. 139–166). New York: Haworth.

Hantula, D. A., & Crowell, C. R. (1994). Intermittent reinforcement and escalation processes in sequential decision making: A replication and theoretical analysis. *Journal of Organizational Behavior Management, 14*(2), 7–36.

Hayes, S. C., Bond, F. W., Barnes-Holmes, D., & Austin, J. (2006). *Acceptance and mindfulness at work: Applying acceptance and commitment therapy and relational frame theory to organizational behavior management.* New York: Haworth.

Hayes, S. C., Bunting, K., Herbst, S., Bond, F. W., & Barnes-Holmes, D. (2006). Expanding the scope of organizational behavior management: Relational frame theory and the experimental analysis of complex human behavior. In S. C. Hayes, F. W. Bond, D. Barnes-Holmes, & J. Austin, *Acceptance and mindfulness at work: Applying acceptance and commitment therapy and relational frame theory to organizational behavior management* (pp. 1–13). New York: Haworth.

Henry, G. O., & Redmon, W. K. (1990). The effects of performance feedback on the implementation of a statistical process control (SPC) program. *Journal of Organizational Behavior Management, 11*(2), 23–46.

Hickman, J. S., & Geller, E. S. (2003). Self-management to improve safe driving among short-haul truck drivers. *Journal of Organizational Behavior Management, 23*(4), 1–20.

Hopkins, B. L. (1995). An introduction to developing, maintaining and improving large-scale, data based programs. *Journal of Organizational Behavior Management, 15*(1/2), 67–10.

Hopkins, B. L. (1999). The principles of behavior as an empirical theory and the usefulness of that theory in addressing practical problems. *Journal of Organizational Behavior Management, 13*(3), 67–74.

Hursh, S. R. (1984). Behavioral economics. *Journal of Experimental Analysis of Behavior, 42,* 435–452.

Hyten, C. (2001). Theoretical issues in the design of self-directed work teams. In L. Hayes, J. Austin, & R. Houmanfar (Eds.) *Organizational change* (pp. 325–343). Reno, NV: Context.

Kahneman, D., & Tversky, A. (1973). On the psychology of prediction. *Psychological Review, 80,* 237–251.

Kahneman, D., & Tversky, A. (1982, January). The psychology of preferences. *Scientific American, 246,* 167–173.

Kremer, C., Rizzuto, R., & Case, J. (2000). *Managing by the numbers.* New York: Basic Books.

Leeson, N. (1996). *Rogue trader: How I brought down Barings Bank and shook the financial world.* Boston: Little, Brown and Company.

Lovelock, J. (1988). *The ages of Gaia: A biography of our living Earth.* New York: W. W. Norton & Company.

Luthans, F., & Kreitner, R. (1975). *Organizational behavior modification.* Glenview, IL: Scott-Foresman.

Malott, M. E. (2001). Putting the horse before the cart: Process-driven change. In L. Hayes, J. Austin, & R. Houmanfar (Eds.) *Organizational change* (pp. 297–320). Reno, NV: Context.

Malott, M. E. (2003). *Paradox of organizational change: Engineering organizations with behavioral systems analysis.* Reno, NV: Context.

Malott, R. W. (1992). A theory of rule-governed behavior and organizational behavior management. *Journal of Organizational Behavior Management, 12*(2), 45–65.

Mawhinney, T. C. (1975). Operant terms and concepts in the description of individual work behavior: Some problems of interpretation, application and evaluation. *Journal of Applied Psychology, 60*, 704–712.

Mawhinney, T. C. (1982). Maximizing versus matching in people versus pigeons. *Psychological Reports, 50*, 267–281.

Mawhinney, T. C. (1987). *Organizational behavior management and statistical process control: Theory, technology, and research.* New York: Haworth.

Mawhinney, T. C. (1992a). Evolution of organizational cultures as selection by consequences: The Gaia hypothesis, metacontingencies, and organizational ecology. *Journal of Organizational Behavior Management, 12*(2), 1–26.

Mawhinney, T. C. (1992b). Total quality management and organizational behavior management: An integration for continual improvement. *Journal of Applied Behavior Analysis, 25*, 225–243.

Mawhinney, T. C. (1999). Cumulatively large effects of small intervention effects: Costing metacontingencies of chronic absenteeism. *Journal of Organizational Behavior Management, 18*(4), 83–95.

Mawhinney, T. C. (2001). Organization-environment systems as OBM intervention context: Minding your metacontingencies. In L. Hayes, J. Austin, & R. Houmanfar (Eds.) *Organizational change* (pp. 137–166). Reno, NV: Context.

Mawhinney, T. C. (2005). Effective leadership in superior-subordinate dyads: Theory and data. *Journal of Organizational Behavior Management, 25*(4), 37–79.

Mawhinney, T. C. (2007, September). *Error sequence and the loss of 88 souls on Alaska Airlines' Flight 261.* Paper presented at meeting of Behavior Safety Now, Kansas City, MO.

Mawhinney, T. C., & Fellows-Kubert, C. (1999). Positive contingencies versus quotas: Telemarketers exert countercontrol. *Journal of Organizational Behavior Management, 19*(2), 35–57.

McSween, T. E. (2003). *The values based safety process: Improving your safety culture with behavior-based safety* (2nd ed.). Hoboken NJ: John Wiley & Sons.

Mechner, F. (2008a). Behavioral contingency analysis. *Behavioral Processes, 78*, 124–144.

Mechner, F. (2008b). *Applications of the language for codifying behavioral contingencies.* Retrieved May 3, 2008, from http://mechnerfoundation.org/newsite/downloads.html

Mekhjian, H. S., Bentley, T. D., Ahmad, A., & Marsh, G. (2004). Development of a Web-based event reporting system in an academic environment. *Journal of American Informatics Association, 11*(1), 11–18.

Michael, J. L. (1993). *Concepts and principles of behavior analysis.* Kalamazoo, MI: Association for Behavior Analysis.

Miller, J. G. (1978). *Living systems.* New York: McGraw-Hill.

Notz, W. W., Boschman, I., & Tax, S. S. (1987). Reinforcing punishment and extin-
    guishing reward: On the folly of OBM without SPC. *Journal of Organizational
    Behavior Management, 9*(1), 33–46.
National Transportation Safety Board (2002). *Aircraft accident report: Loss of control
    and impact with Pacific Ocean Alaska Airlines Flight 261 McDonnell Douglas
    MD-83, N963AS about 2.7 Miles North of Anacapa Island, California January
    31, 2000.* Aircraft Accident Report NTSB/AAR-02/01.Washington, DC.
Olson, R., & Austin, J. (2001). Behavior-based safety and working alone: The effects
    of a self-monitoring package on the safe performance of bus drivers. *Journal of
    Organizational Behavior Management, 21*(3), 5–43.
Olson, R., Laraway, S., & Austin, J. (2001). Unconditioned and conditioned estab-
    lishing operations in organizational behavior management. *Journal of Organi-
    zational Behavior Management, 21*(2), 7–35.
Poling, A., & Braatz, D. (2001). Principles of learning: Respondent and operant
    conditioning and human behavior. In C. M. Johnson, W. K. Redmon, & T. C.
    Mawhinney (Eds.), *Handbook of organizational performance: Behavior analysis
    and management* (pp. 23–49). New York: Haworth.
Rachlin, H. (1989). *Judgment, decision and choice.* New York: W. H. Freeman.
Rachlin, H. (2004). *The science of self-control.* Cambridge: Harvard Press.
Razaee, Z. (2002). *Financial statement fraud: Prevention and detection.* New York:
    John Wiley & Sons.
Redmon, W. K., & Mason, M. A. (2001). Organizational culture and behavior
    systems analysis. In C. M. Johnson, W. K. Redmon, & T. C. Mawhinney (Eds.),
    Handbook of organizational performance: Behavior analysis and management
    (pp. 437–456). New York: Haworth.
Rummler, G. A. (2001). Performance logic: The organizational performance Rosetta
    Stone. In L. J. Hayes, J. Austin, R. Houmanfar & M. C. Clayton (Eds.), *Organi-
    zational change.* (pp. 111–132). Reno Nevada: Context.
Sasson, J. R., & Austin, J. (2004/2005). The effects of training, feedback, and partici-
    pant involvement in behavioral safety observations on office ergonomic behavior.
    Journal of Organizational Behavior Management, 24(4), 1–30.
Schlinger, H. D., Jr. (1993). Separating discriminative and function-altering effects of
    verbal stimuli. *The Behavior Analyst,16*(1), 9–23.
Schlinger, H. D., & Blakely, E. A. (1987). Function altering effects of contingency-
    specifying stimuli. *The Behavior Analyst, 10*(1), 41–45.
Schlinger, H. D., Jr., & Blakely, E. A. (1994). A descriptive taxonomy of environ-
    mental operations and its implications for behavior analysis. *The Behavior
    Analyst,17*(1), 43–57.
Sigurdsson, S. O., & Austin, J. (2006). Institutionalization and response maintenance
    in organizational behavior management. *Journal of Organizational Behavior
    Management. 24*(4), 41–75.
Skinner, B. F. (1953). *Science and human behavior.* New York: Macmillan.
Skinner, B. F. (1957). *Verbal behavior.* Englewood Cliffs, NJ: Prentice-Hall.
Skinner, B. F. (1969). *Contingencies of reinforcement.* New York: Appleton-
    Century-Crofts.
Skinner, B. F. (1972). *Cumulative record.* New York: Appleton-Century-Crofts.
Skinner, B. F. (1981). Selection by consequences. *Science, 213,* 31 July, 501–504.

Stajkovic, A., & Luthans, F. (1997). A meta-analysis of the effects of organizational behavior modification on task performance. *Academy of Management Journal, 40,* 1122–1149.

Sulzer-Azaroff, B., McCann, K. B., & Harris, T. C. (2001). The safe performance approach to preventing job-related illness and injury. In C. M. Johnson, W. K. Redmon, & T. C. Mawhinney (Eds.), *Handbook of organizational performance: Behavior analysis and management* (pp. 277–302). New York: Haworth.

Thompson, A. A., Strickland, A. J., & Gamble, J. E. (2008). Crafting & executing strategy. Burr Ridge, IL: McGraw-Hill Irwin.

Thurkow, N. M., Bailey, J. S., & Stamper, M. R. (2000). The effects of group and individual incentive on productivity of telephone interviewers. *Journal of Organizational Behavior Management, 20*(2), 1–25.

Van Horne, J. C. (1971). *Financial management and policy.* Englewood Cliffs, NJ: Prentice- Hall.

Wikipedia (2007a). Aviation accidents and incidents. Retrieved June 15, 2007, from http://en.wikipedia.org/wiki/Aviation_accidents_and_incidents

Wikipedia (2007b). *List of trading losses.* Retrieved December 20, 2007, from http://en.wikipedia.org/wiki/List_of_Trading_Losses

Wikipedia (2008). *AirTran Airways.* Retrieved February 14, 2008, from http://en.wikipedia.org/wiki/AirTran_Airways.

Zeiler, M. D. (1977). Schedules of reinforcement: The controlling variables. In W. K. Honig & J. E. R. Staddon (Eds.), *Handbook of operant behavior* (pp. 201–232). Englewood Cliffs, NJ: Prentice-Hall.

Zettle, R. D., & Hayes, S. C. (1982). Rule governed behavior: A potential theoretical framework for cognitive-behavioral therapy. In P. C. Kendall, *Advances in Cognitive-Behavioral Research Therapy.* (pp. 73–118). New York: Academic Press.

APPENDIX A: TASK CARD

A. Open access doors. . . .
B. Lube per the following

Item no.	Item description	No. of fittings or areas
1.	MAIN GEAR BOX Check oil level and fill to fill plug with approved jet engine oil. Oil capacity is approximately 0.6 pint.	1
2.	ACTUATOR ASSEMBLY	1
3.	JACKSCREW Apply light coat of grease to threads, then operate mechanism through full range of travel to distribute lubricant over length of jackscrew.	0

(Continued)

APPENDIX (*Continued*)

Item no.	Item description	No. of fittings or areas
4.	SCREW GIMBAL	3
5.	HORIZONTAL STABILIZER HINGE	2
6.	JACKSCREW STOP Fill cavity between screw and stop with Parker-O-Lube.	0

C. Close doors. . . .

Source: NTSB (2002, pp. 29–30).

Role of Communication Networks in Behavioral Systems Analysis

RAMONA HOUMANFAR, NISCHAL JOSEPH RODRIGUES, and GREGORY S. SMITH

University of Nevada, Reno, Reno, Nevada, USA

This article provides an overview of communication networks and the role of verbal behavior in behavioral systems analysis. Our discussion highlights styles of leadership in the design and implementation of effective organizational contingencies that affect ways by which coordinated work practices are managed. We draw upon literature pertaining to complex systems and rule governance to understand how communication networks and verbal rules contribute to the issues involved in reengineering behavioral systems in the face of continued socioeconomic and cultural demands. An analysis of leadership in relation to communication networks in organizations is discussed.

ROLE OF COMMUNICATION NETWORKS IN BEHAVIORAL SYSTEMS ANALYSIS

In the behavioral literature, organizational change is addressed theoretically through metacontingency analysis (Glenn, 1991; 2004; Malott, 2003; Malott & Glenn, 2006; Mawhinney, 1992, 2001, 2009). According to this perspective, when products of organizational practices contribute to the survival of the organization, the practices that generated them are more likely to reoccur. In short, *metacontingency* depicts the contingent relation between

---

Order of authorship is alphabetical.

interlocking behavioral contingencies (IBCs), their aggregate product, and the environmental demand (see Appendix). According to Glenn (2004), "the recurring IBCs comprise operant contingencies in which behavior of two or more people functions as environmental events for the behavior of the others" (p. 144). IBCs can be called cultural practices when a number of organizations are characterized by the same kinds of IBCs (e.g., Japanese car industry vs. American car industry; Glenn, 2004).

Theories of selection and metacontingencies are also applied within the framework of behavioral systems analysis. According to this perspective, which is based on general system theory, organizations are behavioral systems formed by individuals' interactions (IBCs) toward a common goal (production of an aggregate product; Bowler, 1981). This interaction toward a common goal occurs within the context of the organization's interaction with a broader cultural and economic environment (Brethower, 1982; 1999; 2000; Glenn & Malott, 2004; Malott, 2003; Malott & Glenn, 2006; Rummler, 2001; Rummler & Brache, 1995).

In attempting to hold to the parallels between the behavioral contingency and the metacontingency, Houmanfar and Rodrigues (2006) advocated that the first term in a metacontingency be the *cultural milieu* (see Appendix). The cultural milieu is comprised of material resources, overarching governmental policies, as well as organizational policies, rules, traditions, institutions, technological progress, and environmental competition. Even though verbal behaviors associated with cultural milieu are considered important to the development and maintenance of cultural practices and associated metacontingencies (Glenn, 1988; 1989), their role is not explicitly discussed in previous conceptual and empirical work. In that regard, one purpose of this article is to discuss the importance of verbal behaviors, within the context of communication networks in management of IBCs of a given metacontingency. *Communication network* in this context can be defined as a description of the verbal interactions that mediate influences in between components and organized groups (also referred to as metacontingencies; Malott & Glenn, 2006) and among individual members of a given organization.

There are many successful organizational models developed by behavior analysts that discuss the importance of communication networks in organizational change processes (Houmanfar & Johnson, 2003). For instance, Tosti's "Organizational Alignment" model (Kolvitz, 1997) focuses on how the organizational values and practices should apply to everyone, from the front line to the boardroom. Accordingly, the clarification of individuals' roles in relation to organizational change should be tied to the ongoing measurement of progress toward the desired outcomes. The employee has a greater degree of control over changing organizational functioning than does the consumer. Thus, the effects of communication and information dissemination on employees' behaviors and overall performance outcomes are a critical area of organizational change.

Further, organizational stimuli (e.g., rules, policies, mission statement, vision, other organizational members) may influence the maintenance of organizational members' actions. In that regard, the underlying element in this process is the communication system by which top management articulates the organizational goals, polices, rules, etc. (Houmanfar & Johnson, 2003). As antecedents or consequences (or both), these descriptions of organizational contingencies (in a form of instructions, rules or feedback) affect the interrelated behaviors of organizational members within and across the organization.

Thus, behavioral practices of leadership and management are believed to function as important factors in design and implementation of effective organizational contingencies. These leadership practices affect coordinated practices of organizational members that generate products. For instance, leadership and management practices may create an ambiguous environment in terms of work-related information that distorts the stimulus control exerted by organizational rules. This type of ambiguity is in the form of incomplete or inaccurate information that lack clear or accurate description of contingencies and their context (Houmanfar & Johnson, 2003).

The level of ambiguity influences the prevalence of verbal problem-solving behaviors (such as gossip and rumor) that may negatively affect the efficiency by which organizational products are generated through interrelated behaviors of individuals. This phenomenon may be described as resistance to change (Houmanfar & Johnson, 2003; Kolvitz, 1997). The verbal problem-solving behaviors in this context evolve under the absence of antecedent and consequential control of rules (e.g., clear specification of organizational contingencies). This delineation means that the absence of effective action (e.g., complete, clear, and accurate specification of organizational contingencies) is an antecedent for activity that is itself oriented toward the establishment of such actions (Houmanfar & Johnson, 2003). Therefore, to promote a healthy level of problem-solving practices organizations should practice open communication.

In the remaining sections of this article, we will explore how understanding communication networks and the nature of verbal rules may contribute to the successful reengineering of behavioral systems and associated metacontingencies in the face of continued socioeconomic and cultural demands. This discussion will include an analysis of leadership and the associated roles in relation to communication networks in organizations.

A Behavior Analytic Account of Communication Networks in Organizations

In assessing the role of communication in the analysis of leadership behavior, we consider various definitions and descriptions of leadership in the field of organizational behavior management (OBM). For instance, Daniels and

Daniels (2005) state that the role of a leader is to promote conditions that motivate employees to execute the mission, vision, and values of the organization. In doing so, the leader must clearly specify which behaviors and results are critical to the survival of the organization. Similarly, Mawhinney and Ford (1977) write, "We consider the role of the leader to be that of organizing, specifying, and maintaining complex response chains of subordinates by communicating to them the contingencies of reinforcement . . . in the workplace" (p. 406). In addition, Abernathy (1996; 2000) notes that a successful leader makes certain that employees understand what behaviors and outcomes that promote organizational survival are expected of them and provides the resources and means for them to accomplish these ends.

Communication in organizations is usually in the form of verbal products that are passed from upper management to the other parts of the organization. The purpose of communication is often to guide employee behavior to be more efficient and productive while contributing to the overall efficiency and productivity of the organization. This sort of communication comes in the form of rules that the organization assumes will have an impact on employee behavior (Malott, 1992). A *rule* is defined as a contingency-specifying stimulus that details the relationship between an antecedent, a response, and a consequence (Catania, Shimoff, & Matthews, 1989; Schlinger & Blakely, 1987); that is, a verbal description of a three-term (or four- and five-term) contingency. However, the type of rule and learning history of the employee can have a bearing on the behavior of the employee (Weatherly & Malott, 2008).

Pelaez and Moreno (1998) outlined a taxonomy wherein rules may be explicit or implicit, simple or complex, accurate or inaccurate and can vary in terms of their source. Explicit rules detail the contingency in terms of antecedents, behaviors, and their consequences unambiguously, while implicit rules leave out some of these details. The complexity of a rule refers to dimensions or characteristics of stimuli (color, shape, texture, etc.) and higher order relations between stimuli (bigger than, brighter than, shares class membership with, etc.), which in turn can increase the difficulty of comprehending the rule. Accurate rules correspond to the actual contingencies, while inaccurate rules do not describe the contingencies precisely. Lastly, the source of a rule may be oneself, another person, or entity within the organization.

Verbal products that convey effective rules reduce environmental ambiguity and should be promoted as a consistent practice on the part of leadership and management. This influence has been discussed conceptually (Houmanfar & Johnson, 2003) and more recently demonstrated experimentally (Johnson, Houmanfar, & Smith, in press; Smith, Houmanfar, & Denny, 2009), suggesting that implicit and inaccurate rules generate ambiguity and distortion of stimulus control. In these studies, distortion of stimulus control was found to occasion undesirable verbal problem-solving behavior in the form of rumor among the verbal participants. This in turn led to the self-generation of inaccurate organizational rules on the part of participants and decrease in their overall productivity. Conversely, the delivery of explicit and accurate rules through verbal products minimized distortion of stimulus control and produced greater and longer lasting levels of productivity. When these effects are multiplied across a large population of employees, one can extrapolate the communication of organizational rules having a significant impact on organizational performance.

The source of the rules provided to employees can also impact the accuracy and clarity of the rule communication (Agnew & Redmon, 1992). When left to develop their own rules in circumstances where sufficient information has not been provided, workers may self-generate rules that do not support desired behavior. One way to avoid this outcome is through the use of role-specifying stimuli (RSSs) set forth by the organizational leaders (Mawhinney, 2005; Brethower, 1982). These RSSs are descriptions that specify job responsibilities and associated contingencies (see Appendix). Accordingly, they may function as antecedent stimuli to ensure appropriate employee and leader behaviors (Mawhinney, 2005).

With regard to characteristics of rules, a majority of the literature focuses on the topographical characteristics of communication and organizational rules. Even in the case of Pelaez and Moreno's rule taxonomy a topographical as well as a functional view of rule governance is offered. In that regard, to better understand how different types of rules function and interact, it might be worthwhile to examine them from a relational frame perspective.

RELATIONAL ACCOUNT OF RULE GOVERNANCE

Relational frame theory (RFT) makes the claim that humans engage in derived relational responding (DRR) that in turn influences their interaction with the world (Hayes, Barnes-Holmes, & Roche, 2001). DRR is an operant that can be understood in terms of traditional behavior analysis (Stewart, Barnes-Holmes, Barnes-Holmes, Bond, & Hayes, 2006) and can be easily demonstrated in an experiment using three arbitrary stimuli: A, B, and C (see Appendix). In this experiment, a subject's responses of selecting B in the presence of A and C in the presence of B are reinforced. Results show that the subject then goes on to select A in the presence of B and B in the presence of C without reinforcement—this is known as *mutual entailment*. Furthermore, the subject also selects C in the presence of A and A in the presence of C without reinforcement, despite the two stimuli having never appeared together before—this is known as *combinatorial entailment* (Hayes & Hayes, 1989). To extrapolate to the work world, if an employee has established a perception that her company is "team oriented" and is told that a partner firm is similar to her company, that employee is likely to relate the partner firm to the word "team oriented" (combinatorial entailment) despite the employee not being explicitly told that the partner firm is team oriented. This type of relational responding may affect the level of employees' buy-in in terms of adoption of new practices introduced by the partner firm.

Derived relational responding can transform the function of other stimuli. Unlike transfer of function, transformation of function is not merely associative, it is relational. If, for example, C was paired with shock, the subject would show a greater arousal response to A than to C due to the derived relation of A > C despite a history of A not being paired with shock (Dougher, Hamilton, & Fink, 2007). Transformation of function can affect large networks of relations, resulting in a multitude of derived relations based on a few experiences. Suppose that management suggests to employees that their own company is the opposite of a rival firm. Employees may already have established a relation of "good" with aspects of their own company, leading to derived relations of "bad" with aspects of the rival company. This may result in the greater probability of employees resisting a change that they associate with the rival. If the rival uses a measurement system, for instance, and the company is attempting to institute a similar system of measurement, employees may respond negatively toward the system.

RFT suggests that rules are understood by their influence on derived relational responding. Consider a rule that may be communicated at an auto sales company: "The employee who sells the most cars this month will be granted the use of the convenient parking spot right in front of the store." How rules influence employee behavior when the consequence is delayed by a month or when the employee has no history of direct contact with the consequence is difficult to explain as a function of direct contingencies. Although the rule specifies a goal and the consequences that will follow from achieving it, the effect of the rule on the listener is unclear without an appeal to RFT.

Traditionally, behavior analysis has considered rules to be contingency-specifying stimuli (Skinner, 1953; 1957). Rules are thought to affect behavior by their description of a contingent relationship between antecedents, responses, and consequences. This definition of rules, however, does not explain why some rules are effective and why some are not. In short, it does not provide a technical account of rules and their effect on the behavior of the listener (Hayes & Hayes, 1989).

From an RFT perspective, the rule relies on frames of coordination (sameness) between the word "sells" and the behavior of selling and the word "cars" and the actual cars themselves. The rule also relies on an if-then relation between the behavior of "sells the most cars" and the potential outcome of "convenient parking spot" (Stewart et al., 2006). The behavior of selling undergoes a transformation of function due to the relation of "sells the most cars" and "convenient parking spot." During the course of the month, employees might evaluate their sales by placing verbal statements about them in frames of comparison with other employees: "I sold 20 cars in the first 10 days of this month while Sally sold 5 more cars than I did." Statements like these may lead to further DRR that may result in other self-rules such as, "I need to copy Sally's approach and talk about my kids and how they are doing in school" or "It takes less time to sell less expensive cars. Therefore, I should focus on selling cheaper cars so I can increase my overall sales."

Due to the nature of derived relational responding, rules provided by management may have many unforeseen consequences. For example, employees might focus on improving their sales volume by decreasing the time spent negotiating with customers by dropping the price of a car immediately, thus cutting into the company's profit margin. With regards to IBCs, employees may place the behavior of helping another salesperson in a frame of coordination with the outcome of losing out on the parking spot and may refuse to help each other. Employees may give up on achieving the highest sales if they feel they are too far behind other employees in sales made so far. Employees may delay sales until the beginning of next month to get a head start on their sales totals by telling customers that they can give them a better deal if they return next month. It is therefore important for an organization to recognize these unanticipated effects of rules and guard against them. The taxonomy of rules (Pelaez & Moreno, 1998) mentioned earlier may be useful in accomplishing this.

We discussed earlier how Pelaez and Moreno (1998) suggested that rules may vary in terms of such characteristics as explicitness, complexity, accuracy, and source. From an RFT perspective, these characteristics of rules may result in different derived relational responding that may better account for their effect on behavior. The more explicit a rule is, the higher the salience of the relations specified by the rule. When a rule is not explicit, derived relations between the components of the rule and the workplace to which they refer would be based on learning history, not necessarily the present contingency. Thus different employees may come to a different understanding of a rule due to their different learning histories. On the other hand, in circumstances where the contingencies are in flux and one would therefore like the employee to be sensitive to the contingencies, an explicit rule may result in more consistent performance (Hayes, Brownstein, Zettle, Rosenfarb, & Korn, 1986). This functional account of rules demonstrates the effects that derived relational responding of each individual may have on others in a given IBC. In other words, IBCs consist of the sequential behavior of individuals, and the behavior is determined by contingencies prevalent at the individual level of analysis. Accordingly, the adverse effect of a given rule on relational responding of one employee can function as the setting factor (see Kantor, 1967) or context for the behavior of another employee and result in a perpetual effect among a collectivity of employees in a given IBC (see Appendix). In short, the level of consistency or variability of IBCs can be affected by ways organizational information is disseminated via contingency-specifying verbal products.

For instance, the variability of responding that is promoted by incomplete instruction may hinder or promote effective performance, depending on the organizational characteristics. For example, in some organizations (e.g., Sony, Microsoft, and Intel), where creativity and problem solving are the basis for business success, variability of responding and hence utilization of heuristic rules (Chase & Bjarnadottir, 1992) by employees may be a more optimal set of conditions for managers to promote, rather than those conditions occasioned by the use of explicit and complete rules. On the other hand, incomplete rules may have negative implications for management and employees in situations where the consistent recurrence of certain performance patterns (e.g., customer greeting, merchandising, manufacturing) is required. The variability in responding generated by incomplete rules may have a negative impact on productivity in the cases of standardized, repetitive tasks (Johnson et al., in press).

The complexity of a rule may also affect the consistency of IBCs' reoccurrence and the extent to which employees will need to engage in derived relational responding to understand the rule. Thus, complex rules rely on already-established relational networks for their effectiveness. For instance, the inclusion of a metaphor in a rule (e.g., "Customers are like big fish. If you try to reel them in too fast the line might break.") increases the complexity of the rule and requires the listener to abstract the relationship between fishing and making a sale to a customer. Metaphors are effective at promoting variability of responding (McCurry & Hayes, 1992), which may be particularly applicable when employees keep repeating an unsuccessful behavior. These sorts of rules may be more appropriate for employees who have been with the organization for a long time and would likely be confusing and less effective for newcomers.

Although we do not disagree completely with Pelaez and Moreno's definition of rule complexity, we would like to add another dimension to it, namely the number of steps or conditionals referenced in a rule. For example, a complex rule might state, "If a customer asks about the standard package, advise them of the advantages that the deluxe package has over the standard package; if the customer is with a family member and asks for the standard package, refer them to the family package and discuss its advantages; if the customer is there on the weekend with a family member, refer them directly to the deluxe package without mentioning the family package; if the customer refuses the deluxe package, discreetly get the attention of the floor supervisor; if the floor supervisor is unavailable and the customer declines the deluxe package, mention the family package." The rule is complex due to the number of conditionals as well as the number of other rules it references. Thus, from an RFT perspective, the size of the relational network occasioned by a rule, is also a measure of the complexity of a rule (see Appendix). While this latter sort of complexity might be applicable to everyday tasks that the employee engages in, it might be inimical to prompt response in the case of an emergency.

Accuracy is another factor that contributes to the effectiveness of rules. An RFT perspective suggests that the future possibility of following rules would be reduced by their history of inaccuracies. Inaccurate rules result in poor performance, especially by employees with a history of rigid rule following (Wulfert, Greenay, Farkas, Hayes, & Dougher, 1994). Otherwise, employees who come to recognize that the rule is inaccurate are likely to consider management as "inept" or "not knowledgeable" in frames of coordination with each other. This may lead to a decreased possibility that the employee with follow subsequent rules provided by management. Thus, the history with the source from which rules come can affect the probability of employee compliance with the rule.

In an organization, the greater the extent rules from management are detrimental (in terms of accuracy and clarity) to performance, the greater the chance that employees will discard rules from that source and rely on self-generated rules or rules from other sources such as coworkers and friends (Houmanfar & Johnson, 2003; Kolvitz, 1997). Due to the potential of DRR to generate new relations rapidly and efficiently, the characteristics of a rule (such as its source) may come to be related with other perspective toward the rule from the listener's standpoint. Therefore, implicit, highly complex, or inaccurate rules may result in employees' relating of their negative impact to management.

Another characteristic that impacts the effect of rules (Malott, 1992) are the consequences specified by rules. Rules that are ineffective often describe outcomes that are too small or too improbable to matter to the listener. Although the small outcomes are too little to matter in the short term, they may have a significant cumulative effect over time. However, this cumulative effect does not occur until much later, and the verbal description of the distal consequence is ineffective in controlling behavior. The startlingly high rates of obesity might be considered the product of ineffective rules of this sort. We may be aware of the rule that if we eat large quantities of unhealthy food, we will gain weight. The outcome of gaining weight is highly probable, but it is too small, and only in the long run—due to the cumulative effect—is the outcome large. Similarly, the rule that wearing a seat belt reduces the risk of injury is not effective in maintaining seat belt use. Despite the significant outcome of injury, the probability of getting in an accident is miniscule. Hence, the rule is ineffective in affecting behavior.

Malott (1992) and Weatherly and Malott (2008) suggest that when small or distal rules are effective, it is because the listener is affected by aversive emotional states that come to control the behavior through negative reinforcement. Although rules are said to describe a contingency, one may not immediately come into contact with the contingent outcome specified in the rule. From an RFT perspective (Hayes et al., 2001), the distal rules described by Malott (1992) and Weatherly and Malott (2008) might be ineffective because, in the short term, the consequence of engaging in an undesirable behavior is considered less punishing than the small and/or negative outcome that arises from following the rule toward a longer term consequence. In other words, the listener places the two different short-term consequences in a relational frame of comparison with one another, where the positive outcome is framed as being "better than" the negative outcome. It is also likely that the short-term behavior may not be highly predictive or causal in relation to the long-term outcome to be reinforced, even with feedback. Further, we cannot directly manipulate the guilt or aversive feeling that is hypothesized to be related to the behavior. Therefore, for a distal rule to function effectively, the listener must place the long-term outcome in a relational frame equivalent with the short-term outcome as well as in a cause-effect frame with the behavior. In this way, the behavior, through DRR, comes to acquire a relation with both short- and long-term outcomes and may also elicit the same kinds of aversive emotional states that accompany possible negative long-term outcomes.

A final characteristic of rules is the source of their consequence. A rule that specifies a consequence that will be delivered by another person or people (i.e., the consequence is socially mediated), has been called a *ply* (Hayes, Zettle, & Rosenfarb, 1989; see Appendix). If an employee is told that the manager disapproves of loose clothing on the workshop floor, this would be an example of a ply. Alternatively, a rule that specifies a consequence that occurs naturally, as part of the interaction with the environment, has been called a *track* (Hayes et al., 1989; see Appendix). If an employee is told that loose clothing tends to get snagged in the equipment and leads to injuries on the workshop floor, this would be an example of a track. Both kinds of rules can be effective; however, a ply is less likely to be effective when the social context is absent, suggesting a diminished likelihood of contacting the social consequence. A track, on the other hand, ought to retain its effectiveness regardless of the presence or absence of a social context.

Rules specify an if-then or contingent relation between responses and stimuli and therefore are essential in guiding employee behavior. However, not all verbal communication within organizations is in the form of rules. Many of the communications serve to alter the function of stimuli in the workplace, which in turn impacts employee behavior. Rules that change the reinforcing or punishing effectiveness of consequences (in much that same way the establishing operations nonverbally alters the effect of conse-quences) have been called *augmentals* (Hayes et al., 1989; see Appendix). Formative augmentals establish a previously neutral stimulus as a reinforcer or punisher. For example, "If we keep expenses under $100,000 for the month, employees will receive a bonus," will probably result in employees seeking feedback on company expenses, possibly a previously neutral stimulus, and attempting to stay below the specified spending limit. Motivative augmentals, on the other hand, alter the effectiveness of stimuli by altering a consequential function. For example, "Sales are the backbone of our company finances. If we don't sell, we don't make money." This statement takes a stimulus (making a sale) that already functions as a reinforcer for salespeople and increases its reinforcing effectiveness. Augmentals, therefore, are a way to bring about transformation of stimulus functions through DRR and hopefully a subsequent change in employee behavior as a result of the alteration of stimulus functions.

The above-mentioned account of rule governance highlights the importance of functional characteristics of rules in management of IBCs or organized group practices in organizations. With regards to topography and function of rules, organizational rules are institutional stimuli that correspond to a shared response from a group (Kantor, 1982). Therefore, the institutionalized nature of organizational rules requires our focus on not only the shared function they serve among employees but also the topographical characteristics that mediate stimulus control among collectivity of individuals (Kantor, 1982). Organized group practices or IBCs can be defined as learned interactions with institutionalized stimuli (e.g., rules, policies, other organizational members, etc.) acquired under group auspices and shared among members of a given organization (Houmanfar & Johnson, 2003). And, given the coordinated nature of these practices, they can be influenced by verbal products such as rules and augmentals.

Management of Interlocking Behavioral Contingencies

The product or service delivered by an organization does not depend solely on the behavior of a single employee. The coordinated behaviors of many employees from many departments generate the organizational aggregate product (e.g., cars and computers) or service. Thus, successful behaviors of employees within organizations tend to rely on the successful behaviors of other employees. As mentioned earlier, when the product of the behavior of an employee acts as an antecedent for the behavior of another employee, IBCs (Glenn, 2004) are said to exist. For example, within the publishing department, the employee designing the layout of a brochure cannot arrange things precisely until she receives the photographs and product information from the other employee responsible for providing them. This sort of interrelated behavior is often taken for granted in organizations, yet it is essential to proper functioning.

The interlocked nature of contingencies also exists among metacontingencies (Glenn & Malott, 2004; Malott & Glenn, 2006; Houmanfar & Rodrigues, 2006). For example, the publishing department cannot design the brochure until the marketing department has decided on the items that will be going on sale. So, these departments constitute the metacontingencies associated with the internal functioning of the organizations. For instance, when analyzing the IBCs of core departments (e.g., production) and support departments (e.g., human resources) in a given organization, the cultural milieu (e.g., organizational policies, material resources), internal consumer feedback (feedback provided from one department to the other), and the aggregate product of each department (e.g., new employees hired by human resource) are the settings factors that occasion the occurrence of the associated IBCs (assembling of computer parts) that bring about the production of aggregate products that meet the internal consumer (e.g., other departments such as customer service) demand.

In short, departments or organizational teams within and across organizations rely on IBCs to accomplish their duties. Accordingly, managers must ensure that the IBCs are running efficiently and effectively. Just as management can influence employee behavior through verbal products such as rules and augmentals, so too can it influence interrelated employee behavior using the same verbal products.

Fujimoto (2001) provides an account of how Toyota used variations of explicit and implicit rules in its manufacturing plants around the world. Shop floor management was historically governed by explicit rules for plants that did not allow deviation. These rules were considered to be the most efficient because they had been tested in other locations. However, in recent years, smaller Toyota plants had been allowed to try new approaches in dealing with a specific problems pertaining to accuracy and speed of production. If the approach was successful, it was implemented at a few more plants and, if proven useful there, was turned into a standard practice. For instance, one plant used smaller work teams without reliance on explicit rules pertaining to floor operations to increase the efficiency of the assembly process. Based on its success, this management practice was implemented in other plants and soon became a standardized practice in all plants. Thus, by using more implicit rules to encourage variation, Toyota was able to improve its rate of production. This example also demonstrates the importance of evaluating the effectiveness of organizational rules on a continuous basis.

Another example that is demonstrative of the influence of verbal products on collectivity of employees' behaviors and the associated IBCs is Alavosius, Getting, Dagen, Newsome, and Hopkins' (2009) field experiment on a systematic implementation of an incentive system within cooperative associations of 350 companies (inclusive of small manufacturing companies such as boat builders, plating operations, jewelry manufacture, etc.). This process included a series of promotion efforts (facilitated through communication networks across member companies) designed to maximize discussion of safety management by all members of the companies. The authors reported that verbal behavior of many employees was changed by introduction of the promotional materials, incentives, and celebrations. In short, the incentives set the occasion for communications from the shop floor upward through work organizations that solicited and supported active safety management.

A relational understanding of the verbal products that are communicated through organizational networks can enhance our ability to craft the above-mentioned verbal products and so render them more suitable to the needs of specific organizations, departments, and teams. Providing employees with simple, accurate rules that come from a respected source can help to improve the effectiveness of their behavior while reducing the possibility of time wasted on creating (and disseminating) self-rules that may turn out to be inaccurate. Recognizing the nature of different departments and teams and their relation to the organization can guide leadership in presenting formative and motivative augmentals that produce shared goals and hence improved cooperation within the organization. Through recent empirical work in RFT, behavior analysis is increasingly placing itself in a position to theorize effectively and empirically test these educated guesses about the functioning of verbal behavior in organizations.

For instance, establishing shared goals among team members can be accomplished by communicating a clear vision for the team that is in alignment with the goals and mission of the organization. Specifying rewards or outcomes that will result from team success can also mediate an increase in the reinforcing value of the team goals (O'Hora & Maglieri, 2006). If necessary, augmentals can be used to increase the importance of team goals while communicating a clear connection between the team actions and goals—placing desirable team behaviors in frames of "before-after" with the team goals—may help increase team members' prediction of accomplishing the team goals (O'Hora & Maglieri, 2006).

With regard to circumstances where variability of IBCs is promoted by leadership (e.g., Microsoft's design team practices), preparing the team for different scenarios can aid in team success. Ensuring members are aware of the greatest number of potential conditions can be done by generating "if-then" relations between hypothetical scenarios and the proper responses to those situations. If possible, rehearsal of difficult or complex tasks should be arranged so the team has a learning history of performing under different conditions. Problem solving within simulations of various scenarios can also help member skills be identified so role clarity can be established reinforced; these are also factors in successful team performance (Alavosius, Houmanfar, & Rodrigues, 2005).

To increase buy-in (decreased resistance to change) and therefore the effectiveness of their messages, management may want to craft messages to suit the circumstances of the organization as well as the situation of the employees. For that reason, the level of specification of rules can be varied according to the type of team that the employee belongs to. With some groups in organizations (e.g., manufacturing), the rules provided may need to be more specific such that the roles of team members and the goals of the team are unambiguous. With other groups, such as design teams, on the other hand, the goal may be clearly specified, but the manner in which the goal is to be accomplished is loosely defined (e.g., "efficiently"), which gives team members the ability to generate their own rules based on their own experiences as well as some trial and error.

Moreover, in their role as guides, leaders have to create new verbal relations between the current and future state of the organization, between the future organization and its niche in the future environment, and between current employees and the future organization. Leaders have to take into consideration the ever-evolving external environment and verbally evaluate the potential adaptations the organization can make to those possible futures. These relations are based on a verbally constructed future that, for the leader at least, bears some connection with the current situation. However, these relations must be communicated effectively to the rest of the people in the organization if they are to behave in accordance with said relations.

Finally, individuals' histories of relational networks have a significant influence on the way by which a collection of individuals in a given IBC responds to organizational information generated by each other through communication networks. This interaction between relational networks and communication networks can be captured through the phenomenon of self-organization, which is one of the characteristics of social systems.

Characteristics of Communication Networks

As we discussed earlier, the verbal networks formulated by employees in an organization depend on their prior history of already-established verbal relations. New relations are more easily formed if they are in accordance with existing relational networks. Due to the role of coherence (consistency of DRR in the absence of explicit reinforcement) as a reinforcement (Dean, Johnston, & Saunders, 2006; Festinger, 1957; Hayes et al., 2001), relational networks are often created without external input or interference. In other words, the dynamics of relational framing behavior are such that an individual's set of verbal relations tends to become more ordered over time even in the absence of external consequences. This inherent dynamic is referred to as self-organization in other sciences and is one of the defining characteristics of a complex system (Bar-Yam, 1997; Kauffman, 1993). Relational networks as well as the communication networks within an organization seem to display this feature of self-organization. Thus, communication networks may develop in organizations without being specifically put in place by management. People with access to more information, through social links or by virtue of their position within the organization, may act as hubs in these networks (Sandakar, 2009). Similarly, rumor and gossip may proliferate through many parts of the company in the absence of external feedback (Kauffman, 1993).

Communication networks also seem to embody several of the other characteristics of complex systems. Complex systems tend to be sensitive to initial conditions (Bar-Yam, 1997; Kauffman, 1993). From an organizational perspective these initial conditions might be the size of the company, the information given during initial orientation sessions, the nature of the interview process that new employees go through, the history and perspective of the founders of the organization, and so on. These factors may have a significant impact on how information is transmitted differently within one organization compared to another. Interactions in complex systems are often not predictable, which seems to be true of employee verbal interactions within an organization. For example, social contingencies that may serve as the bases for communications, the talkativeness of employees in different roles, and employee reactions or interpretations to official organizational communications are often unpredictable because they may be affected by several factors such as their impression of the organizational culture, events in the news, and their overall impression of the economy.

Since communication networks are unpredictable, sensitive to initial conditions, and often self-organized, it is often unclear how one ought to manage the system. Although the organization's leaders may desire to limit variability and increase the predictability of the verbal relations, such a strategy often does not work (Marion & Uhl-bien, 2001). Disrupting the inherent dynamics of the system often leads to the system self-organizing unpredictably in some other way. For although complex systems tend to have internal characteristics that guide their development, they are also sensitive to their environments. Establishing a system of feedback and clear communication should attempt to limit communication networks from being governed too much by its self-organizational characteristics and be more responsive to the needs of the organization (Brethower, 1982; 1999; 2000; Diener, McGee, & Miguel, 2009; Malott, 2003).

As we move from primarily rule-governed repertoires of some departments (e.g., manufacturing department) to contingency-shaped repertoires of other departments (e.g., design department), self-organization may increase. It would therefore be more effective for management to attempt to provide a modicum of organization to the communication networks while simultaneously recognizing and taking advantage of the communication dynamics that self-organize within the company. To this end, gaining constant feedback from the employees about the effectiveness of management's efforts to influence the content of the communication is necessary.

CONCLUSION

This article provided an overview of communication networks and role of verbal behavior in behavioral systems analysis. The discussion included ways by which leaders' communication of organizational contingencies impact relational responding as well as coordinated and interrelated behaviors in and across metacontingencies. As we see it, the purpose of communication is often to guide employee behavior to be more efficient and productive while contributing to the overall efficiency and productivity of the organization. This sort of communication is generally in the form of rules that the organization assumes will have an impact on employee behavior. In that regard, we addressed the implications that the analysis of rules may have for behavioral systems analysis and more particularly, behavior analysis of organizational effectiveness. Additionally, examples associated with the applicability of behavioral techniques that can be utilized in the analysis of rules, particularly in organizational settings, were provided.

Our analysis also drew upon different behavioral perspectives to demonstrate how communication networks and the nature of verbal rules may contribute to understanding the issues involved in reengineering behavioral systems in the face of continued socioeconomic and cultural demands. In short, we believe that further empirical analyses associated with precise specification and demonstration of the means by which communication networks influence our analysis of behavioral systems is a challenge that is worth the direct attention of behavior analysts—engineers of human behavior—in the field of organizational behavior management.

REFERENCES

Abernathy, W. B. (1996). *Sin of wages*. Memphis, TN: PerfSys.
Abernathy, W. B. (2000). *Managing without supervising: Creating an organization-wide performance system*. Memphis, TN: PerfSys.
Agnew, J. L., & Redmon, W. K. (1992). Contingency specifying stimuli: The role of "rules" in organizational behavior management. *Journal of Organizational Behavior Management, 12*, 67–75.
Alavosius, M. P., Houmanfar, R., & Rodrigues, N. J. (2005). Unity of purpose / unity of effort: private-sector preparedness in times of terror. *Disaster Prevention and Management. 14*, 666–680.
Alavosius, M. P., Getting, J., Dagen, J., Newsome, W., & Hopkins, B. (2009). Use of a cooperative to interlock contingencies and balance the commonwealth. *Journal of Organizational Behavior Management, 29*, 193–211.
Bar-Yam, Y. (1997). *Dynamics of complex systems*. Reading, MA: Addison-Wesley.
Bowler, T. D. (1981). *General systems thinking: Its scope and applications*. New York: North Holland.
Brethower, D. M. (1982). The total performance system. In R. M. O'Brien, A. M. Dickinson, & M. P. Rosow (Eds.), *Industrial behavior modification: A management handbook* (pp. 350–369). New York: Pergamon.
Brethower, D. M. (1999). General systems theory and behavioral psychology. In H. D. Stolovitch & E. J. Keeps (Eds.), *Handbook of human performance technology* (pp. 67–81). San Francisco, CA: Jossey-Bass Pfeiffer.

Brethower, D. M. (2000). A systematic view of enterprise: Adding value to performance. *Journal of Organizational Behavior Management, 20*, 165–190.

Catania, C. A., Shimoff, E., & Matthews, B. A. (1989). In S. C. Hayes (Ed.), *Rule-governed behavior: Cognition, contingencies, and instructional control* (pp. 119–150). New York: Plenum.

Chase, P. N., & Bjarnadottir, G. S. (1992). Instructing variability: Some features of a problem solving repertoire. In S. C. Hayes & L. J. Hayes (Eds.), *Understanding verbal relations* (pp.181–193). Reno, NV: Context.

Daniels, A. C., & Daniels, J. E. (2005). *Measure of a leader.* Atlanta, GA: Performance Management Publications.

Dean, W. C., Johnston, M. D., & Saunders, K. J. (2006). Intertrial sources of stimulus control and delayed matching-to-sample performance in humans. *Journal of the Experimental Analysis of Behavior, 86*, 253–267.

Diener, L. H., McGee, H. M., & Miguel, C. F. (2009). An integrated approach for conducting a behavioral systems analysis. *Journal of Organizational Behavior Management, 29*, 108–135.

Dougher, M. J., Hamilton, D., & Fink, B. (2007). Transformation of the discriminative and eliciting function of generalized relational stimuli. *Journal of the Experimental Analysis of Behavior, 88*, 179–197.

Festinger, L. (1957). *A theory of cognitive dissonance.* Stanford, CA: Stanford University Press.

Fujimoto, T. (1999). *The evolution of a manufacturing system at Toyota.* New York, NY: Oxford Press.

Glenn, S. S. (1988). Contingencies and metacontingencies: Toward a synthesis of behavior analysis and cultural materialism. *The Behavior Analyst, 11*, 161–179.

Glenn, S. S. (1989). Verbal behavior and cultural practices. *Behavior Analysis and Social Action, 7*, 10–15.

Glenn, S. S. (1991). Contingencies and metacontingencies: Relations among behavioral, cultural, and biological evolution. In P. A. Lamal (Ed.), *Behavioral analysis of societies and cultural practices* (pp. 39–73). Washington, DC: Hemisphere.

Glenn, S. S. (2004). Individual behavior, culture, and social change. *The Behavior Analyst, 27*, 133–151.

Glenn, S. S., & Malott, M. M. (2004). Complexity and selection: Implications for organizational change. *Behavior & Social Issues, 13*, 89–106.

Hayes, S. C., Barnes-Holmes, D., & Roche, B. T. (2001). *Relational frame theory: A post-Skinnerian account of human language and cognition.* New York. Plenum.

Hayes, S. C., Brownstein, A. J., Zettle, R. D., Rosenfarb, I., & Korn, Z. (1986). Rule-governed behavior and sensitivity to changing consequences of responding. *Journal of the Experimental Analysis of Behavior, 45*, 237–256.

Hayes, S. C., & Hayes, L. J. (1989). The verbal action of the listener as a basis for rule governance. In S. C. Hayes (Ed.) *Rule-governed behavior: Cognition, contingencies, and instructional control* (pp. 153–190.). New York: Plenum.

Hayes, S. C., Zettle, R. D., & Rosenfarb, I. (1989). Rule following. In S. C. Hayes (Ed.), Rule-governed behavior: Cognition, contingencies, and instructional control (pp. 269–322). New York. Plenum.

Houmanfar, R., & Johnson, R. (2003). Organizational implications of gossip and rumor. *Journal of Organizational Behavior Management, 23,* 117–138.

Houmanfar, R., & Rodrigues, N. J. (2006). Behavior analysis & cultural analysis: Points of contact and departure. *Behavior and Social Issues, 15,* 13–30.

Johnson, R., Houmanfar, R., & Smith, G. S. (in press). The effect of implicit and explicit rules on customer greeting and productivity in a retail organization. *Journal of Organizational Behavior Management.*

Kantor, J. R. (1967). *Interbehavioral psychology.* Akron, OH: Principia.

Kantor, J. R. (1982). *Cultural psychology.* Chicago: Principia.

Kauffman, S. (1993), *Origins of order: Self-organization and selection in evolution.* Oxford University Press.

Kolvitz, M. (1997). Donald T. Tosti, Ph.D. and Stephanie F. Jackson, M. A.: The organizational scan, performance levers, and alignment. In P. J. Dean & D. E. Ripley (Eds.), *Performance improvement pathfinders: Models for organizational learning systems* (pp. 124–141). Washington DC: International Society for Performance Improvement.

Malott, M. E. (2003). *Paradox of organizational change.* Reno, NV: Context.

Malott, M. E., & Glenn, S. S. (2006). Targets of interventions in cultural and behavioral change. *Behavior and Social Issues, 15,* 31–56.

Malott, R. (1992). A theory of rule governed behavior and organizational management. *Journal of Organizational Behavior Management, 12,* 45–65.

Marion, R., & Uhl-bien, m. (2001). Leadership in complex organizations. *The Leadership Quarterly, 12,* 389–418.

Mawhinney, T. C. (1992). Evolution of organizational cultures as selection by consequences: The gaia hypothesis, metacontingencies, and organizational ecology. In T. C. Mawhinney (Ed.), *Organizational* Culture, Rule-Governed Behavior and Organizational Behavior Management (pp. 1–26). New York: Haworth.

Mawhinney, T. C. (2001). Organization-environment systems as OBM intervention context: Minding your metacontingencies. In L. J. Hayes, J. Austin, R. Houmanfar, & M. C. Clayton (Eds.), *Organizational change* (pp. 137–166). Reno, NV: Context.

Mawhinney, T. C. (2005). Effective leadership in superior-subordinate dyads: Theory and data. *Journal of Organizational Behavior Management, 25,* 37–77.

Mawhinney, T. C. (2009). Identifying and extinguishing dysfunctional and deadly organizational practices. *Journal of Organizational Behavior Management, 29*(3/4), 231–256.

Mawhinney, T. C., & Ford, J. D. (1977). The path goal theory of leader effectiveness: An operant interpretation. *Academy of Management Review, 2,* 398–411.

McCurry, S. M., & Hayes, S. C. (1992). Clinical and experimental perspectives on metaphorical talk. *Clinical Psychology Review, 12,* 763–785.

O'Hora, D., & Maglieri, K. A. (2006). Goal statements and goal-directed behavior: A relational frame account of goal setting in organizations. *Journal of Organizational Behavior Management, 26,* 131–170.

Pelaez, M., & Moreno, R. (1998). A taxonomy of rules and their correspondence to rule-governed behavior. *Mexican Journal of Behavior Analysis, 24,* 197–214.

Rummler, G. A. (2001). Performance logic: The organization performance Rosetta Stone. In L. J. Hayes, J. Austin, R. Houmanfar, & M. C. Clayton (Eds.), *Organizational change* (pp. 111–132). Reno, NV: Context.

Rummler, G. A., & Brache, A. P. (1995). *Improving performance: How to manage the white space on the organizational chart* (2nd ed.). San Francisco: Jossey-Bass.

Sandaker, I. (2009). A selectionist perspective on systemic change inorganizations. *Journal of Organizational Behavior Management, 29*(3/4), 276–293.

Schlinger, H., & Blakely, E. (1987). Function-altering effects of contingency-specifying stimuli. *The Behavior Analyst, 10,* 41–45.

Skinner, B. F. (1953). *Science and human behavior.* New York: Free Press.

Skinner, B. F. (1957). *Verbal behavior.* Acton, MA: Copley.

Smith, G. S., Houmanfar, R., & Denny, M. (2009). *Impact of rule accuracy on productivity and communication in an organizational analog.* Manuscript submitted for publication. University of Nevada, Reno.

Stewart, I., Barns-Holmes, D., Barnes-Holmes, Y., Bond, F. W., Hayes, S. C. (2006). Relational frame theory and industrial/organizational psychology. *Journal of Organizational Behavior Management, 26,* 55–90.

Weatherly, N. L., & Malott, R. W. (2008). An analysis of organizational behavior management research in terms of three-contingency model of performance management. *Journal of Organizational Behavior Management, 28,* 260–285.

Wulfurt, E., Greenway, D. E., Farkas, D., Hayes, S. C., & Dougher, M. J. (1999). Correlation between self-reported rigidity and rule-governed insensitivity to operant contingencies. *Journal of Applied Behavior Analysis, 27,* 659–671.

APPENDIX

APPENDIX Glossary of Definitions

Term	Definition
Augmentals	rules that change the reinforcing or punishing effectiveness of consequences (in much that same way the establishing operations nonverbally alter the effect of consequences).
Cultural milieu	comprise material resources, overarching governmental policies, as well as well organizational policies, rules, traditions, institutions, technological progress, and environmental competition.
Derived Relational Responding	operant responding to the relations among properties of two or more stimuli that have not been directly trained.
Interlocking Behavioral Contingency	comprise operant contingencies in which behavior of two or more people functions as environmental events for the behavior of the others.
Metacontingency	depicts the contingent relation between interlocking behavioral contingencies (IBCs), their aggregate product, and the environmental demand.
Ply	a rule that specifies a consequence that will be delivered by another person or people.
Role-Specifying Stimuli	descriptions that specify job responsibilities and associated contingencies that may function as antecedent stimuli to ensure appropriate employee and leader behaviors.
Relational Network	a series of relations between different stimuli (that participate in already established relational responding).
Setting Factors	general surrounding circumstances that operate as inhibiting or facilitating condition in a given behavior-environment interaction.
Track	a rule that specifies a consequence that occurs naturally, as part of the interaction with the environment.

A Selectionist Perspective on Systemic and Behavioral Change in Organizations

INGUNN SANDAKER

Akershus University College, Oslo, Norway

This article provides a discussion of how different dynamics in production processes and communication structures in the organization serve as different environmental contingencies favoring different behavioral patterns and variability of performance in organizations. Finally, an elaboration on a systems perspective on the selection of corporate culture, and the relevance of metacontingencies will be discussed.

A SELECTIONIST PERSPECTIVE ON SYSTEMIC AND BEHAVIORAL CHANGE IN ORGANIZATIONS

Variation in behavioral repertoires with respect to environmental interaction is a prerequisite for the selection of behavior. To be selected, behaviors have to exist within the range of possible behavioral variation or within the population of behaviors. If environments within which organizations interact are stable, organizations can survive at a low level of complexity. However, if environmental complexity increases, demand for organizational complexity will increase concurrently (Bar-Yam, 1997). The range of behavioral variation within systems is constrained by external and internal contingencies. Various constraints on variation and properties of the

The author is grateful to Sigrid Glenn and Gunnar Ree for valuable comments on previous versions of this article. She is also indebted to Ramona Houmanfar for her constructive feedback throughout the publication process.

interaction between behavior and environment (e.g., contingencies of reinforcement) determine what behavioral repertoires are selected.

Contingencies of reinforcement affect the acquisition, change, and extinction of behavioral patterns. Changes in society and working life may usefully be conceptualized as changes in contingencies of reinforcement. When approaching contingencies of reinforcement/interaction at the individual level, refinement of different schedules is possible. In a "top-down" approach to systems, variation will be the main basis for interaction and selection. Moving along a continuum from restricting variation to evoking variability of responses, the range of control may shift from correction of any response deviation to shaping of variation to acquire solutions that are in demand in an unpredictable and continuously changing environment/ market (see Table 1).

During the early industrialization of Western society, standard operating procedures were necessary in order to achieve a high volume of production. Constraining variation, both in product quality and production processes, was a stated objective. Management training and organizational design were developed to control unwanted variation. The environment favored conformity (i.e., a narrow range of variation) by correcting and controlling deviations. Interaction was limited to simple, technology-driven work processes and communication went through strict formal chains of command (Fayol, 1916; Taylor, 1911/1967). Max Weber also describes the emergence and entrenchment of a bureaucratic ideal model, in which the goals of managing public service relate to production volume and standardization of the production process with little or no room for variation or

TABLE 1 Selection of Organizational Behavior

	Objective: standardized processes and products	Objective: match the complexity and competence of the environment
Variation	Constrain variation in behavioral repertoire for maximum standardization of production	Allow high degree of variation to achieve solutions that are in demand in an unpredictable and continuously changing environment/market
Interaction	Interaction limited to "chain of command," that is, influence within the framework of a low number of relatively conformed individuals	Allows a "web of influence," (i.e., facilitating variation in interaction independently of divisions, departments or levels of administration)
Selection	Selection of a limited assortment of behavior patterns governed by the objective of standardizing work processes and products; controlling and correcting for deviations whenever behavior shows too much variation	Sufficient basis for selection of useful behavior under ever-changing conditions; focus on shaping and improving performance

judgment calls. Interactions ideally are limited to formal channels to reduce the risk of unwanted variation through informal interactions (Weber, 1990).

In the new leadership paradigm (Sims & Lorenzi, 1992), we are moving from managing control to facilitating variation in organizational practices. In that regard, contingencies favoring behavioral variation are arranged in a way that differs fundamentally from the contingencies controlling production behavior in early industrialized society. The new paradigms can be discussed in terms of variation, selection, and interaction. Modern, knowledge-based businesses encourage behavioral variation when meeting continuously changing demands in order to increase the probability that appropriate behavior comes about.

This paradigm shift is well described in Burns and Stalker's classic text *The Management of Innovation* (1961), where they describe the transition from "mechanistic" to "organic" organizations as the pace of change in the organization's environment increases. When a once-stable business environment becomes highly dynamic, the business must change its working processes, structures of communication, and degree of interaction with its environment. The shift in organizational paradigm has been described from different perspectives (Rummler & Brache, 1995; Sims & Lorenzi, 1992). These changes in society and working life will be discussed in this article as a systems-level shift in contingencies of reinforcement. Following from this will be a discussion of how different dynamics in production processes and communication structures in the organization serve as different environmental contingencies favoring different patterns of behavior. Finally, an elaboration on a systems perspective on the selection of corporate culture and the relevance of metacontingencies will be discussed.

CHANGES IN SOCIETY AND WORKING LIFE AS SHIFTS IN CONTINGENCIES OF REINFORCEMENT

There are a number of reasons why behavior analysts should take an interest in a systems perspective on behavior change. Important social issues like overpopulation, climate change, or innovation of new technologies demand behavior change on a large scale. Behavior analysts have been concerned with changing large-scale behaviors from different perspectives, including social responsibility (e.g., Biglan, 1995; Mattaini & Thyer, 1996; Todorov, 2005) and organizational efficiency (e.g., Glenn & Malott, 2004; Hayes, Austin, Houmanfar & Clayton, 2001). A systems perspective examines individual behavior as well as behavior of the whole system, including the environment with which the system interacts.

The generic selectionist perspective on change is central to behavior analysis (e.g., Hull, Langman & Glenn, 2001; Skinner, 1981) and to the study of complex adaptive systems (Axelrod & Cohen, 2000; Sandaker, 2003). The learning and maintenance of behavior and the formation and maintenance of systems result from selection by environmental consequences. For the purposes of clarity of communication and stringency of analysis, units of analysis will have to be clearly defined along with factors in the environment or context that influence them. This is not always an easy task, since the system, as a unit of analysis, does not necessarily correspond to the formal boundaries of an organization or institution or to geographical borders. Defining a system as a unit of analysis defines the scope beyond the formal limits of the system. In other words, the unit of analysis is not necessarily defined as a formal entity, like an organization or a department. Rather, the unit of analysis is guided by the use of the system.

Selection processes, whether of individual or systems behavior, may or may not be products of deliberate planning. The process of selection is in itself blind, but through behavioral engineering we try to limit the amount of possible variation, thus directing the selection process. Organizations are usually designed for specific purposes. Systems, on the other hand, may emerge as a result of interactions within and between organizations, but not necessarily for a specific purpose. When approaching social systems, we have to deal both with what is guided by deliberate planning of how the system *should* behave and with the *actual* practical working of the system, which may be a function of contingencies over which there is little or no control. This difference also applies in the structure of the system. Within organizations, the communication system may be designed to serve a specific purpose. A network, considered the architecture of a complex system, may represent an emergent structure selected by consequences of internal interaction.

Theories of organization and management (see model 2 in Table 1) are most often concerned with the goal or purpose of an organization. From the perspective of a rational ideal model, designing a more or less suitable organization is possible. From the perspective of behavior analysis, the organization may be viewed as an environment favorable for various forms of behavior. From the perspective of systems analysis, however, the environment of the organization itself may be favorable for particular systems.

In recent years, a trend has been seen in which organizations are moving away from standardized production processes that constrain the variation in the behavior repertoires of employees and toward a working life that is part of a globalized social structure, with relations among those individuals crossing geographical and institutional boundaries. This trend should indicate that organizations should put effort into achieving great variation in their interactions with their surroundings. Interaction with an environment in continuous change affects the internal workings of the organization and learning of new information by individual employees. For the last couple of decades, the capacity to learn has been held up as the main competitive advantage for a company (e.g., Senge, 1990). The model presented in Table 1 illustrates this paradigm shift.

Behavior regulation and management of variation may be accomplished by rules (Chase & Bjarnadottir, 1992; Houmanfar, Rodrigues & Smith, 2009). Variation may also be prompted by utilizing performance management strategies, positive behavior support, and shaping. The specific character of the actual controlling contingencies for behavior is an empirical question. The systems perspective investigates different functions in the organization in the light of the need to constrain or facilitate variation.

The Company as a Part of Social Change

In 1963, Phillips Petroleum was the first oil company that was permitted to start seismic surveys of the North Sea. The next year, the subsidiary Phillips Petroleum Company Norway (PPCoN) was established. The drilling for oil in 1969 followed by the first North Sea crude oil stored at Ekofisk in 1974 were historical events that changed the international image of Norway (Kvendseth, 1988). All this was accomplished with technology that was new to Norway, though it had been tested in other countries. With an original crew of U.S. rig workers with drilling experience from land wells or the Gulf of Mexico, the technology was put to tough tests and modified to work under Norwegian conditions. For PPCoN, the need for recruiting Norwegian rig workers coincided with a considerable loss of business and revenue for the Norwegian merchant marine, with resulting layoffs. A large number of unemployed sailors were recruited by Phillips Petroleum.

Thus, the first part of Norwegian oil history was shaped by American experts and Norwegian sailors with no experience in oil production. They were pioneers in a high-risk, high-profit business. Coincidentally, "the pioneer" is the nickname of Phillips Petroleum, and they have done the name proud by solving complex technical problems as they occurred. When the sea bottom under the Ekofisk oil field started sinking, the steel platforms were raised by 20 feet to support the rigs and compensate for the sinking. When they started injecting seawater into depleted wells, yield from these wells increased dramatically. The history of those pioneers survives in anecdotes telling of how the Americans used to climb the rigs with no protective gear and wearing wooden clogs. While labor regulations and worker representation on corporate boards were generally accepted in Norwegian companies, the oil company was run as an American business, keeping the reputation of "Phillips the pioneer" alive.

While Phillips was solving technical challenges in the North Sea, accidents occurred that would have a strong impact on the relations of PPCoN with its environment. In 1977, the first uncontrolled blowout from an oil rig occurred, with no personal injuries and a successful termination after 1 week. The same year, a transport helicopter went down with 12 passengers; there were no survivors. Three years later, the helicopter platform *Alexander Kielland* capsized, with 123 casualties. At that time, a number of oil companies were working in the North Sea, and when new drilling concessions were distributed, Phillips competed with other companies, like the Norwegian state oil company, Statoil, which was established in 1972. In short, the Norwegian society and the industrial environment had changed quite substantially since PPCoN started their pioneer enterprise in the North Sea. The Norwegian government wanted to build Norwegian expertise, and there was speculation that Norwegian companies were favored when concessions were distributed. In addition, matters of safety and security were given a lot of attention by the authorities and the media.

Development and adaptation of new technology under novel conditions probably contributed to a large range of behavioral variation and learning. With the challenges of the extreme environment of the North Sea and new competitors in the region, the risks of the oil industry became apparent and the relations between PPCoN and its surroundings changed.

After many years with no drilling concessions, Phillips was awarded new licenses in 1995, including one with operative responsibility. The pioneers remained at the technological frontier, and after heavy investment in safety, security, and total quality management (TQM), the company appeared as credible to the Norwegian Oil Directorate and government bodies. While PPCoN generally allowed great variation and flexible interaction at the individual and systems levels, parts of the company limited the range of variation that was permitted. Safety systems demanded strict standardization and precise routines. There were detailed flow charts where chains of command were described for both accident prevention and handling of emergencies (Sandaker, 1997).

The aforementioned case is an example in which different groups operated depending on the function or designated purpose of the subsystems. Furthermore, this example raises a critical issue concerning the ways in which cultural contingencies exert stronger influences on individual behavior than do the competing individual contingencies and vice versa. This issue will be dealt with in greater detail at the end of the article, when discussing the relevance of concepts like macrocontingencies and metacontingencies.

Organizations as Designed Systems

The noun "design" refers to "a pattern with a purpose." The *American Heritage Dictionary* (2008) provides several definitions of the noun "design," among them, "the purposeful or inventive arrangement of parts or details" and "a basic scheme or pattern that affects and controls function or development." Most common definitions of an organization are variations of "many people working together to achieve a common objective." Robbins and Judge (2007) offer this definition of an organization: "A consciously coordinated social unit, composed of two or more people, that functions on a relatively continuous basis to achieve a common goal or set of goals" (p. 4).

The organization, then, is intentional in its nature. It has been set up or designed to achieve stated objectives, whether it is a manufacturing company, a transport firm, a hospital, or a school. Of course, this also goes for religious and charity organizations and for local, state, and federal agencies. Intentionality (defined as present acts to achieve future results) is a product of human verbal behavior (i.e., verbal governance) involving descriptions of anticipated future reinforcement contingencies controlling behavior in the present. Selection processes are nonintentional by nature; selection occurs based on present conditions. Future selection depends on future contingencies, not present rules. In this way, selection is nonintentional, or blind (cf. Ringen, 1993).

To ensure that the organization is consciously coordinated, management is required: "Managers get things done through other people. They make decisions, allocate resources, and direct the activities of others to attain goals" (Robbins & Judge, 2007, p. 4). The challenge for systems designers is designing for selection by arranging cultural contingencies to select the individual behaviors that ensure total system performance that adapts to unknown selection pressures in the future.

Operating in unpredictable and rapidly changing environments, the design of organizations will not always equip them with the functions that ensure their survival under contingencies that are (sometimes) drastically altered within short time spans. Ideally, organizational design should incorporate functions that increase the adaptability of the organization as a whole system. Structure is important, but so are function and internal processes, the subject of the next section.

A Systems Perspective

A system is an integrated whole whose parts relate to each other and that relates to other systems (Bar-Yam, 1997). According to Ray and Delprato (1989), "The systems orientation presumes that natural events derive localized organizations. Organization itself implies an interrelationship among constituent elements of the system. Thus a system is defined as a set of interrelated (i.e., organized) constituent elements" (p. 85).

Common to most definitions of systems and descriptions of systems perspective is the effort to embrace a whole (Bar-Yam, 1997; Gharajedaghi, 2006). This whole is often summed up by specifying the purpose or objective of the system. I prefer the term *function* to refer to subsystems or units in general systems. Using functional descriptions avoids intentional explanations of systems behavior or terms such as rational (or irrational) behavior. A system may be functional or dysfunctional only in the perspective of the context in which a system operates. The normative terms *good* and *bad* are relevant only when the system's properties are described in relation to the system's interchange with its environment. It is also relevant to consider the goals of the system, which depend on the context in which behavioral norms exist. A terrorist cell may serve its goal of spreading fear to the satisfaction of its members. Still, from a normative point of view, most people would characterize the activity as dysfunctional or bad. A company may be described as a success measured by its goals for profit and growth but may exploit local resources or pollute its environment from another perspective.

A complex adaptive system is defined by its response to changes in its environment. Even if the central nervous system or the metabolic system serves a purpose in an organism, the functions of the subsystem in relation to the rest of the organism define its purpose. The additional characteristic of adaptation indicates that a complex system changes as a function of its interaction with the environment of which it is a part. The selectionist notion of *fit* applies here, and fit determines the probability of the system's survival. The following section provides an overview of the role of function in relation to structure and processes.

FUNCTION, STRUCTURE, AND PROCESSES

A system may be defined by (a) its function, by which the system's properties are defined, (b) its structure, or architecture that tells us how the system is organized to maintain its aggregate function, and (c) the internal processes involved in maintaining its function. All three characteristics are required for an effective systems analysis.

We must be clear as to what level of analysis we are addressing (e.g., Campbell, 1990; Skinner, 1981). A biological system like the liver may be described by its function as a part of the greater metabolic system (cleaning waste and storing glycogen), which in itself has a function as part of another system. All subsystem structure or architecture may change depending on what it is subjected to and on the processes that contribute to maintaining its functions. For example, a religious congregation will have (a) the stated goal, or function, of serving a higher power to ensure eternal life for its members, (b) a structure that reflects who communicates with whom, and (c) a liturgy and articles of faith to describe how devotions are carried out. Even if the structure, function, and work processes of a congregation are considered God-given, the congregation can be analyzed as a social system from a number of perspectives. Structures may have been used as a means of popular enlightenment and dissemination of practical knowledge, as in the lay preacher movements in Protestant Europe.

For function, structure, and processes to contribute to optimizing the resources of the organization, all dimensions must be analyzed. Formulation of goals has been emphasized during the last few decades, as in management by objectives, where function, structure, and processes have been designed to support the objectives. The history of organizational thinking is (naturally) dominated by a deep belief in arranging functions, structures, and processes in accordance with the overall purpose of the organization. From its origin, based on long-term solutions for stable environments, both industry and government were organized for purposes and goals that were expected to last for an infinite future, within stable institutional limitations.

This perspective is seriously challenged by globalization and increasing societal complexity. The power of national government is drastically diminished by international agreements exemplified by the surrender of individual European national legislative powers into the governing bodies of the European Union (EU). And faraway events may have a drastic and fairly immediate local impact exemplified by the financial crises that started in fall 2008, whereby financial problems in U.S. real-estate markets led to collapse in the Icelandic banking system. The emergence and growth of industrial manufacturing sparked interest in the study of structures and process management as tools to create economic prosperity. Based on Adam Smith's *Division of Labor* and the classic organization theories of Taylor and Fayol, there is great confidence that efficiency and productivity are direct consequences of rational organization (Robbins & Judge, 2007).

Roughly speaking, we can see an evolution from the rational ideal model that emphasized structural factors toward an increasing understanding that interaction within and between an organization and the environment selects patterns of behavior that are not necessarily in accordance with the origin and purpose of the organization's goal. This may be a result of suboptimization, when local selecting mechanisms compete with or are opposed to the organization's overall goals or when informal communication in the organization corrupts the formal structures. These selecting processes may be for the good or bad, but they are often difficult to predict and may be seen as opposed to the possibility of making strategic or rational choices.

In the mainstream approach to organization theory, the goal of the system designer is considered a causal factor (Luthans & Kreitner, 1985), along with properties of the agents of the system (Argyris, 1985, 1990; Maslow, 1954; McGregor, 1960). As pointed out by the Nobel laureate economist Herbert Simon (1957), decision processes in organizations are subject to bounded rationality, due to both restrictions in human cognitive capacity and the results of actual interaction between the organism and the environment. Rationality in the sense of microeconomics refers to a belief that human choice behavior and the "economic man" will make optimal choices given all necessary information. In "A Behavioral Model of Rational Choice," Simon (1955) argues against the fundamental notion of "the rational man" as a foundation for microeconomics. Simon argues that this should lead us to seek satisfying solutions rather than optimal ones (March & Simon, 1958; Simon, 1957). In his 1955 article, he also argues that answers to questions about choice-making behavior may as well come from psychology as from microeconomics. He says that "psychologists have certainly been concerned with rational behavior, particularly in their interest in learning phenomena" (Simon, 1955, p. 100) but also that the distance between psychological knowledge and the needs of economy is too large to make rigorous assumptions of choice behavior.

In a similar vein, Lindblom (1959) in "The Science of 'Muddling Through'" describes what he calls anarchic or behavioral decision models. Lindblom emphasizes the limited possibilities of optimizing political decision processes when actual contingencies for decision making are taken into consideration (see Enderud, 1976). Analyzing the political processes of budgets, Lindblom suggests that the behavior of the agents involved in the process is far more influential than the political intentions originally relevant to the budget.

Both economists and organizational theorists agree that human behavior and the development in decision processes seem to be influenced not only by deliberately planned communication structures but also by the selection processes operating in more or less unpredictable ways. There has been a substantial shift from viewing organizations as relatively stable entities more or less independent of their environment to functions developing as the system interacts with an environment of which it is a part. One dimension of a system's robustness may be said to be its ability to match the complexity of its environment (Bar-Yam, 1997). Likewise, formal structures are recognized only as stylized pictures of the internal interaction. Thus, another dimension of systems robustness is the exploitation of the actual network described as going from "a chain of command to a web of influence" that manifest itself only temporarily as structures (Wheatley, 1999, p. 109).

ORGANIZATIONAL DESIGN AND SELECTION BY CONSEQUENCES

The model presented in Table 2 is meant to illustrate how functions, structures, and processes may be described from differing perspectives, depending on whether the intended properties of the system or the selectionist perspective is predominant. One dimension of the model is the continuum from a purely organizational design perspective to the selectionist perspective. The model tries to illustrate the character of (a) the functional relation to the environment, (b) the organizational structure, and (c) the working processes in the organization.

In between the two perspectives, the concepts of "bounded rationality" (Simon, 1957) and "harnessing complexity" (Axelrod & Cohen, 2000) are viewed as attempts to balance selectionist and design perspectives. These are perspectives with no explicit behavior-analytic basis. The matrix in Table 1 shows how different perspectives may have an impact on the organization as an environment favoring a restricted behavioral repertoire or an environment favoring behavioral variation. The effort to design organizations where the

TABLE 2 Dynamics of Systems from the Perspective of Selection and Design

Mechanisms	Function	Structure	Process
Selection	Complex adaptive system; "purpose" judged by the functional relation to environment	Communication patterns as emergent phenomena; scale-free (not random) networks selected by preferential attachment	Self-organizing; emergence; **process control by selection**
Bounded rationality	Hybrid organizations, like matrix organizations	Mixture of "chain of command" and "web of influence"	Exploration of new solutions combined with the exploitation of old ones
Design	Organizations, institutions; defined by intended purpose	Formal structures based on division of labor and chain of command	Production lines, standard operations; process control by correcting deviation

purposes of prediction and control have restrictions on, for example, who can communicate with whom, is more likely to constitute an aversive control regime than is an organization stimulating behavioral variation to secure the raw material for selection matching the complexity of the environment.

When analyzing the system's aggregate *function* from a selectionist perspective, it is important to recognize changes and trends in the environment with which one interacts. From this perspective, the organization is a complex adaptive system that can survive only if it matches the complexity of the environment. Variation is essential, and the functionality of the system can only be judged from its functional relation to external systems with which it interacts (e.g., other companies, cooperating sectors, markets, legislators, and public opinion).

The architecture or the *structure* of the complex adaptive system will be more like a network than a traditional organizational chart. When investigating networks as the structure of complex systems, examples of random networks, in which all nodes are equal, have not been found (Barabási, 2003). Social networks will not be random. Scale-free (as opposed to random) networks are characterized by the phenomenon of *preferential attachment*, which gives different nodes different values and positions in the network. We may say that different nodes have different reinforcing values. Some nodes are selected far more often than others, and hubs are established. A hub is a node with an extraordinary amount of links to the other nodes in the system. They are connectors:

> Connectors—nodes with an anomalously large number of links—are present in very diverse complex systems, ranging from economy to the cell. They are a fundamental property of most networks, a fact that intrigues scientists from disciplines as disparate as biology, computer science and ecology. (Barabási, 2003, p. 56)

The science of networks can help us understand how dissemination of large-scale behavior is facilitated. When it comes to the structure of an organization or the architecture of a system, what matters is if the system was designed for a purpose or has evolved by selection. A formal structure may or may not reflect the actual communication of the system. As the size of the company and the complexity increase, a complete overlap between the formal communication structure and the actual communication channels becomes progressively less likely. At the same time, formal structures may not be the most efficient channels of communication or dissemination for new behaviors.

A network is a dynamic pattern of interaction. Its topology will tell us about how frequently relations are activated, which nodes attract more attention than others, and where to find the real, not the formal, clusters of interaction (hubs). Knowledge about networks as the architecture of complex systems may be used actively in combating diseases. One example is the prevention of spreading avian flu. Instead of initiating traditional mass vaccination programs, in a network approach one would target the hubs where Asia meets the rest of the world (e.g., airports). Information on awareness of symptoms and measures for prevention of spreading the virus is visible at most international airports during periods of high risk.

The different approaches to the work *processes* maintaining the system's functionality will have different consequences for how contingencies of reinforcement are arranged. Organizational design may be intended to restrict variation and probably arrange for correction of deviation, while from a selectionist point of view, the process will resemble a shaping procedure. To put it simply, these two approaches, when compared to each other, will represent an aversive and a positive control regime, respectively. While an organizational design perspective will emphasize the division of labor, trying to match tasks and competencies for stable relations, a selectionist perspective will allow self-organizing through hubs and preferential attachment.

Recognizing the bounded rationality or rather real contingencies of administrative and political decision behavior, as well as the importance of the interactions between systems and their changing environments, we may consider organizations as complex adaptive systems. By combining structures intended to restrict variation with acceptance and encouragement for self-organizing and emergent processes, the advantages of standardization are achieved, while the systems at the same time allow innovation: balancing *exploration* of the unknown with *exploitation* of the already familiar (Axelrod & Cohen, 2000; Porter, 1980, 1985). By analyzing the actual contingencies for interaction, these relations (networks) may be used to disseminate information and innovations effectively instead of being regarded as possible sources of suboptimization or of informal power structures.

THE SELECTION OF CULTURES

Sandaker (1997) described working with Phillips Petroleum, where the differences in corporate culture between "the pioneers" and the Norwegian state oil company, Statoil, a regional competitor that developed its company based on lessons learned from the pioneers. The development of a Norwegian oil industry and the interaction between government bodies and the industry made the pioneers and Statoil more alike as time passed. For a number of reasons, the dress code at the pioneer's land-based activities went from casual/blue collar to more formal codes. Still, in one department in the company, employees collectively insisted on wearing Hawaiian shirts every Friday, demonstrating in a humorous way that the corporate culture of PPCoN had distinct properties different from other oil companies and with roots in the early period. The contingencies had changed and interaction between and within companies gradually shaped new behaviors.

A culture is defined as a complex adaptive social system possessing several observed and agreed upon characteristics prevalent and recognizable over time even though members of the system are replaced by new ones. While aware that this definition may describe a tribe, an organization, an Non Governmental Organization (NGO), or a sports team, I find it useful to define a culture as separated from the context. When working with cultures, whether they are isolated tribes in Amazonia, businesses establishing a "safety culture," NGOs running charity programs, or sport teams working with their "winner culture," we are dealing with observed, agreed upon characteristics that seem to last even though some of the members of the culture may be replaced.

Cultural changes are brought about when contingencies that change the social system are stronger than competing contingencies on an individual level. In the words of Skinner (1981),

> What is good for the individual or culture may have bad consequences for the species, as when sexual reinforcement leads to overpopulation or the reinforcing amenities of civilization to exhaustion of resources; what is good for the species or culture may be bad for the individual, as when practices designed to control procreation or preserve resources restrict individual freedom and so on. (p. 504)

Skinner (1981) introduced the selection of cultures as a third kind of selection. He identified natural selection as the first type, operant conditioning as the second, and then "a third kind of selection by consequences, the evolution of social environments and cultures. It is the effect on the group, not the reinforcing consequences for individual members, which is responsible for the evolution of cultures" (Skinner, 1981, p. 502). Behavior analysts have debated both the nature of the selection process and the necessity of extending the scope from individual behavior to the selection of cultures, organizations, and systems. Some of the topics of debates have included the role of behavioral science in the analysis of culture in terms of individual contingencies, the utility of selection and coevolution as metaphors in our discussion of cultural change (including organizational change), and the importance of units of analysis in these discussions.

The concept of the metacontingency was introduced by Sigrid S. Glenn and refined by her and collaborators in subsequent articles (Glenn, 1988, 1991, 2004; Glenn & Malott, 2004). The point of extending the functional analytical terminology of behavior analysis (interlocking behavioral contingencies stay strictly at the level of individual behavior analysis) to cultural analysis is to establish a technical language of adequate scope and precision to deal with the functions of collectives of people. This definition may be read as a definition of survival contingencies for a *system*: "Metacontingencies, then, are the contingencies of cultural selection. They give rise to organized collections of collective behavioral contingencies that constitute increasingly complex cultural-level entities" (Glenn, 2004, p. 145).

Glenn and Malott (2004) describe the metacontingencies as relations of three components. First are interlocking behavioral contingencies (IBC), where individuals or groups are mutually dependent upon each other to produce the second component: an aggregate product. This product may be concrete (e.g., automobiles) or abstract (e.g., earnings) and is selected by the third component: a receiving system. As cultural selection is argued to parallel the selection of behavior of individuals (i.e., operants), one must distinguish what is selected in cultural selection. Glenn and Malott (2004) suggest that the relations of the interlocking behavioral contingencies are what are selected. Arguing that the "aggregate product" is the only component of the metacontingencies interacting with the environment, Houmanfar and Rodrigues (2006) suggest that the "aggregate product" is the selected unit.

Many evolutionary organization theorists (e.g., Aldrich, 2006; Baum & McKelvey, 1999; Campbell 1965, 1990) and economists (e.g., Bowles, 2004; Easterly, 2007; Nelson, 2007) take selection processes in organizations and cultures for granted but do not always extend the analysis to selection of individual behavior, even if they may reasonably claim to be behavioral scientists. When they *do* consider the behavior of individuals, they do not discuss it in terms of contingencies of reinforcement or influencing behavior change by rearranging those contingencies. Behavior analysis possesses unique strengths in the potential for integrating data across selection levels and in the broad array of intervention tools that come from applied research and practice.

The systems approach in combination with a behavioral analysis perspective may contribute to the understanding of how a system of reinforcers (or interlocking behavior contingencies) constitutes a favorable environment for certain (systems of) behaviors to be selected. Thus, the systems of reinforcers are prerequisites for behaviors to be selected and hence the causal mode for cultural traits or cultural properties to be maintained. To the extent that these properties seem to fit the environment (receiving system), *both* the behaviors *and* the systems of reinforcers are selected.

SUMMARY AND CONCLUSION

In this article I have tried to pinpoint some aspects of choosing between a selectionist perspective and a traditional organizational management approach to behavior in systems. The selectionist perspective capitalizes on generic knowledge from the study of complex systems, emphasizing their functions (as opposed to their structures), and on the implications of this knowledge for influencing large-scale behaviors of individuals through channels of communication and interaction.

From a behavior-analytic position, this is good news since there is a solid body of evidence on how behavior is influenced, selected, and maintained by positive control, in contrast to aversive control and correction of deviance. It is also good news in the sense that huge challenges faced by society through globalization and growing complexity will create a demand for more knowledge of the dynamics in systems influenced by direct contact between agents and their immediate contingencies. While borders are increasingly porous, the "institutional buffers" between agents become less important. Informal communication based on "connectivity by added value" influences behavioral change more than formal structures and networks.

Capitalizing on the knowledge of systems, we may also be able to predict more remote consequences of changes in complex systems. A globalized world, the environment for real-estate businesses, stock markets, energy industry, and all kinds of enterprises may or may not favor the behavior of a specific system. Regarding society as the environment of systems and systems as contingencies of reinforcement, our locus of concern is not the stock exchange or a financial crisis in a vulnerable market. The locus of concern is the behavior evolving as a result of the behavior's interlocking contingencies. As Taleb (2007, p. 225) puts it, "Globalization creates interlocking fragility."

Giving the inspiration to expand the selectionist perspective to cultures, Skinner (1981) wrote,

> Must we wait for the selection to solve the problems of overpopulation, exhaustion of resources, pollution of the environment, and a nuclear holocaust, or can we take explicit steps to make our future more secure? In the latter case, must we not in some sense transcend selection? (p. 504)

In short, to transcend selection and to influence large-scale behavior, we should capitalize on behavior engineering. We will also need to expand the body of knowledge about complex systems, check our impulses to restrict variation, and accept that emergent phenomena are inevitable results of cultural selection.

REFERENCES

Aldrich, H. (2006). *Organizations evolving*. Thousand Oaks, CA: Sage.

American Heritage (2008). *The American heritage dictionary of the English language* (4th ed.). Retrieved April 10, 2008, from http://dictionary.reference.com/browse/design

Argyris, C. (1985). *Strategy, change and defensive routine*. Boston: Pitman.

Argyris, C. (1990). *Overcoming organizational defense: Facilitating organizational learning*. Cambridge: Cambridge University Press.

Axelrod, R., & Cohen, M. D. (2000). *Harnessing complexity*. New York: Basic Books.

Barabási, A. L. (2003). *Linked: How everything is connected to everything else and what it means for business, science, and everyday life*. New York: Plume.

Bar-Yam, Y. (1997). *Dynamics of complex systems*. Boulder, CO: Westview Press.

Baum, J. C., & McKelvey, B. (1999). *Variations in organization science. In honor of Donald T. Campbell*. Thousand Oaks, CA: Sage.

Biglan, A. (1995). *Changing cultural practices: A contextualist framework for intervention research*. Reno: Context Press.

Bowles, S. (2004). *Microeconomics: Behavior, institutions, and evolution*. Princeton, NJ: Princeton University Press.

Burns, T., & Stalker, G. M. (1961). *The management of innovation*. London: Tavistock.

Campbell, D. T. (1965). Variation and selective retention in sociocultural evolution. In H. R. Barringer, G. I. Blanksten, & R. W. Mack (Eds.), *Social change in developing areas: A reinterpretation of evolutionary theory* (pp. 19–49). Cambridge, MA: Schenkman Books.

Campbell, D. T. (1990). Levels of organization, downward causation, and the selection-theory approach to evolutionary epistemology. In G. Greenberg & E. Tobach (Eds.), *Theories of the evolution of knowing* (pp. 1–17). Philadelphia: Lawrence Erlbaum.

Chase, P. N., & Bjarnadottir, G. S. (1992). Instructing variability: Some features of a problem solving repertoire. In S. C. Hayes & L. J. Hayes (Eds.), *Understanding verbal relations* (pp. 181–193). Reno: Context Press.

Easterly, W. (2007). *The white man's burden: Why the West's efforts to aid the rest have done so much ill and so little good*. London: Penguin.

Enderud, H. (1976). *Beslutninger i organisasjoner. I adfærdsteoretisk perspektiv*. Copenhagen: Fremad.

Fayol, H. (1916). *Industrial and general administration*. Paris: Dunod.

Gharajedaghi, J. (2006). *Systems thinking. Managing chaos and complexity: A platform for designing business architecture* (2nd ed.). Amsterdam: Elsevier.

Glenn, S. S. (1988). Contingencies and metacontingencies: Toward a synthesis of behavior analysis and cultural materialism. *The Behavior Analyst, 11*, 161–169.

Glenn, S. S. (1991). Contingencies and metacontingencies: Relations among behavioral, cultural, and biological evolution. In P. A. Lamal (Ed.), *Behavioral analysis of societies and cultural practices* (pp. 39–73). New York: Hemisphere Press.

Glenn, S. S. (2004). Individual behavior, culture and social change. *The Behavior Analyst, 27*(2), 133–151.

Glenn, S. S., & Malott, M. E. (2004). Complexity and selection: Implications for organizational change. *Behavior and Social Issues, 13*, 89–106.

Hayes, L. J., Austin, J., Houmanfar, R., & Clayton, M. C. (2001). *Organizational change*. Reno: Context Press.

Houmanfar, R., & Rodrigues, N. J. (2006). The metacontingency and the behavioral contingency: Points of contact and departure. *Behavior & Social Issues, 15*, 13–30.

Houmanfar R., Rodrigues, N. J., & Smith, G. S. (2009). The role of communication networks in behavioral systems analysis. *Journal of Organizational Behavior Management, 29*(3/4), 257–275.

Hull, D. L., Langman, R., & Glenn, S. S. (2001). A general account of selection: Biology, immunology, and behavior. *The Behavioral & Brain Sciences, 24*, 511–528.

Kvendseth, S. (1988). *Funn. Historien om Ekofisk første år*. Tananger: PPCoN.

Lindblom, C. E. (1959). The science of "muddling through." *Public Administrative Review, 19*, 78–88.

Luthans, F., & Kreitner, R. (1985). *Organizational behavior modification and beyond*. Glenview, IL: Scott, Foresman & Company.

March, J., & Simon, H. (1958). *Organizations*. New York: Wiley.

Maslow, A. (1954). *Motivation and personality*. New York: HarperCollins.

Mattaini, M. A., & Thyer, B. A. (1996). *Finding solutions to social problems: Behavioral strategies for change*. Washington, DC: American Psychological Association.

McGregor, D. (1960). *The human side of enterprise*. New York: McGraw Hill.

Nelson, R. R. (2007). Universal Darwinism and evolutionary social science. *Biology and Philosophy 22*(1), 73–94.

Porter, M. (1980). *Competitive strategy*. New York: Free Press.

Porter, M. (1985). *Competitive advantage*. New York: Free Press.

Ray, R. D., & Delprato, D. J. (1989). Behavioral systems analysis: Methodological strategies and tactics. *Behavioral Science, 34*, 81–127.

Ringen, J. D. (1993). Adaptation, teleology, and selection by consequences. *Journal of the Experimental Analysis of Behavior, 60*, 3–15.

Robbins, S. P., & Judge, T. A. (2007). *Organizational behavior* (12th ed.). Englewood Cliffs, NJ: Prentice-Hall.

Rummler, G. A. A., & Brache, A. P. (1995). *Improving performance: How to manage the white space on the organization chart* (2nd ed.). San Francisco: Jossey-Bass.

Sandaker, I. (1997). *Bedriften som læringsarena. Organisasjonslæring i et komplementært perspektiv*. [The corporation as an arena for learning. Organizational learning in a complementary perspective]. Oslo: Universitetet i Oslo.

Sandaker, I. (2003). Et seleksjonsperspektiv på atferdsendring og læring i systemer [A selectionist perspective on behavioral change and learning in systems]. In

S. Eikeseth & F. Svartdal (Eds.), *Anvendt atferdsanalyse. Teori og praksis* [Applied behavior analysis. Theory and practice] (pp. 417–434). Oslo: Gyldendal Akademisk.

Senge, P. M. (1990). *The fifth discipline. The art and practice of the learning organization.* London: Random House.

Simon, H. (1955). A behavioral model of rational choice. *Quarterly Journal of Economics, 69,* 99–118.

Simon, H. (1957). *Administrative behavior* (2nd ed.). New York: Macmillan.

Sims, H. P., & Lorenzi, P. (1992). *The new leadership paradigm. Social learning and cognition in organizations.* Newbury Park, CA: Sage.

Skinner, B. F. (1981). Selection by consequences. *Science, 213,* 501–504.

System. Retrieved April, 10, 2008, from http://en.wikipedia.org/wiki/System

Taleb, N. N. (2007). *The black swan.* New York: Random House.

Taylor, F. W. (1911/1967). *Principles of scientific management.* New York: Norton.

Todorov, J. C. (2005). Laws and the complex control of behavior. *Behavior and Social Issues, 14,* 86–91.

Weber, Max. (1990). *Makt og byråkrati: essays om politikk og klasse, samfunnsforskning og verdier* [Power and bureaucracy: Essays on politics and class, social science and values]. Oslo: Gyldendal.

Wheatley, M. (1999). *Leadership and the New Science: Discovering order in a chaotic world.* San Francisco: Berrett-Koehler.

Organizational Performance
and Customer Value

DONALD TOSTI

Vanguard Consulting Inc., San Francisco, California, USA

SCOTT A. HERBST

University of Nevada, Reno, Reno, Nevada, USA

While behavior systems analysts have recognized the importance of the consumer of organizational products (i.e., receiving system) in developing models of organizational change, few have offered a systematic assessment of the relationship between consumer and organizational practices. In this article we will discuss how a behavior systems approach can be used to achieve a customer-centered organization through examples and reports from consultation cases. We begin with a performance-based model of customer value, and then consider the general behavioral characteristics of a customer-centered organization. Finally, we will present a seven-phase model of consultation aimed at aligning organizational practices with consumer values.

ORGANIZATIONAL PERFORMANCE AND CUSTOMER VALUE

Arguably one of the most important stakeholders in any business organization is the customer (Ferrell, 2004). The company provides value to customers through products and services, and the customer in turn provides value to the company through revenue. This fact provides a powerful incentive for a company to take a customer-centered view. This approach, however, stands in some contrast to traditional views of organizations. A "pure capitalist" view focuses on owners and financial stakeholders as being of primary importance, while a "pure socialist" view focuses on employees, the wage earners, as the primary organizational stakeholders (Liu, 1982). Recently, models of business combining the capitalist and socialist views of organizations have been proposed (e.g., Abernathy, 2000).

Numerous behavior analysts have discussed how principles of operant selection might be put to use at organizational or cultural levels. In distinguishing behavior systems analysis (BSA) as a field distinct from but derived partially from behavior analysis, Krapfl and Gasparotto (1982) make the case that an understanding of how the behavior of individuals interacts is required to most effectively intervene in organizations. Brethower (2000) extends this idea and notes that, in a systems analysis, it is important to understand the interests of all parties who influence the organization, including investors and consumers as well as those who do its work. Glenn and Malott (2004) provide a framework for understanding the relationships between these parties by identifying the metacontingency as the process by which certain organizational practices and outcomes (i.e., interlocking behavioral contingencies) are selected by the culture at large.

Although the scope of BSA has expanded over the years and the vocabulary has grown more sophisticated, most behavior systems analysts tend to confine their interventions within the walls of the organization, despite recognizing the importance of the broader environment that exists. That is, they do not typically include the customer in the intervention process. In this article we will discuss how a behavior systems approach can be used to achieve a customer-centered organization through examples and reports from consultation cases. We begin with a performance-based model of customer value, then consider the general behavioral characteristics of a customer-centered organization, and finally use a criterion-referenced approach to enable a company to focus on delivering the brand value it promises to customers.

A BEHAVIOR SYSTEMS VIEW OF CUSTOMER VALUE

The long-term success of any organization depends on its ability to deliver value to its clientele. Over the years, marketing professionals have developed a number of models for customer value (e.g., Allenby & Rossi, 1999; Woodruff, 1997). Generally, such models recognize the importance of functionality of a product or service, its price, and behavioral intangibles such as feelings of status, safety, and comfort (Chen & Dubinsky, 2003; Price & Arnould, 1999; Woodruff, 1997).

These models have served marketing professionals well. However, they appear to have been less successful in helping nonmarketing personnel understand what they need to do to ensure that customers actually receive the promised or expected value. The reason for this is not because marketing models of customer value are deficient, but because they are designed to serve a different purpose. Marketing professionals have traditionally been concerned with how to communicate about value (e.g., Dyson, Farr, & Hollis, 1996; Grantham, 2007); operations personnel need to know how to deliver that value.

The worth of any model lies in its usefulness. A model might be considered useful if it allows an individual to make effective decisions or take effective action. A behavior-based model for customer value offers a working model that operations personnel and customer service personnel can use to actually fulfill the promises communicated by marketing.

Customer Value: Quality Versus Cost

Customer value can be broadly defined as quality or benefits to the consumer in relation to cost. In other words, what do customers get in exchange for what they give (Woodruff, 1997)? When customers perceive that the quality of goods or services outweighs the cost, customer retention is likely to result. When cost appears to outweigh quality, customers are likely to go to competitors or even decide to do without the service or product entirely.

A key problem, of course, is how to define "quality" and "cost" in behavioral terms that help people see what they can *do* to increase the quality of goods or services while decreasing costs to the consumer. If product designers, service people, and others in the organization are to deliver maximum quality at minimum cost, they need a clear understanding of how their decisions and actions contribute to customer perceptions.

Quality Factors

We propose that there are two primary factors that contribute to customer perceptions of the quality of a product or service. The first is functional quality, which describes how well a product or service meets the customers' needs. Functional quality is present when a consumer is able to put a product to its promised use. The second is behavioral quality, which relates to how the customer feels about using or owning the product, as well as to the nature of the service experience. Things such as aesthetics, brand recognition, and customer service all influence behavioral quality. There are also two sources that contribute to customers' perspectives associated with the functional and behavioral characteristics of products. The first is the product or service itself, and the second consists of the people who provide the product or service to the customer.

The purchase of a car provides a simple example. The *perception* of "quality" (i.e., how much a customer is reinforced from the vehicle purchase) is based on both the car itself and the people involved in selling

TABLE 1 The Four Quality Factors Matrix

Contact points	Perceptions	
	Functional	Behavioral
Product	How well does it work?	Does it reinforce my behavior?
Provider	How good is their work?	Do they reinforce my behavior?

and servicing it. Both sources can contribute to or detract from the reinforc-ing perceptions of functionality. Dealership personnel who are helpful, responsive, and able to answer questions enhance the perceived reinforcing value of a car purchase. On the other hand, dealership personnel who are arrogant or unresponsive diminish the reinforcement a customer gets from driving a car that otherwise runs well, looks good, and handles beautifully.

The four quality factors (shown in Table 1) represent what goes into the "quality" side of the customer value scale and allow operations personnel to identify opportunities to add to the quality a customer perceives in their product or service. Some marketing experts refer to this division as between the functional and the experiential components of quality (Barnes, 2006).

Cost Factors

Customers' perception of cost is influenced by two factors similar to those that contribute to their perception of quality. Price is the money spent on the product or service. Effort is the difficulty of acquiring, maintaining, or using the product or service. Effort is considered to be the main behavioral component of cost. As with functionality and behavior, there are two sources of the customer's perception of price and effort: the initial acquisi-tion of the product and its ongoing maintenance and use. For example, the price of an inexpensive car may be perceived as high if it turns out to be a gas-guzzler that requires frequent repairs. Additionally, customers may be willing to go to extra effort (e.g., travel farther or spend more money) to acquire a car that is particularly comfortable and easy to drive.

The four cost factors (shown in Table 2) represent what goes into the "cost" side of the customer value scale and, like quality, are divided into

TABLE 2 The Four Cost Factors Matrix

Spending points	Cost factors	
	Price	Effort
Initial purchase	How much money does it take to buy the product or service?	How hard are they to do business with?
Ongoing use	What are the costs of maintaining and using the product or service?	How hard is it to use or maintain the product or service?

functional and behavioral components. Value is enhanced when operations personnel have an opportunity to reduce any of these perceived cost areas. For any given product or service, some factors are much more critical to creating customer value than others. However, neglecting any of them creates an opportunity for competitors to gain an edge.

Recovery

In a perfect world, customer value would be a matter of weighing what customers get against the cost and effort to acquire a product or service. In the real world, things are not as clear-cut. When problems occur, they immediately add weight to the "cost" side of the value scale. The way an organization responds to problems can increase that weight, cancel it out, or even add to the perception of quality. The term "recovery" refers to an organization's ability to respond to problems as they arise in a way that does not decrease the customer value of that product or service. Customers' perception of the value of an organization's recovery from problems is influenced by the same two factors that affect the overall perception of the product or service's quality: How well did they fix the problem, and how reinforcing was it? The former is the customer's perception of the functional value, or their judgment of how effectively the company rectified the problem. The latter concerns the customer's perception of the company's behavior in rectifying a problem and is a function of the staff that deals directly with the problem.

For example, if an airline quickly reunites an anxious customer with lost luggage, it has done a good job of fixing the problem from a functional point of view. However, if the customer is treated abruptly and made to feel like a nuisance, the result will not be reinforcing, and the customer may well choose another airline in the future.

From a behavioral view, how the company responds during recovery is something that can be controlled and treated as a source of value. Likely, you have had an experience that turned you into a lifelong, loyal customer or, alternatively, was so aversive that you vowed never to return. Indeed, the service experience has been shown to greatly affect the probability of repeat business and continued brand loyalty (Schouten, McAlexander, & Koenig, 2007).

Managing Customer Value

In looking for ways to add to customer perception of quality or reduce the perception of cost, it is critical to examine the customer's *total experience* with the product or service. This begins with the initial need and continues through its ongoing use. Customer value is more than a moment of truth; it is the culmination of a great many moments. Delighting a customer is good;

TABLE 3 Customer Value Factors: Product and Provider

	Description	Potential probes
Product		
Functional	How it works: the functional value of the product/service features to the user	The product/service met my needs; it worked the way I wanted it to work; it worked the way the company led me to expect; it performs consistently and reliably.
Behavioral	Is the customer's behavior reinforced by the experience of the product/service?	I feel I made a wise choice in purchasing the product/service; the product/service made me feel: secure/insecure, practical/impractical, in control/controlled, pampered/neglected.
Provider		
Functional	How they deliver: effectiveness of people as they provide the product/service	They did everything I needed them to do, dealt with my requests promptly, were efficient in their work, provided answers to my questions, acted as though they thought highly of the product/service.
Behavioral	Is the customer's behavior reinforced by the experience of interacting with the provider?	The people I dealt with in buying the product/service made me feel: as if my business were important, welcome, confident in their competence, that I could trust them.

however, a few disappointments can easily wipe out value unless they are addressed effectively. The most important step in managing customer value is to assess whether customers felt they received value during the service experience. This can be done by soliciting consumer feedback and should be done at all stages of the service relationship. Questions should target the four sources of customer value (product, provider, recovery, and effort) and address both the functional and behavioral aspects of these sources. Tables 3 and 4 highlight these areas and provide examples of questions that target each source of customer value. Customer responses to questions such as these provide an easy metric for assessing value and a pathway for determining which elements of the service delivery process to target for improvement. Questions can be scaled such that, even when the customer value is generally high, areas can be targeted for improvement and the organization can continuously expand and improve customer value.

CREATING A CULTURE TO DELIVER HIGH CUSTOMER VALUE

All service is experience. One critical element in the service experience is the way people who provide service conduct themselves. This has been demonstrated extensively in literature concerning customer attitudes toward salespeople. Perceived listening behavior (Ramsey & Shi, 1997), use of

TABLE 4 Customer Value Factors: Recovery and Cost, Acquisition Factors

	Description	Potential probes
Recovery		
Functional	How they deal with complaints or problems: the adequacy of the recovery action	They responded promptly; fixed the problem completely, where feasible; offered appropriate compensation; asked appropriate questions to be sure problem/complaint was understood.
Behavioral	Is the customer' s behavior reinforced during the complaint/recovery process?	The people I dealt with in resolving my complaint or problem made me feel: that they were committed to resolving it, that they empathized with me, that my satisfaction was important, that they understood the significance of the problem.
Cost, Acquisition		
Functional	Purchase price	The purchase price of the product is: expensive vs. reasonable, more vs. less than what I was willing to pay; I consider the product/service to be: a major, average, or minor investment.
Behavioral	What effort it takes to locate or access; ease of doing business with us	It was easy to find a place to buy the product/service; I could buy it quickly; it was easy to access the seller.

humor (Bergeron & Vachon, 2008), and salesperson affect (Sharma, 1999; Wood, Boles, & Babin, 2008) have all been shown to influence customers' perceptions of salespeople and their likelihood to engage in business with the provider. As such, the key to providing high value service, along with delivering functional value, lies in the way the organization and its people treat customers. Because of this, ensuring employees exhibit the "right" practices is critical. A behavior systems approach provides a powerful technology for addressing and implementing these practices.

Companies often say they are customer-focused, which presumably means that they believe their processes and their practices are aligned to maximize value to customers from their products or services. Though there has been a trend toward increasing focus on customers, many organizations are still struggling with how to turn the promise of customer focus from words to relevant actions and outcomes. Over 25 years of consulting the question most frequently asked is *"What kind of culture do we need to ensure that we can deliver the value we promise to our customers?"*

Culture has been defined behavior-analytically as "patterns of learned behavior transmitted socially as well as the products of that behavior" (Glenn, 2004). In other words, the differences between cultures can be viewed as the differences in frequency or likelihood of some behaviors over others, as well as the mechanisms in place that shape and maintain those behaviors. The challenge is to first analyze what behaviors are required to

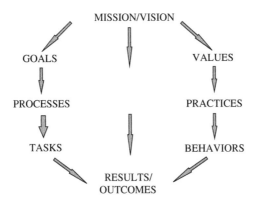

MISSION/VISION

GOALS   VALUES

PROCESSES   PRACTICES

TASKS   BEHAVIORS

RESULTS/
OUTCOMES

FIGURE 1 Our model of organizational alignment derived from behavior systems technology (Tosti & Jackson, 1994).

deliver the desired customer experience and then determine to what extent the frequency of these behaviors needs to be modified or new behaviors need to be taught. For this we use a criterion-referenced approach to cultural analysis (Tosti, 2007). This means we look first at the required outcomes and then, working backward from those outcomes, identify what processes and practices are required to achieve those results (see Figure 1). The important part of this is that all interventions and changes are driven specifically by measurable outcomes. Our analytical process has enabled us to determine the specific cultural practices that are critical to delivering high value to an organization's customers.

The Janus Effect

We have conducted this kind of analysis in a variety of industries throughout the world. One of the things we learned was that every organization has two "faces" that we must be concerned with. There is an internal face that represents how we work with each other and an external face that represents how we work with our customers. This has led us to formulate the concept of the "Janus effect." Janus was the two-faced Roman god for whom the month of January is named (facing both the old year and the new). In our work we often found that an organization's *internal face* was at odds with the desired *external face*.

Ideally an organization's internal and external faces should be congruent. That is, we should treat each other internally in the same way we want to treat our customers. It is hard for frontline people to effectively care for customers if they feel they are treated like second-class citizens by other people in the organization. Too often the result is that frontline people "give up" because they wear themselves out trying to "drag" the rest the organization along with them. How we work with our fellow employees is a critical requirement for maintaining a positive external customer face (Tosti & Stotz, 2001).

Although we have found some differences across businesses and countries, there are certain kinds of cultural practices that seem to be critical requirements for the delivery of a high-value service (Hensey, 1998; Madden, Maul, Smart, & Baker, 2007). As a result we have created an audit instrument that allows us to measure these cultural practices. This audit instrument can determine if a company is truly customer driven and if its internal culture is supportive of delivering high customer value (Tosti & Jackson, 1997). The important thing to note here is that the customer experience is based on more than their exposure to frontline people. The entire organization must "live the value promise."

CRITICAL CULTURAL PRACTICES

We have identified 36 critical cultural practices, which tend to fall into five major categories:

1. *Responsiveness to customers.* This includes keeping in close touch with customers, continuing to learn about their wants and needs, and doing things for the convenience of the customer.
2. *Trust.* A company should behave so that information, recommendations, and commitments made by the company are reliable and that everyone is treated fairly.
3. *Respect.* Taking the concerns of others seriously demonstrates a company's focus on respecting others. Employees should speak respectfully to customers, as well as their fellow employees.
4. *Commitment.* A company must persist in efforts to create and improve value while being willing to be held accountable for performance. Employees on all levels should be willing to admit when a wrong decision has been made and take the appropriate action to correct it.
5. *Personal responsibility.* Decisions should take into account not only the benefit to the business but also the needs of the customer, other corporations, and the resources available. The focus in this category is more on resolving current problems and preventing future problems than on attempting to assign blame. Decisions are based on business priorities and evidence of effectiveness, rather than on personal or political considerations.

Over the years, we have successfully implemented a number of behavioral programs using the Critical Practices Cultural Audit to better align the culture with the desired strategic results (Tosti, 2007). In our experience, engineered cultural change is more likely to take hold when people understand that the change will allow their community to better survive. Since this type of change program focuses on increasing customer value and hence customer retention, people can easily understand how it can benefit the company and themselves as a community. That provides a powerful lever to make the change happen. The cultural audit provides a basis for creating a culture representing an "internal brand." In other words, it provides a promise around how people within the company treat each other that is congruent with the company's external brand promise of value to customers. Often, we find that such a program not only increases customer value and retention but also increases employee value. As a consequence of the change, employees report that they have better working relationships and higher morale. It makes the company a better place to work.

What About Processes?

Most processes are internal and have little direct effect on customer value and, hence, revenue. You can't just improve processes and expect success, just like you can't cost-cut your way to success. A recent powerful example of this is what has happened to Motorola, one of the pioneers in process improvement and the founder of the Six Sigma quality program (see Pande, Neuman, & Cavanagh, 2000). Motorola lost $37 billion in value in only 18 months. There were many factors involved, but a majority of the loss can be attributed to Motorola losing their competitive edge in their marketplace. No doubt their investment in process improvement was valuable, but if Motorola had invested only a small additional amount to create a more customer-focused culture, things might have turned out differently.

Unfortunately, too many organizations and too many behavioral or performance professionals seemed to be fixated on process to the exclusion of other important factors, even to the point of dismissing them. Harrington (1998) notes that the failure of many process-reengineering initiatives was due to the fact that organizations often neglected to fully anticipate effects that targeting a specific process might have on other areas of the company. As such, behavior systems analysts have recognized the shortcomings of focusing squarely on processes and have worked toward developing technologies that focus on outcomes, leaving it to employees to innovate and improve in the service of those critical outcomes (e.g., Abernathy, 2001; Kaplan & Norton, 1992). Focusing on customer value and developing technologies that promote it are innovative and effective ways to avoid this pitfall.

Many organizations define service in terms of the actions of the servers. They clearly view service as a process, but from a customer's viewpoint the service experience is more like a story than a process; it has a beginning, a middle, and an end. Several organizations such as Starbucks and British Airways map out the customer experience and then work to add value along the chain of that experience (Zafar, 2008). British Airways (BA) "blueprinted" their customer experience and noted that going through immigration was part of the travel experience they did not provide. In order to add greater value, they paid for extra government immigration staff and arranged for their first- and club-class passengers to go through a fast-track lane.

How Does Internal Branding Work?

We begin with the brand. Market research is used to determine the "best" value proposition for a product or service. We then use a criterion analysis to determine the required cultural practices. We ask, "What do we have to do to deliver the promise the brand makes to our customers?"

For example, one of our clients, BA, launched its Club World business class service in the late 1980s. The company examined both the features of the service and the customer experience. Their research resulted in a brand promise of "deserved comfort"—that is, business class customers typically felt that the importance of their trip was such that they needed and deserved the comforts of business class. As a result, marketing and advertising materials were crafted to convey that promise, *and* onboard personnel were supported in delivering on the promise. BA then identified onboard behaviors that would show recognition of the importance of customers' business needs. For example, a flight attendant who noticed someone working might say, "I see you're busy . . . can I get you a cup of coffee or tea?" Behaviors like this helped convey the brand message that the airline viewed its passengers as important and was concerned about ensuring their well-being and comfort.

The success of Club World service was overwhelming. In 1 year, it made more profit than all other airlines, in all classes of service. The experience felt special and "different" to customers, and it was the way the BA staff behaved that made it different. In fact, its success quickly spawned imitators who were less successful because they missed the key ingredient. For example, one competing airline carefully copied seat pitch, decor, and meal quality but entirely failed to address staff behavior.

One key factor in this approach lies in the integration of the disciplines of marketing and organizational behavioral systems thinking. Behavioral systems analysis is a body of knowledge using results-oriented principles and methods for improving the performance of individuals, groups, and organizations (Abernathy, 2001; Brethower & Wittkopp, 1987; Malott, 2003). In the past, the marketing and BSA often operated independently, sometimes working in opposite directions. Marketing focused externally on the customer and BSA focused internally on the organization's employees. In coordinating these disciplines, the objective is to optimize the impact of marketing strategies by aligning employees with the promise the brand makes.

An organization can then use a systematic, comprehensive approach that takes into account the range of factors influencing organizational performance—with special attention to the people who must deliver the brand promise. Ensuring that the strategy, culture, and leadership of an organization are aligned is critical to internal branding efforts.

Internal Branding Process

Using a behavior systems approach, we have developed a seven-phase process for internal branding. Phase 1 is the performance analysis. Internal branding begins with research and a criterion-referenced assessment to analyze the external brand promise from an internal performance perspective. The major goals of this analysis are to clarify the brand proposition or promise of value, establish the brand character that will deliver that value and translate it into behavioral practices for the company, and analyze current practices to determine their compatibility with the brand promise.

Often the branding efforts of a company revolve around a slogan or marketing campaign. When this happens, it's not unusual to hear differing perspectives on the brand, the brand promise, and the customer value proposition from people at different organizational levels, including senior management. In one organization, senior managers resisted a promise of 100% satisfaction, which carried with it a money-back guarantee because they felt unscrupulous customers would take advantage of them. Their focus was on the short-term financial risk. They failed to consider the guarantee as a signal of a new level of service to customers that could confidently promise satisfaction. The guarantee was not about customer behavior, but rather how the company personnel must act to meet the promise of value to the customer. External marketing and advertising efforts can attract customers, but it takes an entire company working together to *keep* those customers. The more effective an organization's marketing and advertising functions, the higher its customers' expectations, and the greater the demand on the organization. The saying that "nothing kills a bad product faster than good advertising" applies equally well to branding. It's hard to keep customers if a company's delivery doesn't live up to its brand promise.

The brand character is the way the company wants customers to perceive it and its people. It is first described in terms of behaviors that characterize how the company and its personnel interact with customers while doing business. For those behaviors to become a reality, they must be understood in terms of observable practices. These are developed with input from the top and bottom of the organization using a criterion-referenced approach. This high level of organizational involvement makes it easier for management and employees to understand and buy into the brand. These values and practices become the foundation for the organization's leadership model and the senior management and midmanagement workshops held during phases 2 and 3 of the process.

Finally, the analysis evaluates current organizational practices to determine the extent to which they are aligned with, or deviate from, the required brand practices. This comparison of desired to current brand practices not only establishes the performance gap, it also provides the focal point for the next phase.

Case Example: Nissan North America

NEEDS ASSESSMENT

Nissan's position in the marketplace had eroded over a 10-year period. In part, this waning of popularity was attributed to styling problems. In addition, the organization has historically been "manufacturing driven." That is to say, a major priority was to keep the manufacturing plants in Japan working at full capacity. As a consequence, Nissan continued to turn out cars at the same rate despite the falloff in demand. In order to sell their inventory, Nissan offered large incentives (i.e., discounts and rebates). This eroded the brand position in the marketplace to such a point that by 2001, their cars sold for $2000 less than their Japanese competitors charged for equivalent models. Moreover, the dealers perceived this difference as part of the product's value—the value to the customer is the "deal we offer them is on price not the cars," as one dealer put it. In addition, customer service had seriously eroded, as evidenced by customer satisfaction surveys. In 1999 Nissan was in bad financial shape. It sold Renault an interest in the business and installed a Renault executive as CEO. The new CEO changed the orientation of the company from manufacturing driven to market driven and launched a new line of cars. The cars were newly designed, but the dealers still sold them in the same old ways. This represented a failure of internal branding. While a key process had changed, those changes did not communicate organization-wide in a way that would optimize the benefit of the change for the organization.

INTERVENTION

In the spring of 2001, we undertook a major study to determine what kinds of cultural practices were required to convey the new Nissan brand proposition of "thoughtful cars thoughtful service" to customers. We conducted a series of interviews and focus groups with over 400 employees at the sites, which included corporate headquarters in Southern California and Tokyo, regional offices in New Jersey and Texas, and 20 dealerships.

The interviews were divided into two parts. The first part was a structured interview to probe for systems information around the business and the customer, barriers to increasing or decreasing customer satisfaction, and so on. The second part of the interview was devoted to a criterion-referenced card sort where participants indicated which behavioral practice statements were critical to the delivery of the new brand proposition and how frequently such practices were demonstrated at the time.

At the dealership level, we interviewed both support and frontline people from financing, sales, customer service, and repair. The focus at the dealerships was to determine what practices would be adopted in order to deliver the brand proposition. A sort was also done with a second sample of dealership people to determine what kinds of behavioral practices their local managers must demonstrate in order to support them in those activities. We also interviewed the management of each dealership about the practices that the Nissan corporate people (in the region and at headquarters) needed to demonstrate to support the dealerships' delivery of the brand proposition.

At the regional and corporate levels, we asked them what needed to be done to support the brand proposition. We again use a criterion-referenced approach to define the critical behavioral practices. Thus, we were able to define the common priorities among the three groups and to identify which groups needed to concentrate on which values and practices. We were able to operationally define the kinds of practices to be demonstrated by employees at the dealership level, by managers at the dealership level, and at the regional and corporate levels. We then made recommendations on how these practices could be implemented throughout the organization. In essence, we defined a series of cultural practices that linked the boardroom with the showroom.

Senior Management Orientation

The second phase focuses on senior management orientation. Leaders of the organization must thoroughly understand, support, and actively demonstrate commitment to the internal branding process. Often the pressures of time and other initiatives can cause executives to give initial verbal support but then leave implementation to others. This minimal involvement and delegation of implementation is the first sign that an effort may be headed for failure, particularly when the brand promise represents a substantial behavioral change. When a previously bureaucratic organization decides that taking initiative is a key component of its brand character, lower-level managers and frontline personnel are unlikely to change until there is a visible change in leadership behavior and policies. For this reason, company executives need to be engaged in the change process as early as possible. This starts in an orientation session designed to align and educate the leadership of an organization. The orientation focuses on communicating the results of the phase 1 analysis, developing a commitment to the brand practices; establishing responsibilities for action; and examining the implications of the organization's alignment, approval, allocation, and audit decisions on the success of the process.

An example of a disconnect between current and desired brand practice is a conflict that occurred with BA. The airline's marketing and maintenance departments disputed the time required to complete aircraft maintenance. Marketing applied pressure to reduce maintenance time, because it wanted aircraft available to earn revenue. Maintenance strongly resisted the pressure, citing the need to ensure quality and safety. This conflict between the desire for quick turnaround and the need for adequate time for maintenance created exaggerated demands from both sides. The two departments ended up lying to each other in an attempt to get what they felt they needed. Only when the general brand promise relevant to trust was defined in terms of specific behavioral practices (including "we share information openly and do not mislead others") did the two departments begin to address this internal branding issue directly. Faced with the reality of their brand-destroying behavior, they jointly developed an open process to discuss their perspectives and needs. The result was an increase in aircraft availability *and* improved maintenance, which supported the airline's external brand.

The executive session, which presents the preliminary analysis and offers specific examples of disconnect (such as the BA example above), helps motivate executives to get involved. Realizing that the multimillion-dollar marketing budget is creating an expectation they may not be able to meet, at least not completely, captures the attention of most senior executives.

Middle Management Involvement

The third phase involves the middle managers that lead the internal branding initiative. Top executives need to be actively involved and visibly demonstrate support, but midmanagement provides the day-to-day leadership. It is critical to thoroughly educate, involve, and support this pivotal group. This phase includes three primary activities: preworkshop preparation, workshop participation, and follow-up planning activities, including a review of feedback with direct reports.

These workshops are positioned as working sessions and business meetings as opposed to training. They focus midmanagers on the behaviors necessary to support delivery of the brand promise. The sessions cover the basics of branding, internal branding, and the specifics of the company's own brand. They also include experiential activities that use feedback about the attendees' individual brand behaviors to help them pinpoint behaviors hindering their delivery of the brand promise. This feedback is a key component of the program because it highlights both strong and weak behaviors for each participant in relation to personal averages across all practices. There are no comparisons against others or against a standard. The feedback is exclusively for the recipients' own development; it is never used to evaluate them. This use eliminates recipients' concerns about any impact their feedback may have on their careers or compensation.

The session concludes with each participant drafting a "brand plan" for his or her area of responsibility. Often session members maintain contact later to support and advise each other. These meetings help managers develop working relationships that can develop into valuable sources of feedback and support. At one bank that participated in this workshop, managers historically did not discuss leadership practices and management behavior, and they neither sought nor were receptive to feedback from their peers. The sessions gave them a process and organizational permission to engage each other in constructive feedback. This was a major cultural breakthrough, particularly because it crossed functional boundaries, leading to more effective working relationships.

Communicating Value Proposition

Communicating the value proposition to all employees, not just the managers, is the objective of phase 4. Once management is engaged in the internal branding process and is prepared to support it, employees can start to be enrolled. The use of the term "enroll" is deliberate. It is not enough to educate or involve employees; they must understand how the process affects them and voluntarily enroll. Often information and materials are simply "dumped" on employees, with the expectation that if they are told what is happening and what they need to do, they will do it. This seldom succeeds, for several reasons. First, the context for the change is seldom fully or adequately explained. Second, employees do not have an opportunity to raise their questions. Finally, there is no opportunity to experience the change rather than just hear about it.

During an internal brand launch, employees are typically involved in an all-day session that provides an introduction, explanation, and multiple experiences that personify the core brand values. Only by experiencing the brand firsthand can employees understand its true purpose. One bank built two large brand experience venues in vacant warehouses for its employee activity. These venues were completely staged around the bank's brand and its six brand values. Each day 100 employees were scheduled for small group sessions where each value was described and experienced. At the end of the day, employees not only understood the brand but also could describe the customer experience in their own terms. More important, they reported that they were excited about making sure the brand experience was delivered.

Tactical Planning Sessions

The majority of the employees will still be uncertain of what they have to do to change. They must still receive feedback on their new behaviors. Phase 5 consists of tactical planning sessions, where feedback is routinely provided and discussed. These sessions link midmanagers with their supervisors. First, participants learn about the process and the company's marketing strategy. Next, they review feedback on their group's brand behavior and establish how to better align themselves with the brand practices.

Feedback is the key for changing the existing cultural practices in a work group. Change is not easy because these practices are often part of the group's long-standing routine. Once these existing practices are compared to the desired brand behavior and are openly discussed and confronted, they can be recognized as problematic.

Other key issues are the cultural practices between groups that may inhibit delivery of brand value. In one marketing services company, sales and operations personnel were asked to describe the behaviors of the other group as well as their own. Operations employees were quick to point out that the sales force often promised more than operations could actually deliver. Sales force personnel complained the operations group did not fully provide what clients expected. The gap identified the need for improved communication between the two groups. Often these cross-functional practices are the most fertile area for identifying and eliminating destructive brand practices.

Employee Action

Phase 6 is concerned with employees' direct planning and implementation of brand alignment. The old military saying that "generals make the decisions but sergeants run the army" applies to business organizations as well. Unless supervisors see that changing the culture is their responsibility, little change will happen. To aid them, supervisors are supported in working with their teams to develop specific ways to support the brand proposition at the local level and link these efforts to meeting business needs. This translates the analysis, learning, and process into direct action that employees can take. Frontline teams identify what practices they need to keep or increase and which ones to eliminate. Then they implement their plan.

The direct enrollment of employees through the brand experience, ongoing feedback, and planning activities is a critical component of the process. In service industries, employees directly create and deliver the experience to the customer, so it is imperative to align them with the brand promise. Too often the investment of time and resources in the employee enrollment process is omitted or minimally funded.

A real-estate management company understood the need for making this investment. They implemented follow-up employee meetings at their local community offices and added new corporate logo clothing for their rental and maintenance staff in order to signal the change and its importance. Included in the meeting agenda were materials to record the individual's personal plan to support the brand. Follow-up sessions and feedback reinforced individual behavior critically important to this effort.

Maintenance

The last phase can be considered a maintenance phase. The intention of this phase is to support, assess, and review the ongoing application of the cultural change process. Internal branding needs ongoing attention in order to continue to have a lasting impact on results. As people begin to implement the brand values and behaviors, supervisors and employees will identify inhibitors in the workplace. Generally, removing these obstacles requires resources and management approval. If management is unresponsive, the process will begin to falter. It's also important to periodically assess an internal branding effort and systematically evaluate programs and actions resulting from brand plan implementation.

MOVING FORWARD

We know that there are two major categories of consequences commonly used to impact behavior in the workplace: incentives (Stajkovic & Luthans, 2001; Yukl & Latham, 1975; Yukl, Latham, & Pursell, 1976) and feedback (Alvero, Bucklin, & Austin, 2001; Pampino, MacDonald, Mullin, & Wilder, 2003; Tittleback, Fields & Alvero, 2008). Incentive systems can be powerful but can be difficult to implement effectively. Either behaviors may be difficult to quantify or the wrong behaviors might be inadvertently targeted for incentive (Lawler, 1990). Branding practices are more subjective, but those who observe the performers, like peers and reporters, can evaluate and provide appropriate feedback to individuals and groups.

Creating a customer focus by concentrating on cultural practices and taking a systemic approach to implementation is practical. This process is not a "quick fix," however. It takes planning, commitment, resources, and time—all precious commodities in any organization. However, the significant investment made by marketing to create the brand promise, along with the threat from competitors, makes the work that goes into the process worthwhile. For example, we undertook this process with a property management company. Through our intervention, this large company was able to reduce move-outs by 6% and increase "re-buy" (i.e., when a person relocates yet continues as a client in the new city) by 12% over a 6-month period. These changes resulted in an estimated $123,000 difference in revenue over that period.

To conclude, at their most fundamental level, all organizations are behavioral systems. They are founded and run by people for the sole purpose of delivering value to people. As such, the owners, employees, and the business consumers all have a stake in the organization. A successful organization is able to deliver on a promise to its consumer stakeholders. Traditionally, behavior systems analysts have developed their consultation models from the principle of environmental selection (e.g., Glenn & Malott, 2004). However, while these models recognize the need for the organization to adjust to environment, they do not often include technology that offers systematic assessment associated with the demands of that environment. In this article we have argued that organizations will meet the needs of the consumer more effectively when organizational processes reflect and are aligned at all levels with customer value. In taking a whole systems approach to these efforts, an organization is able to identify what the consumer values, both in terms of functional and behavioral characteristics, and then implement processes and practices that are aligned with those values. In integrating behavioral principles into these interventions, the behavior systems analyst is able to ensure successful implementation and maintenance.

REFERENCES

Abernathy, W. B. (2000). *Managing without supervising.* Memphis, TN: PerfSys Press.

Abernathy, W. B. (2001). An analysis of the results and structure of 12 organizations' performance scorecard and incentive pay systems. In L. J. Hayes, J. Austin, R. Houmanfar, & M. C. Clayton (Eds.), *Organizational change* (pp. 240–272). Reno: Context Press.

Allenby, G. & Rossi, P. (1999). Marketing models of consumer heterogeneity. *Journal of Econometrics, 89,* 57–78.

Alvero, A. M., Bucklin, B. R., & Austin, J. (2001). An objective review of the effectiveness and essential characteristics of performance feedback in organizational settings. *Journal of Organizational Behavior Management, 21*(1), 3–29.

Barnes, J. (2006). *Build your customer strategy.* Hoboken, NJ: John Wiley & Sons.

Bergeron, J., & Vachon, M. (2008). The effects of humour usage by finnanical advisors in sales encounters. *International Journal of Bank Marketing, 26,* 376–398.

Brethower, D., & Wittkopp, C. J. (1987). Performance engineering: SPC and the total performance system. *Journal of Organizational Behavior Management, 9*(1), 83–103.

Brethower, D. (2000). Integrating theory, research and practice in human performance technology. *Performance Improvement, 39*(4), 33–43.

Chen, Z., & Dubinsky, A. J. (2003). A conceptual model of perceived customer value in e-commerce: A preliminary investigation. *Psychology & Marketing, 20,* 323–347.

Dyson, P., Farr, A., & Hollis, N. S. (1996). Understanding, measuring, and using brand equity. *Journal of Advertising Research, 36*(6), 9–21.

Ferrell, O. C. (2004). Business ethics and customer stakeholders. *Academy of Management Executive, 18,* 126–129.

Glenn, S. S. (2004). Individual behavior, culture, and social change. *The Behavior Analyst, 27,* 133–151.

Glenn, S. S., & Malott, M. (2004). Complexity and selection: Implications for organizational change. *Behavior and Social Issues, 13*(2), 89–106.

Grantham, S. (2007). But what do they really think? Identifying consumers' values relevant to adopting biotechnologically produced foods. *Journal of Public Affairs, 7,* 372–382.

Harrington, H. J. (1998). Performance improvement: The rise and fall of reengineering. *The TQM Magazine, 10*(2), 69–71.

Hensey, M. (1998). Essential customer service elements. *Journal of Management Engineering, 14*(4), 12–13.

Kaplan, R., & Norton, D. (1992). The balanced scorecard: Measures that drive performance. *The Harvard Business Review, 70*(1), 71–79.

Krapfl, J. E., & Gasparotto, G. (1982). Behavioral systems analysis. In L. W. Frederiksen (Ed.), *Handbook of organizational behavior management* (pp. 21–38). New York: Wiley.

Lawler, E. E. (1990). *Strategic pay.* San Francisco: Jossey-Bass.

Liu, C. (1982). Managerial objectives and equilibrium outputs in the socialist firm. *Journal of Comparative Economics, 6,* 204–212.

Madden, H., Maul, R., Smart, A., & Baker, P. (2007). Customer satisfaction and service quality in UK financial services. *International Journal of Operations and Production Management, 27,* 998–1019.

Malott, M. E. (2003). *Paradox of organizational change: Engineering organizations with behavioral systems analysis.* Reno: Context Press.

Pampino, R. N., MacDonald, J. E., Mullin, J. E., & Wilder, D. A. (2003). Weekly feedback vs. daily feedback: An application in retail. *Journal of Organizational Behavior Management, 23*(2–3), 21–43.

Pande, P. S., Neuman, R. P., & Cavanagh, R. R. (2000). *The Six Sigma way: how GE, Motorola, and other top companies are honing their performance.* New York: McGraw-Hill.

Price, L. L., & Arnould, E. J. (1999). Commercial friendships: Service provider–client relationships in context. *Journal of Marketing, 63,* 38–56.

Ramsey, R., & Sohi, R. (1997). Listening to your customers: the impact of perceived salesperson listening behavior on relationship outcomes. *Journal of the Academy of Marketing Science, 25,* 127–137.

Schouten, J. W., McAlexander, J. H., & Koenig, H. F. (2007). Transcendent customer experience and brand community. *Journal of the Academy of Marketing Science, 35,* 357–368.

Sharma, A. (1999). Does the salesperson like customers? A conceptual and empirical examination of the persuasive effect of perceptions of the salesperson's affect toward customers. *Psychology & Marketing, 16,* 141–162.

Stajkovic, A. D., & Luthans, F. (2001). Differential effects of incentive motivators on work performance. *Academy of Management Journal, 44,* 580–590.

Tittleback, D., Fields, L., & Alvero, A. M. (2008). Effects of performance feedback on typing speed and accuracy. *Journal of Organizational Behavior Management, 27*(4), 29–52.

Tosti, D. (2007). Aligning the culture and strategy for success. *Performance Improvement, 46*(1), 21–25

Tosti, D., & Jackson, S. (1994). Organizational alignment: What it is and why it matters. *Training, 31*(4), 58–63.

Tosti, D., & Jackson, S. (1997). *Customer value assessment.* Sausalito, CA: Persona Global.

Tosti, D., & Stotz, R. (2001). Building the brand from the inside out. *Marketing Management, 10*(2), 27–33.

Wood, J. A., Boles, J. S., & Babin, B. J. (2008). The formation of buyer's trust of the seller in an initial sales encounter. *Journal of Marketing Theory and Practice, 16,* 27–39.

Woodruff, R. B. (1997). Customer value: The next source for competitive advantage. *Journal of the Academy of Marketing Science, 25,* 135–153.

Yukl, G. A., & Latham, G. P. (1975). Consequences of reinforcement schedules and incentive magnitudes for employee performance: Problems encountered in an industrial setting. *Journal of Applied Psychology, 60,* 294–298.

Yukl, G. A., Latham, G. P., & Pursell, E. D. (1976). The effectiveness of performance incentives under continuous and variable ratio schedules of reinforcement. *Personnel Psychology, 29,* 221–231.

Zafar N. (2008, May). *Indicadores De Experiencia Del Cliente Con Base En Evidencias.* Paper presented a the meeting of Customer Relation Management and Customer Experience Management, Bogota, Columbia.

A Behavioral Systems Analysis of Behavior Analysis as a Scientific System

LINDA J. HAYES, ERICK M. DUBUQUE, MITCH J. FRYLING,
and JOSHUA K. PRITCHARD

University of Nevada, Reno, Reno, Nevada, USA

Behavioral systems analyses typically address organizational problems in business and industry. However, to the extent that a behavioral system is an entity comprised of interdependent elements formed by individuals interacting toward a common goal, a scientific enterprise constitutes a behavioral system to which a behavioral systems analysis may apply. This article outlines the characteristics of behavior analysis as a scientific system, such that it may be conceptualized and evaluated by way of a behavioral systems analysis. Our aim in subjecting this enterprise to a behavioral systems analysis is to achieve a furtherance of its mission. In pursuit of this aim, we suggest actions that behavior analysis might take to increase its share of the psychological market, sustain its veracity, and assure its long-term success.

BEHAVIORAL SYSTEMS ANALYSIS OF BEHAVIOR ANALYSIS AS A SCIENTIFIC SYSTEM

The concepts and methods of behavioral systems analysis are typically applied to business or industry, where the mission of each entity is to increase its share of the market for products of the sort it produces (Brethower, 1982; 1999; 2000; Rummler 2001; Rummler & Brache, 1995; Malott, 2003). Although the products of such entities may be material or service, applications of behavioral systems analysis to material-producing organizations of the industrial sector tend to be favored. Accounting for this discrepancy is the ease with which the constitutional properties of material products may be articulated compared to those of the service variety. Added to this is a difference in the manner by which quality standards are established and upheld across these two types of products. The quality of a material product is a matter of invariance in its constitutional properties. This is to say, the constitutional and quality standards for material products amount to the same thing. By contrast, the quality standards for service products are at least partially determined by their outcomes, whereby the quality of such products cannot be evaluated by an assessment of their constitutional properties alone.

The applicability of a behavioral systems analysis is further challenged when the products of an organization, regardless of their type, are inherently unstable. Such is the case of the products of a scientific entity, where a factor of novelty is entailed by definition (Skinner, 1953). "If a scientific enterprise is successful, something new emerges, something, moreover, frequently incompatible with previous conditions" (Kantor, 1953, p. 7). To put it another way, the quality of scientific products is measured in the degree to which their constitutional properties have been modified from earlier forms. For this reason, some difficulty may be anticipated in the application of a behavioral systems analysis to entities of this sort.

Nonetheless, inasmuch as a behavioral system is an entity comprised of interdependent elements formed by individuals interacting toward a common goal (Malott, 2003), a scientific enterprise constitutes a behavioral system. A behavioral systems analysis is thus presumably applicable to a scientific entity. Accordingly, our plan is to conduct a behavioral systems analysis of the enterprise of behavior analysis. Our aim in subjecting this enterprise to a behavioral systems analysis, as is the aim whenever such an analysis is made, is to achieve a furtherance of its mission.

Our first step in pursuit of this aim will be to characterize the enterprise of behavior analysis as a behavioral system of the scientific variety. The competitive advantages of behavior analysis in the psychological knowledge market, as well as its vulnerabilities in this regard, will be addressed along the way. Having made this assessment, we will suggest some actions that the enterprise of behavior analysis might take to increase its market share, sustain its veracity, and assure its long-term success.

THE MISSION OF SCIENCE

In keeping with the model of analysis characteristic of behavioral systems analyses, we may begin by identifying the mission of behavior analysis as a scientific enterprise. In this regard, we suggest that all scientific enterprises are engaged in the study of relationships of one sort or another, and all are aimed at improving our orientation with respect to those relationships, both autonomously as well as in conjunction with the relational phenomena under study in other enterprises. As the term is used here, being oriented with respect to things and events means being able to characterize their constitutional and relational properties, the implication being that the better oriented one becomes, the more fully are those properties able to be characterized. It is further assumed that the better one knows a thing, the more effective may be one's actions with respect to it, including such actions as predicting and controlling its occurrences.

The Mission of Behavior Analysis

The relationships with which behavior analysis is specifically concerned are those obtaining between the responding of individual organisms and the stimulating of environing things and events. The mission of behavior analysis, therefore, is to achieve an ever-improved orientation to relationships of this type, including their interactions with relational phenomena of other types. It is upon adequate orientation to such events that their occurrences may be predicted and controlled.

The mission of behavior analysis is not fully articulated in this statement, however. Behavior analysis operates in conjunction with a number of other systems having a common goal. While the products of behavior analysis make a unique contribution to the achievement of this goal, they do not do so independently of the products of the other systems involved. Their value in this regard is a matter of their alignment with the products of these other systems. As such, the relationship of behavior analysis to these other systems must be further clarified before its special role in this endeavor, this is to say, its mission, may be fully articulated. A more refined statement of the mission of behavior analysis will be provided upon examination of these issues, to which we now turn.

THE MACROSYSTEM OF THE SCIENCES

Like other behavioral systems, behavior analysis operates within a larger systemic collectivity or macrosystem (Malott, 2003), the nature of which must be taken into consideration if its operations are to succeed. The macrosystem to which behavior analysis belongs is the scientific domain, and one means of revealing its nature is to examine the enterprises contained within it. Toward this end, we suggest that scientific enterprises embody particular characteristics that permit them to be distinguished from human enterprises of other sorts.

One of these characteristics is an element of discovery or novelty, as previously mentioned (Kantor, 1953; Skinner, 1953). The other is a seriousness of purpose (Kantor, 1953). This is to say that the sciences are consequential enterprises, their products affording more effective orientation (Kantor, 1953) or successful action (Skinner, 1957) with respect to the things and events investigated.

This is not to say that neither of these features are present in human enterprises of other sorts. For instance, a seriousness of purpose is characteristic of technology, and an element of novelty is present in the arts. Still, the arts are not consequential enterprises as herein defined, and discovery is neither the aim nor the usual outcome of the utilization of technology. Enterprises of these sorts may be distinguished from those in which both an element of novelty and a seriousness of purpose are present, though, and it is enterprises of the latter sort that are housed within the scientific domain.

These characteristics of the enterprises comprising the scientific domain are engendered by other commonalities among them. Specifically, all such enterprises operate in accord with roughly the same set of general propositions or metapostulates concerning the kinds of things and events upon which their operations are performed and the nature of those operations. For example, all scientists adhere to the proposition that the things and events upon which they operate are aspects of the natural world, the most fundamental of those operations being observation. This "limitation" is imposed by the seriousness-of-purpose criterion upon which their classification as enterprises of the scientific type depends. To put it another way, to become better oriented with respect to particular things or events, as implied by the seriousness-of-purpose criterion, it must be possible to confront them, and it is only when things and events are situated in space-time that it is possible to do so. Kantor's (1958) adherence to this proposition is stated as follows: "No scientific problem is concerned with a 'Reality' beyond events and their investigation" (p. 64).

The adherence of scientists to this proposition is often overlooked by nonscientists. For example, it is sometimes argued that the God problem remains unsolved on the grounds that science can neither prove nor disprove the existence of God. From a scientific perspective, however, there is no God problem to solve. All such problems pit verbally constructed realities, having their sources in cultural tradition, against confrontable things and events. To reiterate, no scientific problem is concerned with such realities.

Likewise, all scientific enterprises adhere to similar propositions pertaining to the sources from which the products of scientific work are derived. The nature and logic of these propositions may be illustrated in an examination of their implications for scientific products of especially high value, among which are verified laws and theories (Kantor, 1953, p. 25). Inasmuch as products of these sorts are descriptive of the constitutional, developmental, relational, and other properties of things and events of the natural world, derived from direct or indirect observational contacts with them, it is generally agreed that their expressions should exclude references to entities and processes not found among the things and events investigated.

This "limitation" is imposed by the novelty or discovery criterion upon which enterprises of the scientific type are identified. By way of explanation, there are only two sources from which products of these types may be derived, namely, the matrix of things and events comprising the natural world, and the accumulation of nonscientific understandings comprising the intellectual traditions of the culture. Hence, when theories and laws contain references to entities and processes not found among the things and events investigated, it must be assumed that the source from which they are drawn is cultural tradition, which, by definition, is anything but novel (Kantor, 1953).

For example, a theory of action making reference to the psychic powers of a transcendent mind is not a theory derived from the investigation of action as an aspect of the natural world; rather, it is one constructed in accord with cultural tradition. The same holds for a theory of memory making reference to storage or a theory of imagining making reference to internal representations, as for countless other historical as well as contemporary theories.

In addition to limiting the source from which authentic scientific products may be derived to things and events investigated, satisfaction of the novelty or discovery criterion, by which enterprises of the scientific domain are identified, requires agreement among such enterprises as to the temporary status of their products. New understandings of phenomena arise from their investigation, and subsequent investigations of those phenomena give rise to newer understandings still. This is to say, the products of scientific enterprises are corrigible and cumulative. To presume otherwise, as when the products of science are deemed absolute, ultimate, or final, overlooks the source from which they are legitimately drawn and actual activities by which they are achieved.

Moreover, given that the sciences are distinguished from enterprises of the technological sort by their embodiment of an element of novelty, failing to appreciate the temporary status of scientific products affords enterprises of the latter sort membership in the scientific domain. To the extent that the achievement of an enterprise's mission depends on the congruence of its aims and operations with those of the macrosystem within which it operates, ambiguity as to the nature of the latter is ill-advised. We contend, therefore, that for the sciences to achieve their missions, the temporary status of their products must be acknowledged.

To reiterate, it is only when the products of an enterprise are derived from observations of things and events, absent impositions upon them from nonscientific cultural sources (Kantor, 1953), that they entail the element of novelty or discovery that is characteristic of the enterprises comprising the scientific domain.

The Macrosystem of Behavior Analysis

We have identified the propositional foundations of enterprises exhibiting both a seriousness of purpose and an element of novelty or discovery. Inasmuch as products of these sorts do not arise from other sets of propositions, we may, for the moment, consider these foundations to constitute the processing system for enterprises of this type. Further, while we have yet to identify the receiving system for these products, for the moment we may take it to be the culture at large. With these admittedly preliminary descriptions of the relevant processing and receiving systems at hand, we may identify the macrosystem to which behavior analysis belongs, namely the scientific domain, as that collectivity of enterprises in which observational contacts with things and events of the natural world give rise to new and more effective interactions with those things and events. Implied by the concept of effectuality in this statement is the satisfaction of the culture's needs for products of this type.

As was the case of our attempt to identify the mission of behavior analysis, a more precise definition of the macrosystem to which this enterprise belongs awaits further analysis. We turn, then, to these considerations.

THE PRODUCTS OF SCIENCE

It is conventional to characterize the products of scientific enterprises as materials of information or knowledge, such as the records of specific investigations and more comprehensive treatises, which comprise the library of science. Undoubtedly, materials of this sort are products of such enterprises. However, they do not comprise the totality of such products. Also included are definitions, postulates, instruments, apparatuses, methods, and techniques, among many other items. It is therefore not useful to characterize all of the many and different products of scientific enterprises collectively as "materials of knowledge."

The products of scientific enterprises resist identification for another reason as well. Unlike the products of nonscientific enterprises, which undergo periodic modification in response to systemic feedback, the products of scientific enterprises are inherently unstable. This is the case because their corrigibility does not arise from systemic feedback alone. It is also a function of the cumulative nature of scientific enterprises.

Still, a scientific enterprise is not subject to a behavioral systems analysis until the products of such enterprises are identified, and one means of doing so is to consider them in relation to their consumers. Products of different sorts are consumed by different groups, in other words. Moreover, unless the products of science are identified and differentiated in terms of their relevant receiving systems, the feedback to which their changes are at least partially attributable, in not being properly circumscribed, will not be maximally effective.

Hence, we suggest that the products of any given scientific enterprise are of at least three sorts, namely, those consumed by members of its own community, those consumed by members of other scientific communities, and those consumed by nonscientists, be they members of the culture at large or of its more specific segments.

Products of Behavior Analysis Consumed by Behavior Analysts

The products of a scientific enterprise that are of particular relevance to members of its own community are those pertaining to the characterization of its unique subject matter. As discussed above, all sciences are engaged in the study of relationships of one sort or another. The relationships with which behavior analysis is specifically concerned are those obtaining between the responding of individual organisms and the stimulating of environing things and events. The products of behavior analysis consumed by members of its own scientific community, thereby, are characterizations of relations of this type, including such items as the conditions under which they arise, actualize, develop, change and dissolve. Products of this sort, otherwise known as laws and principles, in having been abstracted from observations of the events comprising the unique subject matter of a particular scientific enterprise and are therefore descriptive of those events alone, are of interest only to those engaged in that enterprise. The principle of reinforcement is a case in point: the only consumers of this product of the enterprise of behavior analysis are behavior analysts.

Before relations can be characterized, the factors involved in those relations must be identified. The products of identifying operations with respect to these factors are definitions; and inasmuch as the factors involved in the relations characterized by different sciences are different, these definitions are of interest only to those for whom the factors so defined are relevant. For example, how stimuli and responses are defined in the enterprise of behavior analysis is of no concern to anyone but behavior analysts. In short, subject matter definitions comprise another class of products for which scientists' own communities constitute the relevant receiving system. Added to these are formal assumptions or propositions relevant to particular subject matters. Constructions of these sorts are representative of the types of products that are particularly relevant to the scientific community responsible for their production.

Products of Behavior Analysis Consumed by Other Scientific Communities

The products of a scientific enterprise consumed by members of other scientific communities operating within the same macrosystem are of a different sort.

The latter may be distinguished by their applicability to circumstances beyond those under which they were originally developed. For example, mathematical formulations developed with respect to the relational events under investigation in one science may be applicable to the relationships investigated in another. Other such items include techniques, methods, apparatuses, and instruments.

Products of Behavior Analysis Consumed by Nonscientists

The products of scientific enterprises may also be relevant to the nonscientific community. Generally speaking, though, the products consumed by nonscientists differ from those consumed by scientists. By way of explanation, scientific products must be verified in nonscientific circumstances prior to their consumption by nonscientists, and what emerges out of this process are not the original products but rather derivations of them adapted to the exigencies of ordinary living. For example, fixed procedures are derived from conditional principles.

More to the point, as previously discussed, the products of science are corrigible, a characteristic that is only partially attributable to systemic feedback. As predicated by the cumulative nature of scientific enterprises, their modifications also arise from their prior configurations. The products of science have, as such, a temporary character that is not fully realized in their derivations, and inasmuch as scientific products are defined by this characteristic, we contend that the products consumed by nonscientists are something other than those consumed by scientists. The derivations consumed by nonscientists are static technologies. In the case of behavior analysis, these are technologies by which relations between behavior and stimuli may be changed in one way or another.

THE PROCESSING SYSTEM

Because the elements of a behavioral systems analysis are interrelated, individual elements are able to be identified only by reference to the other elements involved in the analysis. Hence, in our initial attempt to identify the macrosystem to which scientific enterprises belong, it was necessary to formulate a preliminary description of the processing system for enterprises of this sort. We reasoned that the propositional foundations of enterprises exhibiting both a seriousness of purpose and an element of novelty could be conceptualized as the processing system of such enterprises on the grounds that products of these sort did not arise from other sets of propositions. A more refined description of the processing systems of scientific enterprises is called for at this point.

In the context of a behavioral systems analysis, the processing system may be understood as the set of operations through which resources are turned into products (Malott, 2003). Having already identified the products of science, we may focus on the resources upon which this system operates in the sciences. Included among these resources are societal circumstances favorable to scientific work, the accumulated products of that work, scientists familiar with those products, and the whole of nature. Of these, only favorable societal circumstances and knowledgeable scientists are worthy of further scrutiny. However, given that their scrutiny would require detailed analyses of relevant component systems, a better understanding of the processing systems of scientific enterprises may be able to be achieved by examining the actual operations of these systems rather than the resources upon which they operate.

Toward this end, we may begin by acknowledging the fact that scientific enterprises are exceedingly complex entities. They are at once comprehensive scientific systems and collections more specifically focused subsystems. The primary subsystems of scientific enterprises are centered on particular phases of scientific activity, namely, those of investigation, interpretation, and application. Taken together, they comprise the processing systems of scientific enterprises.

The relationships between these more specifically focused subsystems and the comprehensive scientific systems in which they are embedded are relations of part to whole, wherein it is implied that the subsystems of given scientific enterprises are connected by shared features. Their shared features are not commonalities of practice, outcome, or aim, though. Investigative, interpretive, and applied subsystems differ in these respects, and these differences prevail regardless of the comprehensive system to which they belong. Instead, their shared features pertain to the types of events upon which the comprehensive system is focused and that further distinguish it from other scientific enterprises. More specifically, shared across the subsystems of a comprehensive scientific system is an adherence to a common set of definitions and postulates pertaining to a particular subject matter.

Further clarity as to the character of the processing system might be achieved were it possible to categorize the products of scientific enterprises on the basis of their relations to distinguishable components of this system. However, the products of each of the three primary components of the processing system of a scientific enterprise, namely, its investigative, interpretive, and applied subsystems, are meaningful only in relation to the products of the other components. For that reason, if the character of the processing system is to be clarified by a description of its outcomes, the latter are best articulated in somewhat general terms. Accordingly, we suggest that the processing system of a scientific enterprise may be conceptualized as a set of interrelated operations that are such as to render the enterprise capable of pursuing its mission, a capacity assured by qualities of validity and significance. As understood in this context, the validity of a scientific enterprise is a matter of internal consistency or coherence, while significance is a matter of its congruence with other members of its macrosystem (Kantor, 1958). The notion that a scientific enterprise, by virtue of its validity and significance, has the capacity to pursue its mission raises the issue of progress in science. To be clear, we are not suggesting that the eventual outcome of mission pursuit is mission accomplishment. On the contrary, the missions of scientific enterprises, namely, ever-improved orientation to relationships of particular types, are not of the sort that can ever be accomplished. In other words, the products of science have temporary status. For that reason, progress in science is productivity, and the productivity of a scientific enterprise is enabled by its validity and significance. We turn now to the processes by which these characteristics of scientific enterprises are assured.

As stated above, the relationships between the more specifically focused subsystems of scientific enterprises and the comprehensive scientific systems in which they are embedded are relations of part to whole, and when the nature of these relations is recognized as such, common ground among the subsystems of a comprehensive scientific system is assured. This is not a trivial matter. Quite the contrary, it is this commonality among the subsystems of a scientific enterprise that make the products of the work undertaken in any one subsystem relevant to the aims of any other. At stake in the absence of coordination of this sort is the validity of the comprehensive system.

Operations Assuring the Validity of Scientific Enterprises

COORDINATION OF THE INVESTIGATIVE AND APPLIED SUBSYSTEMS

When the investigative and applied subsystems of a scientific enterprise become disconnected, neither is capable of achieving its objectives. For the products of investigative subsystems to have value in the context of their comprehensive scientific systems, they must be subjected to verification; and the operations by which they are verified, along with the products of those operations, constitute the applied subsystems' primary contributions to scientific enterprises (Kantor, 1958).

Added to this, the operations and products of applied subsystems give rise to technologies pertinent to various domains of human activity, and ill-informed applied subsystems give rise to mundane practices of these sorts. This is the case because the only source other than the verified products of scientific investigation from which these technologies may be derived is cultural tradition or common sense. Practices derived from this source are mundane. They may also be inept. Inasmuch as cultural support for science is owing to efficacy of the technologies spawned by it, the unqualified inter-mixture of these technologies with inept practices derived from cultural sources put the support for science at risk. Fostering the integration of the investigative and applied subsystems of our science is the best defense against this threat.

COORDINATION OF THE INVESTIGATIVE AND INTERPRETIVE SUBSYSTEMS

Equally important for the validity of a scientific enterprise is the relationship between the system's investigative and interpretive subsystems. This is the case because interpretative operations are performed on the products of investigation. More specifically, investigative operations, such as observation and experimentation, are performed with respect to the things and events of the natural world comprising the subject matters of their comprehensive scientific systems. Among the products of investigative operations are descriptions of those things and events as well as propositions concerning them. Taken together, these products are the things and events upon which the operations of interpretive subsystems are performed.

Interpretive subsystems consist of sets of propositions pertaining to particular features of events of these sorts, namely, their interrelations with other events, their significance, and their orders or degrees of abstraction. The operations of interpretive subsystems include such practices as defining, classifying, sequencing, analyzing, abstracting, and generalizing, the products of which are hypotheses, theories, laws and explanations pertaining to the products of investigation.

The investigative and applied aspects of comprehensive scientific systems are more readily partitioned into distinct subsystems than are their interpretive aspects. Indeed, interpretation is a prominent part of these subsystems as well. However, the aims, operations, and products of interpretation, wherever it occurs, are different enough from these features of investigation and application to warrant its separate coverage. Moreover, the interdependence of interpretation and investigation is more likely to be appreciated when the specialized practices and unique contributions of interpretation are conceptualized as a separate subsystem, and problems arise when this relationship is overlooked. These problems are of two sorts, the first of which threatens the validity of scientific systems, the second threatens their significance.

Validity is an issue of consistency, and coherence among subsystems of a scientific enterprise is required for consistency. By way of illustration, a scientific system purporting to study the mind is necessarily incoherent because there is no possibility of coordination between its investigative and interpretive subsystems. This is to say, the products of its interpretive subsystem, namely theories of the mind, cannot be the result of interpretive operations with respect to relations among the products of its investigative subsystem, namely descriptions of observed things, because the things related in such theories are not possible of observation and they are thereby not described. When the interdependence of the interpretive and investigative components of a scientific system is violated in this manner, the system is rendered invalid.

The preservation of the interdependence of the investigative and interpretive subsystems also depends on their being acknowledged as distinct components, as a relationship of any sort requires the participation of at least two entities. Hence, the coherence of a scientific system is also impacted by the stature of its subsystems in this regard. Accordingly, threats to a system's coherence, and therein its validity, are present whenever either of these subsystems is enlarged beyond its boundaries to incorporate the other. Specifically, when the propositions unique to specific subsystems become intermingled under such circumstances, their pertinence to particular types of operations becomes ambiguous. If this ambiguity gives way to improperly constrained operations, particularly of the subordinated system, free constructions are the result.

Operations Assuring the Significance of Scientific Enterprises

Significance is a matter of a system's capacity to interact effectively with other scientific enterprises. This capacity is a product of two sets of conditions. First, only a valid system is capable of effective interactions with other valid systems. To put it another way, incoherent systems interact with other systems in incoherent ways. As discussed above, the primary source of incoherence in scientific systems is incongruity between their investigative and interpretive components.

Roughly speaking, the interpretive subsystem of a scientific enterprise occupies a middle ground between the investigative subsystem of that enterprise on one side and its system-level foundations on the other. As discussed above, the validity of a scientific system depends on there being a coordinative relationship between its interpretive and investigative subsystems, and the validity of a scientific system is a necessary condition for its significance.

The significance of a scientific system also depends on there being a coordinative relationship between the propositions of its interpretive subsystem and its system-level presuppositions. This is to say, the focused propositions of the interpretive subsystem must have been abstracted without contradiction from the presuppositions of the system proper. The latter pertain to matters of wider scope, namely the scientific enterprise as a whole, and these, in turn must have been abstracted without contradiction from presuppositions pertaining to the enterprise of science more generally, articulated at the macrosystem level. In short, the significance of a valid scientific system is a matter of how closely aligned its presuppositions are with those of other scientific systems.

SYSTEMIC FEEDBACK

The unique characteristics of scientific products make it difficult to distinguish feedback from their receiving systems from that of their processing systems. Hence, feedback from both of these sources will be taken as one. To illustrate the function of systemic feedback in a behavioral system, the validity and significance of behavior analysis are examined.

The Validity of Behavior Analysis

The validity of behavior analysis is being challenged by a lack of coordination among its three primary subsystems. Its productivity, and thereby its progress toward the achievement of its mission, is being diminished by this circumstance.

COORDINATION OF THE INVESTIGATIVE AND APPLIED SUBSYSTEMS

Not only is a lack of coordination between the investigative and applied subsystems of behavior analysis evident, its absence is not universally recognized as a problem. Support for this claim comes from a number of sources. Among them are the terms of the long-standing debate as to the relevance of the experimental analysis of behavior to applied behavior analysis and vice versa (Poling, Picker, Grossett, Hall-Johnson, & Holbrook, 1981). At issue in this debate is the fact of relevance, not the value of it. In other words, recognizing and redressing the incoherence that has been developing across these subsystems for decades has not been the primary focus of these efforts, and "bridge" studies notwithstanding, the gap between remains wide. Few citations of basic works by applied scientists, and vice versa, illustrate this circumstance. For example, Elliott, Morgan, Fuqua, Ehrhardt, & Poling (2005) found that 7.8% of the citations in *Journal of Applied Behavior Analysis (JABA)* were from works published *Journal of Experimental Analysis of Behavior (JEAB)* and only 0.6% of those in *JEAB* were from works in *JABA*.

Trends in graduate education in behavior analysis provide another example of the lack of coordination between its investigative and applied subsystems. Graduate programs in behavior analysis have seen significant growth over the last several years. Most of these new programs are focused exclusively on applied science and technology, however. For that reason, most of the students earning graduate degrees in behavior analysis have had no training in the basic science of behavior. The oddity of our discipline in this regard is hard to overlook when we are faced with analogous circumstances in other scientific enterprises. By way of illustration, whether or not engineering students need training in physics is not under consideration in departments of engineering, nor is anyone in the biomedical field pondering the wisdom of having medical students study biology.

No doubt circumstances of an extrascientific sort (e.g., extramural funding, faculty expertise, and personal preferences) have contributed to the growing lack of integration between these two subsystems in our field. Still, in our haste to accommodate to such circumstances, we should not overlook the serious consequences of this trend for behavior analysis.

COORDINATION OF THE INVESTIGATIVE AND INTERPRETIVE SUBSYSTEMS

As discussed above, incongruous interpretive constructions tend to arise when the interdependence of interpretation and investigation is overlooked. Problems of this sort are relatively rare in behavior analysis, and for good reason: the primary source of incongruous interpretive constructions is cultural tradition or, more precisely, institutionalized dualism, and opposition to this institution is foundational for behavior analysis (e.g., Skinner, 1953; 1974).

Still, such practices are not altogether absent in behavior analysis (e.g., Staddon, 1997), and wherever such practices are tolerated, they proliferate. Furthermore, it appears that the historical conflict between the radical naturalists of the field of behavior analysis and the dualists of every other scientific system has become less pointed over the past several decades. While each of the parties continues to preserve its identity, each also appears to have incorporated a sufficient quantity of useful bits of the other's formulation into its own as to have obscured their differences, so it has become convenient to trivialize their fundamental conflict as a matter of "semantics."

In our estimation, the most serious problems of this sort are seen in the investigative subdomain. Only in this domain is it considered acceptable to knowingly invoke explicitly dualistic constructions in the interpretative phases of scientific activity on the grounds that such practices serve strategic purposes. For example, it is not uncommon for basic scientists in our field to appeal to such things as "internal clocks" and "memory traces" as explanations for behavior. It is conceivable, though doubtful, that these so-called "useful hypotheses" may have some immediate utility as guides to significant subsequent research. However, so long as a contribution to the understanding of behavior as a natural phenomenon is the aim of our work, such practices are necessarily and inevitably misleading. In short, the presence of incongruous interpretive constructions in the context of behavior analysis is reason to believe that the institution of dualism is moving inside; and if we operate from this location, its capacity to obstruct the progress of our science is enormous.

Further, the interpretive subsystem of behavior analysis tends to be absorbed by its investigative component. Evidence of this circumstance comes from the articulation of prediction and control as the aims of the scientific enterprise as a whole (e.g., Skinner, 1974). These are not the aims of the comprehensive system of behavior analysis, though. They are rather the aims of its investigative and applied subsystems in particular (Kantor, 1953). The interpretive subsystem has a different aim, namely explanation, and the aims of the system as a whole are inclusive of the aims of all of its subsystems.

Processes Assuring the Significance of Behavior Analysis

The significance of behavior analysis is difficult to assess because its presuppositions have not been fully formalized or adequately systematized. In other words, the definitions and assumptions essential to and characteristic of behavior analysis are nowhere articulated with sufficient precision and authority to permit identification of its boundaries as a scientific enterprise, clarification of its relations with other sciences, or promotion of adequate scrutiny of its constructional practices and their products. The result is incoherence. For example, even the definition of as fundamental a concept as *behavior* lacks clarity. It is at once the action of the whole organism and the action of its parts considered separately (e.g., Skinner, 1953; 1957). The same lack of clarity applies to propositions concerning this concept: Behavior is held to originate during the lifetimes of individual organisms and to be innate (e.g., Skinner, 1974). As such, it is also difficult to identify the broader philosophical position with which behavior analysis is aligned; it appears to be aligned with one position in which the events of one science are not presumed to be reducible to those of another science as well as with another in which they are.

It might be argued that a better indicator of the significance of a scientific system than the alignment of its presuppositions with those of other scientific systems is the magnitude of its mutually beneficial interactions with other sciences—that the proof of the pudding is in the eating, so to speak. That the science of behavior fares well by this criterion is a hopeful thought. However, the relative isolation of our discipline suggests otherwise (e.g., Critchfield et al., 2000). Added to this, there is a tendency for our discipline to be subordinated in our interactions with other sciences. This is to say, other sciences benefit considerably more from these ventures than does our own. Moreover, while it is possible to make an assessment of the significance of our science by this criterion, it is of little use as a means to enhance it. The latter, we believe, will depend on our becoming better oriented with respect to the nature and value of system building in science. (See Clayton, Hayes, & Swain, 2005 for a review of Kantor's system-building procedure.)

The preceding comments are not intended to suggest that system building is an end in itself or that the presuppositions of behavior analysis, once articulated, will be forever fixed. Like all other components of scientific systems, system-level definitions and postulates are products of observational operations, and they are modified as further contacts with relevant events demand. However, due to the generality of system-level constructs, the demands pursuant to their reconstruction are of an unusually high order. It is only after enormous quantities of subsystem products (e.g., data, theories, laws), pertaining to a myriad of more specific events have been accumulated that system-level definitions and postulates become subject to reconstruction, and then only if these products, when taken together, resist formulation in their terms. For that reason, changes of this sort occur relatively infrequently. When they do, though, a massive reorientation of the scientific enterprise in which they operate is entailed.

Because paradigm shifts are outcomes of scientific productivity, and tend to be facilitators of it, their occurrences in particular scientific systems are interpreted as signs of progress in those systems. The same is not implied of the paradigm shuffle our science is likely to experience in the absence of greater efforts toward its systemization.

CONCLUSION

In many regards, behavior analysis is a thriving scientific system. For example, the applied technologies developed within the system of behavior analysis are of unmatched effectiveness and demanded by many within the culture at large. Furthermore, the increasing specialization within the field may be viewed as an indicator of productivity. That is to say, the fact that knowledge has accumulated such that specialization is required for expertise within various subsystems suggests that behavior analysis is indeed making significant progress. While progress has been made, some important concerns remain.

As we have described, the validity of scientific systems depends upon internal coherence. In other words, the validity of behavior analysis depends upon the extent to which its various subsystems interact in a consistent manner so that their products may contribute toward the same overall goal or mission. Of particular concern here, as we have described, is the lack of clarity regarding the exact definition of the subject matter. When clarity regarding the subject matter is lacking, internal inconsistency is the inevitable result. More specifically, under these circumstances the products of various subsystems are likely to be incoherent and overall productivity threatened. Further, disciplinary boundaries between other sciences (e.g., biology), as well as cultural institutions (e.g., dualism), remain unclear, such that the discipline of behavior analysis risks being reduced to other sciences, or common practices within the culture. Given this, one important system-building effort in behavior analysis continues to be the identification of a unique subject matter that may be differentiated from those in other sciences as well as cultural institutions more generally. Subject matter clarification is of utmost importance toward scientific validity and productivity.

These issues also pertain to the scientific significance of behavior analysis as a scientific system. Significance pertains to the extent to which individual systems cohere with the larger metasystem of science, such that interactions with other disciplines may be coherent and productive. When validity is compromised, as is the case in behavior analysis, the potential for productive interdisciplinary interactions is prevented. In other words, when disciplinary coherence is absent, coherent interdisciplinary interactions are not made possible. Valuing coherence not only promotes disciplinary productivity but also enhances interactions with other disciplines, such that interdisciplinary relations may be more valuable.

It was our goal to conduct a behavioral systems analysis of the scientific system of behavior analysis. In doing so, we have identified reasons to believe that behavior analysis is thriving in many regards, as evidenced by increased demand for behavior analytic services and the growing knowledge base within the field more generally. However, we have also identified reason for concern, particularly when the validity and significance of behavior analysis is considered. It is our hope that in doing so, we have prompted further interest in the system of behavior analysis as a whole and facilitated continued efforts toward systemization. Behavior analysis offers a unique contribution to the field of the sciences, and its continued productivity in this regard may depend upon more serious consideration of the scientific status of the discipline as a scientific system.

REFERENCES

Brethower, D. M. (1982). The total performance system. In R. M. O'Brien, A. M. Dickinson, & M. P. Rosow (Eds.), *Industrial behavior modification: A management handbook* (pp. 350–369). New York: Pergamon.

Brethower, D. M. (1999). General systems theory and behavioral psychology. In H. D. Stolovitch & E. J. Keeps (Eds.), *Handbook of human performance technology* (pp. 67–81). San Francisco, CA: Jossey-Bass Pfeiffer.

Brethower, D. M. (2000). A systematic view of enterprise: Adding value to performance. *Journal of Organizational Behavior Management, 20,* 165–190.

Clayton, M. C., Hayes, L. J., & Swain, M. A. (2005). The nature and value of scientific system building: The case of interbehaviorism. *The Psychological Record, 55*(3), 335–359.

Critchfield, T. S., Buskist, W., Saville, B., Crockett, J., Sherburne, T., & Keel, K. (2000). Sources cited most frequently in the experimental analysis of human behavior. *The Behavior Analyst, 23,* 255–266.

Elliot, A. J., Morgan, K., Fuqua, R. W., Ehrhardt, K., & Poling, A. (2005). Self- and cross-citations in the *Journal of Applied Behavior Analysis* and the *Journal of the Experimental Analysis of Behavior:* 1993–2003. *Journal of Applied Behavior Analysis, 38,* 559–563.

Kantor, J. R. (1953). *The logic of modern science.* Chicago: Principia.

Kantor, J. R. (1958). *Interbehavioral psychology: A sample of scientific system building.* Chicago: Principia.

Malott, M. E. (2003). *Paradox of organizational change.* Reno, NV: Context.

Poling, A., Picker, M., Grossett, D., Hall-Johnson, E., & Holbrook, M. (1981). The schism between experimental and applied behavior analysis: Is it real and who cares? *The Behavior Analyst, 4,* 93–102.

Rummler, G. A. (2001). Performance logic: The organization performance Rosetta Stone. In L. J. Hayes, J. Austin, R. Houmanfar, & M. C. Clayton (Eds.), *Organizational change* (pp. 111–132). Reno, NV: Context.

Rummler, G. A., & Brache, A. P. (1995). *Improving performance: How to manage the white space on the organizational chart* (2nd ed.). San Francisco: Jossey-Bass.

Skinner, B. F. (1953). *Science and human behavior.* New York: Free Press.

Skinner, B. F. (1957). *Verbal behavior.* New York: Appleton-Century-Crofts.

Skinner, B. F. (1974). *About behaviorism.* New York: Knopf.

Staddon, J. E. R. (1997). Why behaviorism needs internal states. In L. J. Hayes & P. M. Ghezzi (Eds.), *Investigations in behavioral epistemology* (pp. 107–119). Reno, NV: Context.

Index

Page numbers in *Italics* represent tables.
Page numbers in **Bold** represent figures.

For Product Safety Concerns and Information please contact our EU
representative GPSR@taylorandfrancis.com
Taylor & Francis Verlag GmbH, Kaufingerstraße 24, 80331 München, Germany

www.ingramcontent.com/pod-product-compliance
Ingram Content Group UK Ltd.
Pitfield, Milton Keynes, MK11 3LW, UK
UKHW011454240425
457818UK00021B/819